LORD OF THE I

EXPLORING THE ASTROLO

Haydn Paul has spent many years exploring the transpersonal way, and has been a practising astrologer since 1978.

By the same author

Phoenix Rising:
Exploring the Astrological Pluto

Revolutionary Spirit:
Exploring the Astrological Uranus

Visionary Dreamer:
Exploring the Astrological Neptune

Queen of the Night:
Exploring the Astrological Moon

LORD OF THE LIGHT

EXPLORING THE ASTROLOGICAL SUN

Haydn Paul

ELEMENT BOOKS

First published in Great Britain in 1991 by
Element Books Limited
Longmead, Shaftesbury, Dorset

Typeset by Selectmove Ltd, London
Cover design by Max Fairbrother
Printed and bound in Great Britain by
Billings Ltd, Hylton Road, Worcester

British Library Cataloguing in Publication Data
Paul, Haydn
Lord of the light : exploring the astrological sun.
1. Sun. Astrological aspects
I. Title
133.53

ISBN 1–85230–188–0

Contents

1.	Sol: Lord of the Solar Dance	1
2.	The Mythological Sun: God's Eye of Fire	12
3.	The Astrological Sun	23
4.	The Sun and Planetary Aspects	55
5.	The Sun in the Natal Houses	146
6.	The Sun in the Natal Signs	171
7.	The Heroic Quest: Paths of Light	194
8.	The Esoteric Sun: The Heart Mandala of Light	215
9.	Communion with the Sun	228
	Index	232

Lord of the Light is dedicated with appreciation to:

John Mason: a living spirit of iconoclastic Zen, a close friend and companion for many years along the lighted way.

Maidie Mason: whose support, tolerance, encouragement and faith in the endeavours of the 'Kitchen Table Brotherhood' has always been recognised by us.

In Memoriam: Osho Rajneesh, dissolved in the universal buddha-field of light, 19 January 1990.

CHAPTER 1

Sol: Lord of the Solar Dance

In the beginning, God created the heaven and the earth . . .

And God said, Let there be light: and there was light.

And God saw the light, that it was good: and God divided the light from the darkness. . . .

And God said, Let there be lights in the firmament of the heaven to divide the day from the night; and let them be for signs, and for seasons, and for days, and years:

And let them be for lights in the firmament of the heaven to give light upon the earth: and it was so.

And God made two great lights; the greater light to rule the day, and the lesser light to rule the night: he made the stars also.

And God set them in the firmament of the heaven to give light upon the earth. (Genesis 1:1; 1:3–4; 1:14–17)

THE SUN IS THE SOURCE OF LIFE in our solar system. When the nuclear combustion of the Sun begins to fade and diminish, so also will the release of light, life, and warmth to our planetary family. As the Sun dies, so will the life of the solar system be gradually extinguished. When the solar dance is completed, silence will descend, as the performance of time and our solar creator reaches its destined apotheosis.

The Romans named the Sun the god *Sol*, derived from 'solus' meaning the One, or He alone. Sol is a star, the nearest one to us, and is not a large one, but is sufficient to vitalise our existence with solar radiation, and is the central governing force for our planetary system, around which all planets orbit.

One of the earliest recorded insights into the idea of the Sun as the centre of our solar system was during the ascendancy of the Greek culture and rise of the philosophical mind which has so influenced our Western development. In 450 BC, Anaxagoras additionally proposed that the Sun was in fact a red-hot stone larger than the Peloponnese; his reward for this suggestion was expulsion from Athens!

During the sixteenth century the Polish astronomer, Copernicus, created his heliocentric theory that the Sun and not the Earth was the centre of the solar system, and this revolutionary idea established a new era of astronomy. Yet it would take until the seventeenth century for more realistic measurements to be made regarding the Sun. The German astronomer Johann Kepler codified the three laws of planetary motion after 1600, which confirmed the theory of Copernicus and would also provide the basis for Isaac Newton's later work on formulating the laws of motion and gravitation. In 1666 Newton also split sunlight into the colours of the spectrum through displacement via a glass prism.

Modern science now recognises that the Sun is a gaseous body, whose surface is never still, due to the ceaseless nuclear transformation and burning of its hydrogen mass, where under immense pressures hydrogen nuclei combine to form helium nuclei which release energy through this process and keep the sun shining, periodically erupting and shooting out huge fiery geysers (solar flares) thousands of miles into space. These solar flares cause the phenomena of solar winds, which drive particles from the Sun to hit Earth, affecting the ionised layer above Earth and changing ionospheric conditions. Part of this inner pressure and friction within the Sun is caused by the mass rotating at different speeds, and as a result of its burning of the hydrogen mass, the Sun is self-luminous. The Sun's dimensional volume is 1,300,000 times greater than the Earth's, and although the Sun's mass is only 330,000 times greater, the actual density is lower than the Earth's. The Sun's core is extremely dense and concentrated, but most of its matter is highly tenuous, making the Sun mainly gaseous, unlike the planets which are formed of more solid matter. The diameter is some 864,000 miles, and its gravity is 28 times that of the Earth.

The actual distance varies between the Sun and the Earth, from 91.5 million miles on 4 January, to its mean distance of 92.9 million, and its maximum distance on 5 July of 94.5 million miles; this depends on the relative rotational positions.

Our galaxy or local star-cluster orbits through the Milky Way system, which perhaps contains in excess of one billion stars, moving towards the constellation of Hercules at a speed of 12 miles a second. The diameter of this galaxy is estimated to be 100,000 light years, with a breadth of 20,000 light years. To the human perspective, this scale is staggering, but in the context of the known universe this is not a large galaxy. The Sun revolves eastwards around its own axis, following a defined orbit in space, currently towards the constellation of Hercules, and also orbits around our galactic centre with millions of other Solar System stars. The duration of a 'galactic circuit or cosmic year' is 225 million years.

The Sun has an apparently annual orbit through the twelve signs of the heavenly zodiac, although this is the perspective from Earth, as it is in fact the circle that Earth's revolution makes around the Sun, the ecliptic and its own rotation around the polar axis. The constellations whose names correspond to the zodiac signs are the 'backdrop' to the perception of the Sun's position from our angular relationship on Earth, and determining the Sun-sign is dependent on the time of year. One visual impression from our geocentric position is that because the Earth moves eastwards along the ecliptical path and rotates on its axis, the Sun is apparently moving westwards across the heavens.

During our planetary day, the dawn sunrise is on the eastern horizon, and sunset at evening descends into the West. In individual natal charts for births near dawn, the Sun position is close to the Ascendant; at noon, the Sun has moved nearer to the Midheaven; at sunset it is near the Descendant, and by the Nadir at midnight.

Due to the orbital regularity of the two luminaries, the Sun and Moon, ancient man used their positions as calendrical guides, establishing the concepts of duration and periodic seasonal changes. The time of a day became determined by the rate at which the Sun rose in the East and then set in the West; this also dictated the period of light when human activity and social involvement was at its peak, prior to the more recent development of artificial lighting which offers more options for lifestyle flexibility. For the agrarian cultures, the Sun's light was the controller of their life, with its daytime warmth, and its seasonal indications which determined their planting and reaping cycle, and so the Sun's movements were carefully monitored for 'heavenly guidance'. Over centuries of patient observation and recording, the regular pattern of the solar cycle was clarified, becoming predictable and enshrined in a variety of legends, myths and religious invocations to the power of the Lord of the Solar Dance.

While the older civilisations were more biased towards the power of the divine feminine principle, evoking the source of life through the matriarchal images of Ishtar, Isis and Aphrodite, a shift in the perception of the supreme cultural deities was made as the recognition of the solar eminence dawned within consciousness. In Egypt, this saw a transference of power from Isis to Osiris and the Sun-Child Horus, which eventually resulted in the attempt by Akhenaten, 'the glory of the sun', in the fourteenth century BC to usher in the new supremacy of the solar deity Ra, the falcon-headed Sun-god.

The more peaceful agrarian matriarchal cultures were increasingly challenged by the wandering nomadic tribes, led by fierce warrior chieftains, who gained power and lands through force of arms. The dominance of the masculine principle began to spread and the more martial expression of male strength was soon embodied in their solar father-gods, who 'supported' their attempts at conquest and social supremacy. The importance of the dynastic power of kingship began to emerge, and the foundations for our present patriarchal culture were slowly established by replacing and oppressing the older matriarchal societies based on the lunar principles of the Moon Goddess.

Eventually, the religious spirit re-emerged associated with the solar light, the light of day and discriminative consciousness when applied on its lower levels of understanding. The image of the Father-God ruled the heavens, and a masculine priesthood became the only holders of spiritual knowledge, mediating the light to man.

Between the cycles of the Sun and Moon, the sequence of hours, days, months and years became developed, forming a structure for cultural activity and days of ritualised celebration. Observational stone markers were raised in the Celtic world, as a means of measuring the Sun's position during its annual 'heavenly pilgrimage' across the zodiac, and these would also indicate the transitional days of seasonal change. Knowing these was vital to guaranteeing an adequate food supply, and to prepare for the onset of winter cold. Ancient man was much more attuned to the vagaries of nature than we are now, and had a more reverent relationship to natural cycles than currently exists in modern society, which because of technological advances can virtually ignore the seasons in many respects as both food and warmth are readily available.

Of particular importance to the solar cycle were the equinoxes and the solstices, which were culturally conceived in terms of the rhythms of natural growth and decay, the polarity of the universal life–death process. The equinoctial points are determined by the passage of the Sun path along the ecliptic until it crosses the equator, moving from South to North at the vernal equinox (20 or 21 March, the cusp of Aries), or from North to South at the autumnal equinox (22 or 23 September, the cusp of Libra). The solstices are determined by the Sun's maximum position away from the equator, when the ecliptical path cuts the equator at an angle of 23½°. The Sun appears to stand still and pause in the sky at the Summer Solstice (21 or 22 June, Midsummer and the cusp of Cancer) and the Winter Solstice (21 or 22 December, Midwinter and the cusp of Capricorn). The greeting of the dawn on Midsummer is still popular among those of pagan and Druidic beliefs, and currently Stonehenge is the site of modern clashes between followers of the old ways of Albion and contemporary attitudes as to the 'preservation of heritage'.

Both equinoxes and solstices represent the relationship and relative balances between the lights of day and night, the Sun and the Moon, within the nature cycle and the consciousness of man. The equinoxes are points of balance, when the times of day and night are equal and mutually harmonious. The psychological importance of this is considered in my book *Queen of the Night* (Element, 1990) in terms of the personal integration of both Moon and Sun energies within the individual. The solstices are points where there is inequality between the forces of day and night. At the Summer Solstice, the forces of the Sun are dominant in the Northern hemisphere, and its creative and generative power is at a peak and warmth ignites the world of nature to flower, blossom and give fruit. At the Winter Solstice, the Sun is moving away into the Southern hemisphere, and the forces of the Moon and night become more dominant, as the light and heat fades away and cold and darkness spread over the land.

The Sun and Moon form an axis of light, periodically tipping and readjusting to influence the seasonal transitions, and yet they also have inner effects on human psychology. In astrology, Sun and Moon correspond to the conscious and unconscious levels of mind, and summer is traditionally a time to be active in the external world, while winter is a time for withdrawal into the home and reconnecting to the deeper inner nature.

The Vernal Equinox commences the new zodiacal year at Aries, and is the period when the Sun re-enters the Northern hemisphere, stimulating intense activity in the organic growth of nature's abundance. New life begins to stir under the soil surface, new shoots begin to emerge into the increasing light as the life potency of Earth is revitalised. Nature shakes off its winter's decay and hibernation, entering its new annual cycle of productivity and displays of beauty. This is the springtime, when the hidden seed within the darkness of the fertile soil gives birth to the new leaf, declaring its independent existence.

The Summer Solstice is the start of Cancer and the peak of the phase of fertility which started at the vernal point, and is the temporary apex of the solar forces over the lunar forces. The world is ablaze with colour, verdancy and natural scents, and vegetation and insect life flourish. Man's attention is attracted to the external world, and the growing crops of food soak up the radiant solar light, turning it into a fuel for fruition and later human consumption.

The Autumnal Equinox is the movement back to restoring equilibrium, as is indicated by its sign of Libra, where the phase becomes that of harvesting the ripe crops and the completion of the objective growth process. The green leaves of the trees start to brown and fall as the Sun's vitality diminishes, and the night/lunar forces assume a greater dominance as nature reverts to the period of gathering its forces for the next gestation cycle.

The Winter Solstice at Capricorn sees the apex of the night forces, where the seed of latent promise enters the black womb of the earth, awaiting the time for re-emergence. From this point, the balance slowly begins to change again, as the night force steadily declines until the renewal of the solar day force at the following Vernal Equinox, and the repetition of the cycle.

Embodied in this is the natural human cycle of birth–maturity–death, as we are equally part of the universal process. It is likely that by perceiving this annual pattern and by conceiving the renewal and rebirth of the solar god, man was considered also to be an integral part of this, an attitude that would lead to the doctrines of reincarnation, personality continuity, and a form of physical immortality.

THE POWER OF THE INNER SUN

There are interesting correspondences between the Sun and the human cell, as both perform roles as a central nucleus around which other parts are gathered, collected and organised. The Sun is the nucleus or heart of the solar system; the eventual death of the Sun means the inevitable disintegration of this planetary system. The macrocosmic correspondence to this is the nucleus of the galaxy, the galactic centre of the Milky Way. The microcosmic correspondences are the nucleus in the cellular structure of the human being, where, by 'extracting' the nucleus of the cell or the operative cessation of the physical heart, the human organism dies. The importance of the cell is that it is a unit which structures living matter into predictable shapes, and this is a mass of protoplasm which is bounded by a membrane wall and which contains the essential nucleus, the bonding and unifying agent. The nucleus contains the formative chromosomes (the continuity of the procreative parents and hereditary tendencies) and is the internal core of the atom which is surrounded by electrons and holds the positive charge of the electrically neutral atom.

The emanation of light from the Sun has been a major field for scientific research during this century, and these investigations have provided a basis for understanding the nature of light itself. Light has been measured as constantly travelling at a speed of 186,000 miles per second, and the time taken for the Sun's light to reach Earth is 8.3 minutes. Light waves travel across 'empty space' between the stars and the planets, and it was the originator of the Quantum theory, Max Planck, who conceived that light was composed of atoms of energy. At our current stage in understanding, light is recognised to be a rapidly alternating electromagnetic field which is transmitted through space in the form of waves, and that visible light registered by the human eye is only a fraction of the whole transmission of this electromagnetic spectrum. Light is understood to have a dual nature: it is both particle and wave simultaneously when viewed from different standpoints, and the light quanta are actually 'energy packets', termed *photons*.

What does this imply? Perhaps simply stated, the foundations of matter are light derivatives, which correspond to the biblical creation myth and similar religious symbolism; and the axiom of the Ancient Wisdom that 'Spirit is Matter vibrating at its highest pitch, and Matter is Spirit vibrating at its lowest pitch' is to be equated with the power of light to be both creator and created, forming the universe and being the universe, including our own natures. Light is both spirit–matter, wave–particle manifesting as the appearance of the universe.

Scientific investigation of the sub-atomic levels of our material sense-reality reveals that matter does not exist with certainty at definite places in time and space, but that it shows 'tendencies to exist'; and that atomic events do not either occur at definite times in definite ways, but display 'tendencies to occur'. The modern 'laws' of atomic physics are now conceived in terms of 'probabilities', where the scientist can never accurately predict atomic events with certainty as though the universe follows inviolable laws, but can only suggest how likely something is to happen.

Through this examination of light and quantum physics, a new science of the 'probabilities of interconnections' is slowly forming. One reflection of this is the Mandelbrot series of equations which unlocks the theories of Chaos science, where a popular image is of the butterfly beating its wings which could activate a late hurricane elsewhere in time and space. Like Quantum theories, a basic oneness of the universe is being scientifically revealed, one that embodies a complex web of relationships between all parts of the universal whole, and in which these relationships always include the observer as an essential part of this interaction.

Astrology too is an exploration of 'probabilities' and 'tendencies to occur/exist' through its interpretative analysis of natal factors in the individual chart. Skilled astrologers recognise that their analysis cannot be guaranteed to be totally accurate, but they expect their insights into the nature of individual tendencies to be fundamentally correct, even when evaluating deeper levels of that personality. They can see the basic conditioning attitudes and psychological patterns that will determine choices and decisions in life, and through their astrological perception can 'predict' issues that will occur, and the likely responses to dealing with them. So from one perspective, interpreting an astrological natal chart is similar to the scientific exploration of the sub-atomic levels in determining what is likely to exist and occur.

This underlying unity of life which is being explored by modern science has been the essential realisation of mystics in all cultures, and is also the basis for the relevance of astrology. Astrology is a science of relationships, between spirit and matter, between the planets and Earth, between the human microcosm and the universal macrocosm, between the inner worlds and the reflected external reality. Similar to the role of the physical Sun, the astrological Sun performs the task of planetary cohesion and focused relationships; similar to the physical light serving as the foundation for physical reality, the inner spiritual light of the inner Sun is the foundation for being. Indeed, the electromagnetic interplay and relationship between the Sun and the planets is the basis for the astrological insight into planetary influences on life and human nature. Like modern genetics, astrology proposes that character, intelligence, inclinations are present at birth; and astrology has been present in cultures much longer than the existence of genetic research. But it is at that level that the solar symbol of the circle and point is indicative of the correspondences of Sun–heart–cell–atom. These are repeated again, through the DNA nucleic acids present in the chromosomes of the cells of higher organisms, that store hereditary genetic information and other building blocks for the human being.

Lord of the Light is concerned with a deeper astrological understanding of the solar principle in the individual and society, especially exploring the sphere of spiritual experience and insight. Entering this dimension of the Sun through opening to inner enlightenment is the key to a new rebalancing that is vital as we progress towards the Aquarian Age.

Today, we stand at a cultural crossroads, confronted both by our social strengths and weaknesses, striving to perceive the direction that collectively we should move towards. Our world is a clash of contrasts, and these polarities between the standards of living in the Western world and the Third World nations are starkly revealed in the light of modern media communications. Our global eye looks into all human experience, impassively recording our triumphs and failures for all to see. The recognition of the world family is slowly dawning, and collective concern for all members of humanity is rapidly increasing as is an ecological awareness of our planetary home.

Technologically, we have entered a solar age, through experimentation with nuclear energy and the exploration of the subatomic world. Soon, there will be major breakthroughs into understanding the components of life and further developments in more safely tapping atomic and solar energy supplies. Parallel to this external advance, there is the growing need of people to look within their own natures, 'modern man in search of soul' as Jung could see. *Queen of the Night* examined this trend by reference to the astrological Moon and the reawakening of the lunar principle of self-nurturing, and by examining the insights offered by initiation within the Goddess's Moon Temple. *Lord of the Light* continues this exploration by considering the search for the Sun-centre within the individual – the doorway to the spiritual sun – through the application of the masculine heroic quest, or the mystical path to enlightenment.

It is by the reintegration of both solar and lunar principles within the individual or society that a new regenerated balance can be achieved, one which reflects a holistic perspective and vision, both to the nature and potential of the individual, and to how this can be culturally expressed so that our quality of life is improved by moving more in harmony with the oneness of life. By contacting our solar centre, we can begin to unite our different psychological patterns (the planets) under the cohesive and integrative qualities of our astrological Sun, prior to progressing deeper into the solar mysteries of its heart. We should remember that this inner Sun is the creative heart of our inner solar system, and learn how to work with it more effectively as a means for self-development. Discovering and following our solar path is one such route, whereby our potential can become manifested in life. Studying our Sun position in the natal chart, by house, sign and aspect can indicate a sphere of our nature that can serve as an integrative force. Evoking the light of the solar

Lord can illumine our way forward into the mysteries of universal life; this is the Aquarian path, and may involve a redefinition of our masculine principle expressed through society. Solar power is highly transformative, but as all those who have acted as pioneers along their own individual solar journeys know, this is the path that promises 'life more abundantly'.

If a richer and more fulfilling life is what we desire, not just for ourselves but for everyone else, then we can share in the process of universal resurrection and rebirth that is promised by the solar mysteries. We need to discover the power of the inner Sun, and open our minds and hearts to the penetrative rays of the Lord of Light. Then we can consciously participate in the ongoing task of universal creativity and the return journey to the overshadowing light of the evolutionary process.

CHAPTER 2

The Mythological Sun: God's Eye of Fire

THE ROOTS OF EARLY SUN-WORSHIP lie lost in the mists of time, but as ancient man looked to the sky, the light, energy and warmth of that golden orb illuminated his mysterious world. He was awed by that heavenly eye of fire gazing down and revealing the nature of the world in which humanity had been born. He was fearful when the sun set in the West, and the ebony dark night cast its distorting and veiling shadows across his world, as the darkness and cold descended with nightfall. He called out for the light to return, and each day the dawn light rose in the East as the chattering and singing of the animals and birds woke him to greet another day. His invocation had been successful; the light responded to his worship, his god had heard his pleas to return.

The Sun is the most personified of the planetary lights, assuming the central role in the pantheon of planetary deities that mankind has generated or recognised during his evolutionary progression. Over time, the Sun has been perceived as the source of the creative power of nature, of life and light, and associated with the masculine principle of the Father-God, in distinction to the Moon and the Mother-Goddesses of the feminine principle, of darkness and the mysteries of shape-shifting and birth.

Initially the physical Sun was actually worshipped as God, but later developments of religious insight were modified by the realisation that the physical form of the Sun was just an objective manifestation and representation of the principle of God in our universe. Many of the ancient religions personified the solar disc. Hinduism conceived the Sun as the deity in whom Brahma, 'the

Lord of Life dwells', with the sun as 'the source of all souls and of all life' and Agni representing the Divine Fire. Brahma is the God of universal creation, forming part of a trinity with Vishnu, the Preserver, and Shiva, the Destroyer. Each religion and culture had their solar deities. The Persians had Mithras, a cult which later became popular among the Romans spreading across much of their European empire during the first three centuries after Christ, and which became a rival for followers with early Christianity. The Zoroastrians had Ahura-Mazda (Ormazd), the Sun-God, Light and Life-Giver, being their supreme deity of goodness and light in perpetual conflict with the dark Ahriman. Chaldea and Babylon had Bel, and the Phoenicians called the Sun Adonai, a term used by the Jews to mean 'Lord', but they adopted Yod as their solar deity. The Egyptians had Aton (Aten) and Amun-Ra; Rome had Sol, the Greeks Helios; the Druids Hu; and the Aztecs had Quetzacoatl, who was the giver of the arts and civilisation to man, and whose symbol was the plumed serpent. Dragon imagery is associated with both Chaldean and Phoenician solar deities, and in China, the dynasty of their Sun Kings parallels their own cultural affinity to dragon symbolism.

There was a triple aspect to the solar worship in Persia, Egypt and Babylon, a trinity of the God as 'Supreme-Intelligence-Motivating Creative Force' representing the main qualities of the God-Head. This threefold pattern is repeated in the Christian doctrines of the Trinity and has correspondences to other religions, as well as to the Triple Goddess of Maiden-Mother-Crone. For the solar cults this probably arose from the perception of the three phases of the daily Sun, those of dawn and sunrise, noon and the apex of the Sun, and of sunset and the fall of the Sun over the horizon. Sunrise was the beginning, the new birth of light, and corresponding to God the Father, Brahma, the Creator. Noon was maturity and the peak of the daily light, the source of natural growth and human activity, and corresponds to God the Son, Vishnu, the Preserver, and the fruit which falls to the ground to release its new seeds. Sunset was the ending of the day and the light, the descent into the darkness of the underworlds, corresponding to the Holy Ghost, Shiva the Destroyer, and the gestation of the seed prior to the new birth at the perpetuation of the solar cycle.

The balance of religious power and influence changed from the matriarchal cultures and the worship of the Moon-Goddess, towards that of the solar principle and the supremacy of the patriarchal and masculine Father-God. It was this shift in man's religious perception that resulted in the attempts of Akhnaten 'the glory of the Sun' to replace the existing cults by that of Ra the Sun-God, and the efforts of Moses to introduce a new solar religious conception to the tribes of Israel, casting down the symbols of their older cults by the imposition of the tablets of the new dispensation. The realisation that may have stimulated this change came from a secret knowledge that the light of the Moon was only a reflection of the real Sun light, and that of the male's importance in generating new life. This was sufficient to generate a movement within the collective consciousness towards acknowledging the solar deity, and patriarchal societies developed: the child became the son of the father, instead of the child of the mother, and lineage and heritage became transformed as social power was transferred into masculine hands.

Solar myths have several major themes, recurring across continents and cultures, and in ways similar to those of the Moon, they symbolise the natural processes at work within the world and the human being. These include the phases of human physical and psychological development, seasonal changes, and heavenly movements, associated with the ongoing transformations within life; birth, growth, maturity, death, and the achieving and passing away of ideas, aims, plans, relationships and work over the full cycle of experience. Then comes the continuation of the fertilised seed and the renewal of human and natural life, the ever-born, ever-becoming, ever-dying cycle of existence, with the continuity of life through different forms revealing true immortality and the process of rebirth.

The solar myths which will be considered are mainly those of the Egyptian, Greek and Celtic worlds, as these are the ones that have influenced our Western traditions and social development. But there are many more in other world cultures, as the light of the Sun shines equally on all without discrimination or condemnation; it is the light of the planet and of all humanity.

EGYPT

In the Egyptian myths and legends, the solar deity was known as Ra, Atum, Amon and Aten at different times, although the two most associated with the Sun-God are Osiris and his son Horus. Osiris was originally a Moon-God, consort of the Goddess Isis, but as the new solar cult began to grow he was transformed into a solar principle through the mystery of his resurrection. The adversary of Osiris was Set, which reflected the ancient dualism of opposite twins or complementary principles in nature. Osiris became the 'bright Son of Light', and Set his dark twin, a pattern of relationship that was repeated in the biblical story of Cain and Abel, or in the temptation of Jesus by Satan-Lucifer, and indicated the ever-present Shadow that accompanied the hero on his spiritual and transformative quest towards his destiny.

Osiris was murdered and dismembered by Set, his body scattered across the world. He was a verdant nature God undergoing the traditional sacrifice, and in order for the new life to flourish he had to die upon the land, so that the new seed could be released and be regenerative. His wife Isis scoured the world, seeking each part of his mutilated body, eventually locating all except his phallus which had 'disappeared into the land'. Through the magical power of Osiris's vizier, Thoth, Isis created a wooden phallus and successfully impregnated herself with the seed of Osiris, giving birth to Horus, the Sun-Child. Osiris had been recreated through this magical act, and was resurrected as the Sun-God, ascending to assume his rightful position in the heavens with Isis, his Goddess of the Moon at his side.

Osiris became a symbol of the incarnating supreme solar deity, taking the Lion as his image, becoming the universal lord and teacher of the solar religion and laws, building giant temples of worship and offering the secrets of culture and civilisation to his followers. In his roles as priest–king–father, he oversaw the process of nature from seed, to growth and fruition, ensuring the cyclic continuity. He was aided by the Lord Thoth, whose symbols of the crook and the flail indicated the rule of order and discipline, and he is associated with the power of intellect and the magical knowledge of the occult path.

At the sacred solar city of Heliopolis, the Sun-God Ra was dominant, and the Hymn to Ra echoed around the temples, intoned by the priesthood at the daily phases of the Sun. 'Homage to Thee, O Thou who risest in Nu, and who at thy manifestation dost make the world bright with light: the whole company of Gods sing hymns to Thee after Thou has come forth each day . . .' Heliopolis (the Greek name for Sun City) was the centre of the Egyptian solar cult, and was where the priests of the falcon-headed Ra proclaimed their Sun-kings, pledging that at death the king would rejoin his heavenly father Ra. Suggestions have been made that the pyramids are solar monuments dedicated partly to the resurrection and rebirth of the solar priest-kings. Across Egypt, the blazing light and heat of the Sun poured down each day with little cessation; apart from the fertile strip of land adjacent to the Nile delta, the power of the Sun denuded the land of vegetation, creating vast desert areas. At night, the cool light of the crescent Moon cast deep shadows over the enigmatic face of the Sphinx and the towering pyramids.

Horus was conceived by the magical union of Isis and Osiris after his father's death and dismemberment, and born after the resurrection of Osiris as the Sun deity and the renewal of his fertility. Horus is known as the Lord of Force and Fire, the Child of the Aeon, and his time of divine ascension has been associated with the dawning of the Age of Aquarius, especially in the connection between the power of the Sun and our modern ability to generate nuclear fire. Horus appears as a child, seated in an opened lotus flower, with his finger to his lip, signifying silence, reminiscent of certain Buddhist imagery. As an adult, he is the hawk-headed God, his symbols being the two eyes of Sun and Moon, indicating his all-seeing nature. He is associated with being an avenging warrior, combating Set to restore again his father's kingdom; a healing saviour and a lord of oracular prophecy; a god of music, art, and patron of beauty, home and family. An invocation to Horus summarises several of his attributes:

> Radiant Horus, let harmony pervade our beingness. Don your armour of light and fight on our behalf in the cause of freedom of spirit. Heal our sicknesses and wounds and revive us. Restore the kingdom of your father here on Earth, so that all living things may dwell in the aura of Heaven.

Horus became the fiery eye of God looking down on humanity, one of the warrior-gods whose sword of light is unleashed to fight for truth and light.

Solar deities assumed great social power in the Egyptian society, and Osiris and Horus were honoured and worshipped across the land. Sekhmet the daughter of Ra was a fierce lioness goddess, crowned by the solar disc, and she also gained her own followers.

GREECE

The Greek myths generated the heroic Olympian pantheon of the major twelve Gods and Goddesses, who were dominated by the All-High Zeus. His home was the luminous sky, and his temporal abode was on the peak of Mount Olympus. It appears that he was an original solar deity, son of Kronos, and regarded as the King and Father of gods and men, the dispenser of good and evil, the giver of laws and defender of hearth and home. He had a special sanctuary in Arcadia on Mount Lycaeus, a name which has its root-derivative meaning 'light', and there a circle of sacred oak trees grew, providing him with his crown of oak leaves. Zeus was known as Jupiter in the Roman empire, and both the astrological attributes of Sun and Jupiter are ascribed to the *animus* projections from this aspect of divinity and transpersonal reality. Zeus becomes a patriarchal figure, embodying distinctly masculine energies, force, power and strength, the male as king and law-giver, the creator of social order, justice, leadership and royal charisma. In addition, Zeus became the divine lover, choosing many women to receive his divine attentions, serving as the generative force of a successive phase of new gods and heroes. The Sun was known as the 'Eye of Zeus/Jupiter'.

The Greeks personified the Sun's orb as Helios, meaning 'most high', the god of the physical Sun, who drove his chariot across the sky from east to west, drawn by a team of magnificent winged white horses. These symbolised the need for purified passions, so that all personal energies were mastered, understood and controlled by the solar powers of the centre of the psyche, in order to be correctly, safely and creatively used. Across the night sky, Selene of the Moon drew her lunar chariot in the blackness, lit only by the silvery light of the Moon breaking through the dark clouds.

The major Greek Gods associated with the Sun are Apollo, Orpheus and the hero Hercules. Apollo was the son of Zeus and Leto, a daughter of the Titans, and he was a solar or light god in all aspects. In particular, he emphasised the *anima* aspect of divinity in the male form, those receptive, artistic abilities and appreciation. The corresponding *animus* embodiment in the female form was made by Apollo's twin sister, Artemis. His solar rays were healing, stimulating the body's own natural healing and purifying abilities. Asclepius, the god of healing, was a later son of Apollo. One of Apollo's symbols was the lyre, which he had received from Hermes in exchange for his own caduceus; this lyre had seven strings, one for each of the notes of the planets, indicating that he was the Master and Lord of universal knowledge and mysteries. He also had a bow and arrows, revealing his skill at hitting his target through his solar energy, rays and fertilising power.

In Apollo's aim for the centre of the target was reflected a search for the centre of Self, and through that ceaseless journey, new spheres of human knowledge and exploration were discovered to add to the wonderment of life. The oracular Apollo was contacted at the Oracle of Delphi, where the command of 'Man, Know Thyself' overshadowed the entrance into the shrine and created a context for the delphic pronouncements by the sacred channels. From the Apollo cults were derived the Apollonian Mysteries, which were more related to reason, logic, and the natural order of the heavenly and planetary relationship. These were in distinction to the wilder Dionysian Mysteries, which included rites of 'sacred inebriation' in order to enter 'ecstatic trances' and divine possession, and from which many of the concepts of the sacrificial king entered Western religious ritual due to the dismemberment of Dionysus by the frenzied Maenad Bacchantes.

The later Orphic Mysteries were a combination of Apollonian and Dionysian, trying to join the lyre and gift of music with a more disciplined ritualised dance and theatrical performance of assumed god-forms, invoking the mantle and possession of the inner divinities. These mysteries were derived from the legends of Orpheus, a son of Apollo and Calliope, the muse of harmony and rhythm, who also possessed or inherited the secret of the seven-stringed lyre of universal knowledge and of the seven creative rays of the spectrum. The image of Orpheus is as a master of the muses, singing in the natural wilderness, surrounded by enchanted wild animals, and he became a psychopompos image and spokesman for the gods, who respected his gifts of divine harmonies, his gentleness and beautiful spirit. For the sake of his love for Eurydice, his wife, he had to enter the underworld of Hades attempting to rescue her from death by a poisonous snake-bite. The condition for her return to life was that Orpheus should refuse to look at her during the journey back into the light. Eurydice failed to understand this, and her entreaties and persuasion to look at her with love succeeded. By failing the condition imposed by Hades, Eurydice had to remain in the underworld. Orpheus had followed his feelings of love and surrendered to the Goddess's demands. He returned alone and dejected to the world, and one version of the story has Orpheus's failure causing fury in the Thracian women, who then proceeded to tear Orpheus apart in a manner parallel to the destruction of Dionysus by the Maenads.

The main themes of the Orphic Mysteries were those of the dangerous descent into the underworld (the unconscious mind), taking the light down into the darkness to illuminate that realm, and then re-emerging again into the light of day, transformed by the sacred journey into the inner mystery. This poses the question asked of the prospective initiate at the start of his search for the absolute truth, or God: if you cannot find God in the outer world, then where can you turn next? If successful, the realisation is that man and gods are interrelated, that both human and divine consciousness can merge in the form of the God-man, and that this is the heart of the Great Work and the aim of true religious endeavours. Like the quest of Isis for her lover Osiris, Orpheus follows Eurydice to free her from the underworlds of dark ignorance and lack of comprehension through the light entering the darkness.

Within mythic symbolism much esoteric teaching has been communicated about the divine life process by means of stories and simple imagery. The twelve labours of the hero, Hercules, are examples of such a transmitted teaching. Hercules as the solar hero passes through the trials of each zodiac sign on his path to mastery and realised divinity, enabling him to become the 'father of all' and 'the Selfborn' by his eventual descent into Hades, his claiming of the sacred golden apples from the Tree of Life and his slaying of the dragon of darkness. This legend is considered more deeply in Chapter 7, The Heroic Quest.

Celts and the Western Solar Mysteries

The Celtic legends follow a similar pattern of solar myths, those of the 'Wonder Child', the 'Priest-King', the 'Holy Warrior' and 'Sacrificed Hero-God' who choose to descend into the black hidden depths, in search of knowledge, redemption, rescue and liberation of all trapped in the underworld. The incarnated saviour theme is not exclusive to Christ and Christian doctrine, and is a universal pattern within Sun symbolism. The resurrection of the light is always attained within the context of entering the darkness.

The Western Mysteries still retain an understanding of the balance needed between both masculine and feminine principles; Wiccan and pagan teachings give rightful places to God and Goddess or harmony within the psyche as the necessary state to achieve for spiritual insight and illumination.

Ancient Irish myths indicate a phase when a radical change occurred in the matriarchal culture, as the inner religious perception shifted from the polarity of Goddess-preference to that of the incoming solar force through Celtic Europe. This was the newly powerful solar cult emerging into social dominance and usurping religious allegiances, and was probably allied to force of arms by the masculine warrior tribes which were migrating across Europe, in which brute strength and war skills took precedent over more gentle forms of social relationship. In such groups, the patriarchal warlord held sway, and over time more masculine deities and religious symbolism gained hold over the collective psyche, as the animus-dominated tribes grasped social power through aggression and resorts to violence.

The 'Chief Sun God of Celtica' became Lugh, who replaced Nuada of the Silver Hand and Moon associations as the leader of the 'Danaans' in Ireland. Lugh was a warrior, healer, smith, poet, harpist and carpenter, similar to Apollo and Horus. The Danaan Treasures recur in later Grail mythology, and were known as the Lia Fail, the Stone of Destiny; Lugh's Sword, Lugh of the Long Arm; Finias, the Magic Spear; and Murias, the Cauldron of Dagda, the magic cornucopia and vessel that perpetually remained full and capable of satisfying all.

There is considerable evidence in Celtic relics and artistic symbolism of the importance of the sun-disc in their religious beliefs, and this is highlighted in the earlier construction of the Stonehenge stone circle, which is positioned in ways which indicate solar alignments to astronomical movements, studying the 'universal clock' to note the changing of the seasons and to develop calendrical patterns of time. The Hele stone at Stonehenge is a marking point for sunrise on Midsummer's Day.

In the Celtic pantheon of deities were the Sacred Five, comprising the Triple Moon Goddess, her Solar Consort, and the God of the Underworld. The Threefold Goddess is the Maiden/Mother/Wise Woman-Crone, and is discussed in my *Queen of the Night*; her consort is a benign solar deity, and his dark twin is a magician and Lord of the Regions of the Dead, sometimes referred to as the 'Dark Tanist'.

The Solar Lord is perceived as a bringer of light and fertility, a healer to the land, and rejuvenator of the impulse of life. He is the 'Son of the Mother', serving as her consort, lover, husband, and father of her children. After his annual mating with the Goddess at the summer solstice, his energy wanes until he fades away into the Underworld prior to his new birth again at the Winter Solstice, becoming the resurrected Child of Promise, the reborn Star Child. And then the cycle is annually repeated.

One theme that recurs with solar deities or heroes is that of the dark twin, the light and the shadow. The Celts had the Summer King and Winter King, whose respective symbols were the oak and the holly, embodying the ritualised sun-cycle, and the periodic transfer of power and function between them. The order of Druids were Sun-priests, who gathered in their sacred groves of oak trees (Sun and Jupiter associations), and they were the custodians of Celtic wisdom and nature rituals. The Celtic male gods of light tended to express their anima–animus natures in an extroverted manner, combining an artistic, creative and poetic sensitivity with prowess as a warrior, which was suited to their culture and society. The dark tanist and magician was the opposite polarity, expressing the anima–animus natures in an introverted manner, containing them within himself and using his powers for personal gains and power over others, functioning more like a negation of light ('a black hole') rather than in a positive and revitalising way. Yet he also signified the fact that the solar hero has to enter the darkness of his own nature, in order for transformation and redemption to occur. Parallels to this can be noted in the conflict of Osiris and

Set, Ormazd and Ahriman, Jesus and Satan, Arthur and Mordred, among others.

In Wales, Gwyn ap Nudd was their god of light, who also ruled over the Underworld and was a huntsman and warrior type. One of his cults reappeared later in the area of Glastonbury, renamed as Herne the Hunter, one of whose tasks was to collect the souls of all dead heroes for his shadowy kingdom of the Underworld. Later Welsh tales tell the story of Gwydion, a deity of light and science, who defeated the Underworld God and slayed the Moon Goddess Rhiannon, a tale indicating the triumph of the solar power. Gwydion raised the sun-hero Llew/Lugh, who was the son of Arianrhod, which again implies the growing supremacy and masculine responsibility in that culture. Here, Gwydion symbolises the power of reason becoming more dominant than the intuitive feminine quality of the anima inspired Arianrhod. The relationship of Gwydion and Llew/Lugh is repeated in the legends of Merlin and Arthur, who took him away from his mother for special training, preparing him to face his destiny. The tales of the Merlin cycle also reflect the 'Son of Light' pattern, being a magical child who descends into an underworld to gain his magical powers and the art of prophecy, prior to his outer emergence as King-maker and advisor to the throne, and his eventual disappearance through his love for Nimue/Vivienne and his ritualised death by sacrificial binding in either the tower of glass, a thicket forest, or trapped within the earth cave.

Arthur represented the Solar King, forming his circle of the Knights of the Round Table who, through valour, imposed order and peace on the land until they were dispersed on the quest for the Holy Grail – which is a symbol of the Moon Goddess – in order to restore balance to nature and to redeem the wasteland. The Round Table is often portrayed with the twelve signs of the Zodiac inscribed, suggesting that the qualities of each sign were embodied in the Knight who sat at his appropriate seige. Arthur probably took his place at Leo, the sign of kingship, and eventually the centre of the circle saw the descent of the veiled Grail, summoning the Knights to their quest for self-realisation. The role of the hero is considered further in Chapter 7.

CHAPTER 3

The Astrological Sun

IN THE NATAL CHART, the astrological Sun symbolises the central archetype of self, both in its superficial reflection as the ego, and in its innermost nature as the individual being. It is important to recognise this apparent dualism of sun symbology, because it is through the dilemmas and painful dichotomy between egoic consciousness – which operates as a surrogate and separated centre – and the inclusive archetypal Self that the path of self-discovery is forged by experience.

As life revolves around the physical centre of the Solar System Sun, being dependent on its self-generated transformation for existence, we too must learn how to refocus ourselves into alignment with the solar centre within our psyche. The astrological Sun becomes our personal star, a higher Self and the principle for integration and wholeness of being through the search to recognise our deepest inner centre. The Sun functions as a magnetic and guiding force around which all the complexities of our psyche 'revolve in orbit', sustaining the egoic structure in a state of cohesion and continuity of consciousness.

This function of the Sun persists through most lives without the need for a greater awareness of the process, yet the issue of individual purpose can unlock a further door into the solar mysteries. The questions of meaning, purpose and direction in life are stimulated by our 'Star-being', which teaches us that to live more fully by developing latent potential we need to discover a more stable centre than our egoic identification. The limitations of the ego become apparent when facing the storms of life. Tragedies or losses can destabilise through emotional flooding, creating nervous breakdowns or the shattering of ideals and faith which can destroy our intellectual certainties and foundations, or the flow of creativity may become too powerful and artistic genius tip us over the brink into insanity. Our fragility is extremely vulnerable, if based on the egoic level that society encourages us to perceive as our whole nature. In the majority of lives, there must have been times when each of us have wondered if we are going mad, as life fails to conform to our expectations and dreams, and we undergo the painful experiences of our resistance to the facts before us; the collapse of relationships, the loss of loved ones, the piercing of illusions and dreams.

One potential of the solar centre is the process of indicating purpose. From this indication, we can derive a focus that concentrates our energies and become one-pointed towards our goals. These can be purely material objectives, or ambitions for social status reflecting the level of activity of the egoic Sun; but a deeper level of connection to our inner depths is possible. Through a search beyond the superficiality of life, contact can be made to one's archetypal purpose. The transferring of the personal centre of identification from the peripheral 'I am' to the central 'I am That' is the way of integration and the emergence of the spiritual Sun. Exploring this dimension is the intention of this book.

The dualism of the Sun, like the intimate relationship of light and shadow, is indicated by the lesser light of the ego (the consciousness of separation) and the hidden, inner, greater light of the Self (the inclusive consciousness). By the interplay of the solar polarity, the evolutionary path in time and space is woven through the strands of human life. A point comes when awareness dawns that 'I must arise and be about my Father's work' and the journey commences to discover our real purpose and individuality. This awareness can be born when each recognises that what they had previously considered to be their self is just a sequence of passing thoughts, emotions, and feelings, forming a pattern of discontinuous moments generated by a constantly changing personality. The questions of 'Who am I? What am I doing here?' haunt the mind like permanent ghosts, tainting enjoyment and life absorption until, somehow, they can be resolved.

The issues of the ego–Self relationship involve questions

arising from 'the personal myth', the individual dream that we are attempting to manifest through our lives, and which embodies significance and purpose. This myth is the ongoing journey to apply solar life-energy to unfold all potential and to utilise all resources so that we respond to the magnetic attraction of our destiny, which is perpetually calling us to rediscover our true whole nature. By becoming increasingly conscious and creatively expressive, we can open our limited egoic filter so that it serves to release our unique individual expression of the group function and potential indicated by our Sun sign. This sign also represents our life path and goals, and the particular characteristics of the personal Sun sign form individual aspirations and conditioning facets of the personality which almost unconsciously lead us towards certain directions and experiences. In this way, the Sun operates on both unconscious and conscious levels, mirroring the interplay of ego and Self. Through the birth imprint of our Sun sign (our sharing in the collective group psychological type), the embryonic path to awakened solar consciousness is also present and waiting for activation.

In astrology, the meaning of the Sun has been associated with the ego-personality, the individuality or Self, seeing it as the source of will, vitality and personal power, the 'will to be' and 'the will to express creative purpose and potential'. This is fine, except that the majority of people fail to know how they can direct this power, or even what direction to aim towards. Without attaining a higher centre, most people's power is unconsciously dissipated, resulting in just following well-worn social lifestyle patterns, never realising that they have been disempowered by misidentification with the lesser light. Humanistic and transpersonal astrology focuses on the principles of the solar centre and the opportunities for self-actualisation, in an attempt to inspire the unfolding of a strong unifying Sun, capable of integrating the psyche (the various planets) and forming a channel for creative expression. Once the individual purpose is discerned, then energies can be directed by the harmonising Sun into specific directions; the Sun is restored as the inner ruler, Master of the house.

The Integrated Sun

Integrating the Sun within the individual psyche is a definite step in evolutionary development, and is associated in Jungian psychology with *individuation*, and in psychosynthesis, spiritual and magical paths with contacting the *higher Self*. There are progressive stages of solar integration, and these involve physiological and psychological transformations. Currently, there is still a minority in the world who are capable of such changes, although with the dissemination of the many paths towards the inner light now being available, there will be an increasing number of people who can attest to the nature and value of the inner reality as being the forward direction for humanity.

Any personal work to integrate the inner Sun is highly beneficial, as the conscious centre is strengthened so that its cohesive nature begins to unify all disparate tendencies of the psyche (the planetary characteristics). The value of this cannot be overemphasised, nor can endeavours to resolve stresses, tensions and energy leakages from any challenging aspects of the Sun to the planets. The positive benefits of solar alignment result in clarified life directions, self-sufficiency, strength of will, self-awareness, unity of perception, more meaning, purpose and self-confidence; and in equal measure to the healing of a fragmented personality, so does the individual path forward begin to form as a lighted way to follow.

Through accessing the positive energies of the solar centre, the sense of identity is reshaped into enhanced solidity, offering an awareness of potential and a refined will capable of manifesting this into tangible form. Life options increase in proportion to the realisation of self-responsibility and freedom of choice. One of the earlier touches of solar contact stimulates the recognition of lifestyle creation, which may necessitate the release from traditional socially accepted life-paths as a first step of individual assertion. A later phase of solar integration involves the fusion of the individual will with the 'universal will' or intention of the higher Self, although this occurs on the transpersonal path, and requires a reorientation away from a personal focus towards types of social involvement and contributions to benefit humanity.

In a colloquial sense, evoking the Sun makes the individual feel 'more together', a unity of personality rather than a battlefield of clashing and conflicting inner voices. Energy can then be directed towards self-chosen aims, instead of being dissipated in opposing inner demands from differing personality tendencies. Self-confidence increases, as does a sense of well-being, and this intensifies personal vitality and enjoyment of life, which is then transmitted to others through friendliness, goodwill and the 'radiation of light and love' without discrimination. The centres of the solar plexus and heart become more activated and important in regulating body energy flows, and as these centres of individual 'gravity' become more powerful, shifts in perception and responses to life also occur. The egoic centre of personality begins to open to the influence of the higher Self, whose qualities of balance, harmony and clarity commence the inner rearrangement of characteristics, enlivening the positive natures of the planets and transmuting the negative tendencies.

A higher perspective of individuality and relationship to the world emerges, in which the spirit of co-operation and sharing predominates. Issues of power over others fade away, as there is little need to assert the self by an imposition of status, power and will, and the challenges then become those of expressing potential and of aiding others to discover their own life paths. The integrated Sun is a path of conscious self re-creation, where by inclusive insight the inner light seeks to kindle all other hidden lights, in mutual enrichment. The search for self-fulfilment is not primarily selfish now, but through an awareness of others attempts to resolve social needs too. By the assumption of the solar roles of leadership, the individual with an integrated Sun works to guide and direct people to make those steps of progression, whereby they, too, can release their personal creative expression. Mere egoic assertion generates roles of superiority and inferiority, but a solar leader is intent on elevating all to share equally in his power and role.

The Unintegrated Sun

Indications of an unintegrated Sun can be revealed in a lack of self-confidence and social assertion, where awareness of an inner disunity and conflicting messages fragments the personality and diminishes the experience of well-being and certainty of life direction. Insecurity is continually present, underlying all self-expression, although this can manifest in two different styles.

One is a passive, withdrawn nature, feeling helpless, insignificant, timid, and shy, lacking self-confidence in social situations and often evading relationships through fears of inadequacy and exposure, or being taken advantage of by someone less scrupulous. Potential remains latent and unrecognised, and life persists in being disappointing and disillusioning, yet effort is not made to change things either. A passive acquiescence to the dominance and leadership of others is common, as is an adherence to socially traditional lifestyles. Within this type of personality, a short-circuiting of the solar power has occurred, and to such a degree that they are willing to surrender their freedom of choice in life. They might dream and indulge in personal fantasies, yet never make any effort to realise them in real life. In many ways, their Sun has descended over the horizon and back into their unconscious minds, leaving them unfocused and lacking a dynamic personality centre.

A second type of expression is the overtly egoic overcompensation for an underlying insecurity. Here, the emphasis is on social power and the need to impress others. Self-esteem is connected to social position and status, perhaps in employment or in tangible material possessions, and issues of command, leadership, control and self-satisfaction dominate. Images of self are derived from the responses of others, and attaining 'superior positions' is often a driving motivation for such types in an attempt to bolster a less stable sense of identity; strip them of such roles and often the personality falls apart, because of their misidentification, for instance with managerial roles. Often the quality of relationships is seriously affected by these expressions, and the emphasis is placed much more on self than on any awareness, consideration and concern for others; self-centredness dictates most choices, and a need for an approving audience is often present, where the ego prefers to remain as a centre of attention. Sometimes an over-assertion of self-sufficiency may occur, where the solar influence is misapplied to cut away the need for relationship in life, and when this occurs, the quality of interpersonal contact is severely diminished, or the need to dominate and control becomes paramount, and personal demands have to be satisfied. Like a child, the need for approval by others is essential, and often life turns into an ongoing performance, designed to grasp centre-stage and reap the applause. In the spotlight, the self is glimpsed, but once the light is switched off, the sense of identity returns to its real, vulnerable state.

With these types of unintegrated solar expression, one cause of the distortion of the Sun centre may be related to the early parental relationship, especially with the father. Both of the above are extreme types of reaction, and many who lack a solar centre may display either tendencies or a less defined personality expression, which can vary between characteristics of both types. The need, however, is a rebalancing of the egoic centre through self-assertion and creativity that also includes due regard for the needs of others, which can then lead to the path of the higher Self. By remaining with an unintegrated Sun, the individual is choosing a life which will inevitably disappoint, as aims will remain dreams, relationships will fail or be unsatisfying, and inner conflicts will persist as the many inner voices continue to demand that their needs are met.

SUN AND THE ELEMENTS

The elemental relationship of the Sun's natal position can be suggestive in indicating the type of 'fuel-energy' that the individual requires to maintain feelings of well-being, focus and life purpose, and which should be consciously sought in order to deepen this solar connection.

With the Water element, Sun in Cancer, Scorpio and Pisces signs, the individual emphasis is placed on sensitivity, feelings and emotional responses to life, and these offer a renewal of vitality and a type of psychic guidance over choices, the 'gut response' to people, situations and environments. Individuals with these elemental Suns need to *feel right* in all aspects of their lives, and unless that feeling-tone is correctly engaged, their experiences can become painful and oppressive. All perceptions of the world are conditioned by underlying feelings, and it is often the case that this level requires careful cleansing, purifying and healing before it is integrated more successfully. The challenge is to create a lifestyle that suits these essentially individual response patterns of their psyche. A balance needs to be attained and maintained, or else excessive Water can tip the personality into imbalanced emotional reactions which ignore common sense or rationality; equally, tendencies towards emotional repression should be transformed, or else the 'life-fuel' begins to run out in an emotionally atrophied inner wasteland. Often those with heightened sensitivity can attempt to repress emotions, and this too becomes detrimental to well-being. Each element has its own challenges which are ultimately part of the individual solar quest, and while the Sun in Water signs emphasises a heart response to life, the lesson lies in how to live with those acute feelings and how to open the heart even wider to embrace all universal life compassionately.

With the Air element, Sun in Gemini, Libra and Aquarius signs, the individual emphasis is placed on mental activity, intellectual concepts and social communication. The need here is for mental stimulation, a variety of interests, changes of environment or friends for that sense of renewal. Air signs inhabit a world of mind, and are the 'Thinker' signs of the zodiac. They can be liable to imbalance by over-valuing this level of the human personality to the exclusion of the other aspects. Logic and rationality can dominate, and the individual may need to ensure that this does not diminish the exploration of life by closing mental doors towards experiences that fail to fit into such a world view. The Air element can be a natural searcher, due to that innate tendency to question and wonder, and if this side can be evoked more it can become very important for the solar quest. The Sun in Air signs emphasises a mind approach to life, and the lesson lies in how to direct that mental ability and curiosity and how to open the mind to a synthetic insight and understanding into the universal mind.

With the Earth element, Sun in Taurus, Virgo and Capricorn signs, the individual emphasis is placed on the five senses and the material level of life, the enjoyment and use of physical existence. The need is to feel materially secure and stable, creating a safe and ordered lifestyle to feel well-being. Earth inhabits a world of action, providing the 'Builder' signs of the zodiac, yet can become imbalanced by excessive reliance on physical reality and the need to acquire possessions. While such needs motivate the individual to pursue their life-path, adjustments may be required so that life does not just become physically focused; the awareness needs to be opened to the other dimensions of life too, or else the result becomes an eventual limiting prison of being 'earthbound'. An innate practicality needs to be redirected beyond self-satisfaction, and the lesson and path lies in the challenge to direct those organisational and pragmatic abilities so that they can benefit all physical life, forming structures for solar potential to be unfolded within all universal manifestation.

With the Fire element, Sun in Aries, Leo and Sagittarius signs, the individual emphasis is placed on an assertive exploration of life, viewed from a basically optimistic and intuitive perception of the richness of opportunities that are available. The need is to create a lifestyle in which the individual can feel free, enabling those leaps of spontaneity, enthusiasm and intuition to be made without undue restriction. The direction of such leaps emerges from dreams, fantasies and visions. Conformity to static living patterns of work, relationships and obligations is not a step that Fire enjoys making. Focusing and directing this restless energy becomes a challenge to self-discipline; leaving options open is essential not to feel trapped. Clarity of purpose needs to be gained, or else that vital energy can be easily dissipated through incessant but fruitless activity. The lesson lies in the challenge to break free from a self-centred perspective, and to use that intuitive insight to generate new horizons, and possibilities for yourself and your fellow men, so that the destined solar nature can shine forth. It becomes essential for Fire signs to follow their dreams, because otherwise the inner spark is slowly extinguished through a wilful ignoring of its presence, and when that fuel-energy fades then the restrictive nature of the world inexorably descends to imprison the light.

The Sun and the Transpersonal Planets

The three outer planets of Uranus, Neptune and Pluto are extremely important in supporting attempts to manifest solar power. It is often their influence that stimulates the individual to commence searching to discover a permanent inner centre, more robust and powerful than the ego which is subject to the volatility of life, outer influences and the vacillations of temporarily dominant inner subpersonalities.

The qualities of the transpersonal planets will be focused through the solar centre, although personality reactions to their heightened vibrations are variable and often can appear more negative than positive in nature. Once the solar alignment is made, then the transpersonal qualities begin to be reperceived and operate more positively. Activation of the three transpersonal planets – either by influential natal aspects, or by transit/progression aspects – has a real impact on the stability of egoic identity and life structures. It is often noted that breakdowns of lifestyles, marriages, or personality are connected to transpersonal planetary stimulation, especially when the Sun is relatively unintegrated and unable to withstand the stresses and impulses that are agitating within the unconscious mind.

Solar contacts with Uranus often imply the probability of periodic life changes, as the impulses for individual freedom look to escape from any oppressive limitations and restrictions that have been created. An unpredictability characterises this contact, fuelled by a need for spontaneity, excitement and variety which can often manifest as impulsive behaviour. There can be issues related to selfish and selfless actions, which require a resolution and new direction to pursue in order to release the positive dimension of this planetary relationship. The attraction of future potential is highly stimulating, even to the detriment of failing to appreciate the present, and there is the continual impulse to shatter existing structures for the freedom of the new, especially when the inevitable obligations of duty and responsibility begin to feel onerous.

One challenge is to absorb this urge to become free within the existing lifestyle, so that changes are made without destroying the value of previous efforts. Relationships can be renewed and revitalised, employment can be changed, new interests developed, intellectual study can be chosen, or attempts to release talents, gifts and potential can be consciously made. These actions help to redirect this Uranian energy into forming a solar path of expanded opportunity, where a concentrated approach to fulfil aims and the satisfaction of solar achievement can offset the Uranian urge for perpetual freshness. The problem is to settle into a productive life direction, so that creativity has a clear focus and a variety of channels to be expressed through. Otherwise, these energies will overflow and create disruptions in life and relationships, destroying what could have been good foundations by the impulse to search for the chimera of the new.

Sun contacts with Neptune can be very important in the unfolding of the solar path, especially within the mystical and humanitarian dimension. The main danger with Neptune is its quality of distortion when activated within an unintegrated personality, or when its energy impinges on an unstable personality. The Neptunian vibration has an effect of dissolving, and if this is activated then the cohesion of both personality and lifestyle can be damaged. Neptune gravitates naturally to the Achilles' heel of the individual, and if the solar centre has not been realised, then the effects can be most disconcerting as the person becomes prey to glamours and illusions, distorted self-perceptions and delusions and often sows the seeds of their own downfall.

However, if the solar centre is strong and based on living the heroic quest, then Neptune can add qualities of vision, idealism, creativity and compassion. From Neptune can come qualities of imagination and artistic sensitivity which may form part of the solar path of expressing potential, as well as awakening the individual to relationship responsibilities in life as his compassionate nature expands through awareness.

Sun contacts with Pluto imply an impulse for self re-creation and transformation, and these needs will provide an underlying dynamic to the personality that may not always find their presence to be comfortable or reassuring. This indicates that unconscious patterns and motivations will be influential, and becoming aware of the nature of these is highly important for the personal quest of self-knowledge, by the liberation of repressed energies and compulsive tendencies.

Pluto also serves to undermine the power of established structures of personality and lifestyle, in order to allow a new vitality to come through, and this reflects the traditional battle of the assertive hero and the ageing king. The issues of power and domination are present, especially in the context of exerting individual will over others, and these can form a testing ground for the planetary relationship between Sun and Pluto.

Intensity of feelings will be looked for in life, and sexuality may be highlighted in the individual nature as influential in defining a self-image. Periodic crises are likely as the old patterns resist the new impulses, especially when there is a need for 'something else' in life, or a need for further self-expression. Relationships can be a fertile ground for transformation and the unfoldment of a solar path, as through failure they can strip the individual of any personal certainties, forcing them to pursue greater self-understanding as a means of living with themselves, particularly in coming to terms with their sensitivity of feelings and power of emotions.

Each of the transpersonal planets brings radical change in their wake, often against the conscious volition of individuals prone to their unconscious activity. Uranus, Neptune and Pluto can 'destroy' lives when their contribution is resisted, ignored or misapplied by the ego, struggling to retain its spurious dominance within the personality. Equally, they can remake lives, by their contribution to forming three major strands of the integrated solar path in individuals who succeed in attaining greater consciousness. The unifying factor is the role of the Sun, which can shed light into the darkness of the personal unconscious mind, liberating repressed energies and the Shadow-self into new life.

If there are any natal solar aspects to a transpersonal planet, then a positive, constructive and creative expression of that energy is crucial to self-integration, and effort should be made to ensure that any negative characteristics are modified or transmuted; the alternative is to remain liable to subtle influences and unresolved compulsions that have a power to overturn a life virtually overnight if the pressure for their release intensifies. Acknowledging that inner tensions exist is the initial step towards a transformative path, and enables the old patterns to be released with less attachments when they are recognised to be now unsuitable and restrictive. The Sun has the power to control these energies, because of the innate flexibility of movement from the separated egoic self to the higher Self; taking that path is the real intention of transpersonal activity and manipulation of life, and in so doing both the solar and transpersonal purposes are united.

Sun and the Father Archetype

In the natal chart, one of the Sun's correspondences is to the archetype of the Father. This is an intrinsic pattern which exists as a formative structure or imaging matrix within the psyche from the time of birth, becoming operative in infancy and continuing to exert an influence throughout the adult life in varying ways. As this archetypal imprint resides within the individual unconscious, there is a simultaneous connection with the collective pattern of the Universal or World Father-Parent, which in recent cultures has become embodied within common religious imagery as the patriarchal God of the Bible or the Koran.

Emerging from this archetype are the conditioning images for collective masculine development, those specific ways of expressing physical masculinity within each society that evolve as cultural norms; for instance, homosexual male behaviour is still not fully accepted within our Western societies, yet in the influential Greek culture this became an acknowledged part of the importance of masculine peer bonding.

Within our childhood experiences the role of the mother is usually dominant, due to the time spent more exclusively in her company and through her greater involvement in the child's early life. This can relegate the father and the masculine principle to the background of consciousness, yet as children mature they will grow into a patriarchally dominated culture, where the pre-eminence of men and masculine power is enshrined in all areas of life and within the social hierarchical structures, although this is slowly changing as the feminine principle is now regaining power. One conflict can occur through confusion within the mind, as for current social adaptation the more unconscious masculine image is expected to become recognised within the child's conscious mind as the power, authority, law and justice in society, and conversely, the feminine image which once included those attributes for the small child is forced to become 'socially subservient and second class'.

An additional complexity emerges today by the breakdown of traditional static family units, where through divorce and separation the primary parental pair dissolves, and children spend time probably living with one parent – often the mother

– and the domestic atmosphere of polarised archetypal principles becomes imbalanced, with the child losing one of the sexual and archetypal role models.

One of the major challenges facing us as we move deeper within the Aquarian Age is to develop a 'new' archetypal image which can take us beyond the polarities of either masculine or feminine patterns, an image that evokes our common human nature. This is often represented by the symbol of the androgyne, a transsexual inner pattern slowly rising through the collective mind into a greater social recognition, although the potential of this has been prefigured by the hermaphrodite image, and the importance of attaining the *mysterium coniunctio* of the inner divine marriage.

Through the medium of astrology, we can study the Sun to discern the activities of the masculine pole of the personality, to gain insight into the influence and importance of the physical father on the formative childhood development. This includes the nature of the relationship with the father, operating on both conscious and unconscious levels. Solar aspects to the Moon can indicate the parental relationship, and challenging aspects to Saturn or Uranus (as archetypal patterns of Father-Gods in mythology) can also suggest difficulties within the child–father relationships, which may need healing and resolution within the adult psyche. In such cases, archetypal patterns can become intertwined with the actual family relationships or the childlike perceptions of parents.

The Sun or planets in either the 4th or 10th houses are especially significant in this context. There is a difference of opinion whether the 4th house is more identified with the father than the 10th; modern psychological astrologers favour the 4th house, and traditional astrologers prefer the 10th house. Deciding which is left to each astrologer and the approach they prefer, as there are persuasive arguments for each preference. In our culture, the masculine principle is given primary position, so as the 4th house is associated with roots and foundations, we could justifiably relate the Sun and father archetypes to this house. Taking this position offers an experimental opportunity to examine our subjective images of father through the 4th house cuspal sign, or by the nature of any planets located in that sphere, especially if there is a single planet in that house.

Studying the Sun's influence in this archetypal context can lead to considering issues of patriarchal authority, tyranny, economic controls, sexual potency, intellectualism, emotional expression, rationality, and power over family direction. Exploring such realms may offer insights into how our own 'natural expression and attitudes' have been formed or conditioned, and into our reactions when faced by these issues in our social lives. One major example of the father archetype operating is the social tendency for projection, creating representatives of the dominating father-figure through hierarchical leaders in politics, business, schools and religions who assume the powers of archetypal collective and group projections. Our tendency to submit to authority is almost instinctive, be they our social rulers or priests, and one of the hardest challenges of individuation and the search for self is the casting away of this submissive acquiescence to whatever we are told is right. We need to discover for ourselves; yet, paradoxically, as parents we tend to perpetuate social conditioning for our own children, as we simultaneously recognise that social acceptance demands social conformity. The challenge is to balance such necessary conformity with an equal assertion of individual freedoms, expression and potential.

SUN AND RELATIONSHIPS

The dynamic impulse of the solar principle within relationships is the heroic quest to discover one's 'missing half' in order to feel whole; this need manifests both as a psychological search for enlightenment or more commonly as a physical relationship between masculine and feminine principles, either as the external social marriage or the inner sacred marriage, physical or psychological union.

For men, as representatives of the masculine Logos, the need is to unite with the feminine Eros for completion, and this requires the conscious integration of the anima archetype, which is the embodiment of the unconscious female pattern within the male psyche, and is often related to his early experiences of his mother and women. Solar aspects to the Moon are significant in suggesting the nature of this archetypal imprint, as are secondary aspects and the sign positions of Venus and Neptune, which can reflect partner preferences and tendencies towards projected archetypal idealisation and romanticism, the perfect dream-lover. The issue for men is the degree to which they can integrate this inner feminine, transforming any urge to be overly dominating – as justified by social traditions – and how far they can modify and sensitise any aggressively assertive tendencies arising from a fear of the absorptive quality of the feminine nature.

For women, the Sun tends to symbolise the nature of the father imprint that has been absorbed, the formation of her archetypal animus pattern and male image that is influential in her relationships and attitudes with men. Within the woman, it is Eros who searches for the vitalising Logos principle for completion and individual balance. It is often a psychological cliché that both men and women look for partners who serve as surrogates for mother and father images, and yet this is a true insight. From positive child–parent relationships, the impulse is to discover a partner who reflects those favoured qualities, and from more negative relationships, the need is for a partner to embody qualities that may have been lacking during childhood experiences. The issue for women is the degree to which they can integrate their inner masculine pattern, as through their animus they can develop an objective self-reflection leading to greater self-knowledge.

For men, integrating and dealing with Moon aspects can be problematic and challenging, but for women the same is true of their efforts with solar aspects, which can be easily misapplied to become imbalanced masculine traits. Often, the woman's Sun remains latent within her unconscious mind, as she ignores ambitions for social recognition and outer achievements, preferring to live exclusively in accordance with female conformist social roles of domesticity and motherhood. Aspects to the Sun then pose problems, such as with Uranus, where a need for independence, freedom and self-assertion may be felt, or with Pluto which can often have associations with the father or men, where a lack of adequate love in childhood can re-emerge in patterns of either submission to masculine power and authority, or overt attempts to 'repay' men by being manipulative, wilful and dominating in an archetypally inspired matriarchal personality. For women, squares and oppositions to their Sun reflect these inner and outer stresses that require resolution, and which often retain at their core psychological patterns resonating with their father imprint, sometimes resulting in distinct complexes or obsessive relationship choices.

Within men, the anima archetypal images form female guides, the tarot Empress and High Priestess or various Goddesses when following the heroic quest; the Grail legends in particular are full of such feminine figures in relationship to the knights. Within women, the animus archetype generates male guides, the Emperor, Magician, High Priest, Hierophant, or various God images, when following the quest of the heroine. As Jung recognised, and ancient esoteric mystery schools knew long ago, it is only by the reabsorption of unconscious archetypal projections on to the opposite sex that a path to inner harmony and balance can be discovered, through the conscious individual integration of the archetypal polarities of anima and animus. Both Sun and Moon in astrology strive for mutual completion and wholeness, and by working in such a way with their astrological relationships to unfold the one that is less conscious in the individual nature, then progress can be made.

THE SUN–SATURN POLARITY

Where there are planetary aspects between the Sun and Saturn, the implication is that the individual will have to face certain tests and challenges in life, feeling that they have something to prove or achieve. Often this inner motivation will be related either to the individual's childhood relationship with their father, or to a deep conflict within their psyche.

The Sun–Saturn polarity indicates both opportunities and limitations for the person, those tensions between expansion and contraction which, over time, help to shape a unique self-expression. The Sun will encourage the unfolding of latent potential and the movement towards the solar path of personal destiny; Saturn will restrict, limit and test the quality of the person who is determined to walk the solitary path. This is not a negative constraint, but one designed to confront the individual with everything that they need to transform and modify, enabling them to walk the solar path with ease.

Saturn is known as the 'Great Teacher', 'The Dweller on the

Threshold', and guards the transpersonal path from those who are ill-prepared for its rigours. This Sun–Saturn polarity is similar to the myths of the twin gods of light and dark, where the hero is tested by his dark twin prior to his resurrection, or where the conscious self is shocked to discover the existence of the shadow-self, perpetually present within his nature. Saturn can appear as a dark figure, sepulchral and black, casting a shadowy veil over dreams and ambitions, and standing fixedly in the way. It is his duty to reflect the unintegrated aspects of the psyche, to prompt individuals to learn those lessons that they may prefer to avoid; otherwise, the way is temporarily barred. In every life there are phases when we become 'stuck', facing an impasse, those apparently inpenetrable brick walls. We may even recognise what our aim is beyond that barrier, but fail to see the means to move onward. Often this process is vitally necessary. A free passage may not really benefit us, and it is through the challenges of life that our real qualities and abilities are evoked. In this way, the restrictions imposed by Saturn force inner changes if we are to progress. If we choose to surrender to the impasse, and turn around without accepting the challenge, then we declare ourselves unready for further progress. Saturn is a wise teacher; he does not condemn our failings, but carefully allows each to travel at their own pace.

For many, Saturn becomes the dark side of ourselves, the darkness before the golden dawn of sunrise. He represents the unredeemed, repressed, unawakened aspects of our nature, parts which may be denied and thrust away from conscious acceptance. His threshold is the shifting parameters of the conscious and unconscious mind, and the intention of his dominion is the gradual raising to consciousness of the dark self, the liberation into light. The apparent adversary of the 'hero' is really his friend, guiding him to actualise his solar potential. But it is only when the hero acknowledges the dark Saturn, and allows him entrance into his opened nature, that the way becomes clear. What occurs is a deeper stage of unifying integration, through an act of resolving separated parts of the individual psyche, where by standing within a personal centre, the dual aspects of light and dark of the individuality are recognised and equilibrated.

As this is an ongoing process, such encounters are periodically renewed because the task of bringing light into the darkness is the 'Great Work'. This is known as the 'path of inclusiveness', where we can progressively open to embody the promised life of abundance, and which enables us to embrace the complexity of life and humanity more comprehensively. Our astrological work can prepare us for this, as we deal with the conditioning planetary energies and psychological types of humanity. We should become much more open-minded, tolerant and understanding of our fellow man as a result of our studies.

The encounter with Saturn is an inevitable consequence of attempts to follow the Sun-path of development. It depends on our rate of progress as to how often Saturn appears in our way, but each time is a point of crisis and potential inner change. As our movement intensifies, we confront Saturn more regularly, yet it always assumes a different garb to suit the appropriate lessons, and at each stage the lesson becomes more inclusive in its implications.

In the natal chart, Sun–Saturn aspects highlight this polarity and ensure that it will be activated during our lives. We can feel the impulse to move 'onwards', and sense the restraining barriers circumscribing our options. Time constraints are Saturnian obstacles, which are often felt by those following development paths. Intuitions of 'what we should be doing, and where we should be' are registered, immediately facing us with the actual life situation, and the problem of 'moving from here to there'. Why the delays, we ask? Inevitably, the answer is that we are not ready, even though we may believe we are. With experience and hindsight, we eventually acknowledge the aptness of the higher insight and understanding of our nature.

With the positive aspects of sextile and trine, we should find Saturn to be more amenable to smoothing the path for our Sun-destiny, with the hurdles less difficult to cross. The conjunction aspect poses a mixture of obstacles, some quite within our capabilities, and others demanding considerable stretching to pass without falling. Here, Saturn and Sun stand like very close friends, and the stark truths of Saturn can be accommodated within the intimate nature of their friendship; although the occasional friction can be extremely abrasive, the result is beneficial and ultimately strengthening. With the square and opposition aspects, the challenges are more direct and appear insuperable, demanding resolution or the individual faces the likely collapse of their dreams and direction. The square is experienced as inner stress, pressure and tension, where the struggle can be either to integrate disparate personality tendencies or to actualise latent potential. The opposition projects this tension onto the external reality which is a manifestation of Saturnian restrictions, and the struggle is fought in the outer world, pending a conscious transformation of the inner dichotomy of dualistic perception. Where there are no Sun–Saturn natal aspects, the urge to assert individuality and make a personal mark on the world is often less developed, and there may be a diminution in the need to attain autonomy.

The Sun–Saturn polarity offers an opportunity to reshape the individuality, to make it more whole, complete and self-determined, so that through a focused and directed will, the ability to express the solar potential is increased.

There are certain tendencies that are often associated with Sun–Saturn contacts, which can include a wariness and lack of trust in the goodwill of life, and an attitude which is confrontational in essence, seeing life as a challenge to be overcome by an assertion of individual strength. For the Saturn–influenced person, 'nothing is free', and everything must be worked for; anything that comes easily can be distrusted. 'Where's the catch?' is the unspoken query. Working with the principles of spiritual manifestation is not usually Saturn's manner, unless a substantial transformation has been experienced.

The individual respects discipline and control in life, preferring the virtues of order to spontaneous freedom and impulsive choice. Yet this energy is of great value to unfolding that solar ambition, as it confers perseverance, forethought and caution, ensuring that the signposts are read correctly and the right route taken. Responsibility and life duties are taken seriously, and in some cases can be used as an excuse for a lack of progress, allowing them to become imprisoning barriers rather than a structural framework to expand within. The inner need is to create something out of life, to impose something of the individuality on society and life, to make that imprint; in so doing, a greater degree of self-esteem and recognition is achieved. Effort and hard work are highly valued qualities to be emulated, and assuming that attitude implies that time for relaxation and frivolous pursuits will be at a minimum.

The Sun–Saturn polarity is often associated with the individual's father and parental relationship. The reality and perceived image of the father has probably been a major influence in shaping the personal attitudes, and where such aspects exist, there may be good reasons to look closely at that relationship to discover the underlying patterns for later adult attitudes and values, especially when they are acting as inhibiting limitations.

While the sextile and trine aspects indicate a more positive type of relationship, one that is basically supportive, encouraging and loving, the conjunction, square and opposition can indicate a much deeper imprint that has proven to be more influential on the developing child's personality and outlook. These three aspects are more problematic, and can be the roots of compulsive adult tendencies.

What often emerges is a limitation of the quality of the parent–child relationship, where emotional disappointments and failures of expectations occur. Part of this can emerge from the father's failure to engage with his children emotionally, perhaps through an inner reaction against acknowledging his feelings, or through other preoccupations absorbing his energy and time. He may be pressured by adult stresses, such as lack of money, an unsatisfying marriage or job, and so becomes unable to offer much of himself to his children. He may lack emotional sensitivity and empathy with the child, and fail to understand the childlike perception of the world. He may favour the security and stability of a well-disciplined, ordered, and controlled lifestyle, which the child tends to disrupt in various ways. Emphasis may be placed on material values and possessions, and parental directions are given only to encourage the child to satisfy that area of life; this may inhibit a child's natural inclination to pursue more imaginative and creative paths, or to explore the world of intellectual knowledge. As most parents tend to encourage their children to follow their own adult preferences and to reflect their view of the world, this may not always match the developing child's perception and interests; conflicts, disagreements and misunderstandings can follow.

For some, the masculine image that is psychologically absorbed can be distorted. The father can be undermined by a dominating mother, and though he may be loving can be perceived as weak, passive and ineffectual, especially if he is failing to achieve his aims and this becomes a source of contention between parents.

A distinct father image is required during childhood, so that the psychological balance is correctly adjusted. These Sun–Saturn aspects are sometimes associated with the father's ill health or with cases where there is a definite gap between parents, caused by marital friction, or where the father leaves the family home through divorce or separation.

Whatever the specific nature of the unfulfilling father–child relationship, its effects spill over into the later adult life. For men, this often stimulates ambitions and fears of failure. The drive for visible success, prosperity and status can be an attractive antidote to that inner insecurity, by proving their personal value to the world, and simultaneously to the father, who may have failed fully to recognise the value of the child. The challenge of such an operative pattern in the psyche is either to use it as a spur to overcome all obstacles to success, or in the passive acceptance of an inner inadequacy and destiny of failure, especially when progress is not being made. As children are a creation of the parental relationship, there is a tendency for them to feel responsible when that relationship is disharmonious; if the marriage dissolves, they can adopt feelings of guilt and failure which then taint their adult lives, devaluing their self-esteem.

If this happens to a young boy, whose parental relationship collapses, then he can lose the masculine image of his father, the inner and outer role model for his male development. A structure for his unfolding identity is then lost, and he is forced into the situation of having to create his identity himself. Depending on the domestic circumstances, the age of the child, and the strength of their character, this situation can be either highly beneficial or destructive. Compulsions to prove personal success can develop, and life is perceived as a challenge to be overcome, with the inner struggle for development and integration being projected externally. It is by an assertion of a type of masculinity, – the discovery of an independent identity, self-worth and self-reliance – that the travails of life may be withstood. The positive consequence of this is that he could become the conscious director of his own destiny, reflecting his solar power by transcending the Saturnine restrictions. The negative consequence is that relative failure can shatter an unstable and insecure self-confidence, and agitate those unresolved tendencies of non-acceptance and self-rejection that can still be present in the unconscious mind.

Accompanying psychological patterns to this tendency of self-rejection include an inability to relax easily, to be frivolous and play, to feel happy and contented. There is the fear of 'What is lying in wait around the corner?' which can spoil the enjoyment of the present. Types of self-denial are common, and these can often unconsciously generate personal failures, until the deep causes for them are recognised; these can be noted in unwise actions, lack of judgement, perception and discrimination, or psychosomatic illness. Saturn corresponds to a certain type of religious deity, often seen as an unbending biblical Jehovah image within Western society, who utters clear commandments of right behaviour and threatens punishments for all who fail to conform to the divine fiat. The Saturn individual has an ambivalence towards religion, often accepting the moral commands and restrictions on life, yet finding a monotheistic deity unsympathetic to their inner quest to establish a unique identity. External success and self-integration rarely occur before the Saturn return around the age of twenty-eight, and even then only with considerable exertion and focus.

The influence of Sun–Saturn on women is related to their adult relationships with men and their expression of the part of the psyche which reflects the masculine principle of their nature. If the contact with the father was unsatisfactory, then the woman's adult self can be restricted in several ways. She may lack the ability to be self-determined, to express initiative, will and decisiveness; she may feel uneasy with men, acting either as passively subservient to the dominating masculine image, or hostile to any threats of usurping her freedom and individuality. The tendency can be either to repress her inner animus, or to assert its presence in an unbalanced manner, by imitating exaggerated masculine characteristics of dominance and assertive power over people. There will be an attraction (or unconscious rejection) towards men who offer an impression of a 'surrogate father', perhaps strong, protective figures whom she could surrender to or rely on, to whom her emotions could freely flow and who will respond properly to her sense of relationship. A deeper understanding of her psychological patterns and adjustments within her attitudes may be needed, or else conflict, ambivalence and fluctuating emotions may exist within her adult relationships. One beneficial aspect to this Sun–Saturn challenge can be the stimulation to explore her nature more intensely, as a response to her inner disquiet, enabling her to unfold her creative potential more effectively, and to integrate the masculine potencies of her animus and so balance her psyche by discovering a unifying wholeness.

Solar Returns and Solar Transits

The annual transiting movement of the Sun around the natal chart is symbolically a contacting of all conditioning patterns within the personality – on both conscious and unconscious levels – by the power of the Self, indicating a renewal of the potential for individual purpose and life direction. This movement can be viewed as both a stimulation and a sustaining of the disparate personality facets as indicated by planetary placings and aspectual relationships, generating the network of cohesiveness that forms the structure of personality consistency.

The solar cycle, or solar return is an annual pattern where the revolution of the Sun over the 365 days cyclic duration reiterates and activates the full potential of the static natal horoscope, by its journey across each house until arriving back at the solar degree of the day of birth. In this way, solar movements reflect the annual heroic cycle (see Chapter 7) of birth–maturity–decline–death and renewing resurrection, and offer a new opportunity each year to make some progress towards the underlying solar life purpose. Effectively, each adult year recapitulates the challenges and prospects that are innate in our individual charts from birth, confronting us with those inner and outer patterns that either aid or hinder our self-development.

The Sun's mean motion is almost one degree per day, and it is the only transiting body which makes the same aspects annually on approximately the same day, allowing for a slight variation leading to the leap-year adjustment.

Both conjunctions and oppositions are made once to each planet, and twice annually for transiting solar sextiles, trines and squares, excluding the retrograde motions of the more distant planets. Solar transiting aspects have a variable influence of some two days from applying to separating, although individual resonance to solar effects varies, and any immediate transit impact may be felt slightly before or after that period, irrespective of any longer-term consequences. As the Sun indicates both outer ego and the inner Self, all solar aspects made by transiting movement can signify points of opportunity, both for ambitions of the separate self, and for inspirational contacts or signposts from the inner Self.

Solar transits to the natal Sun may open channels within the psyche which could be used by individuals trained in meditative skills, where the separate self deliberately attempts to align with the higher life purpose, perhaps even ritualised in the form of a personal consecration to seek the lighted way. Such transits, especially those forming conjunction, trine or sextile, can be applied either to develop or extend self-expression and potential to incorporate an inclusive consciousness of the interrelationship between self and society. There may be intuitions of ways to improve well-being, or the glimpsing of latent talents or directions to explore, or even the gaining of a new perspective on life ambitions and purpose. Taking each birthday as a particularly potent point to re-establish a solar cycle is especially effective; we can enjoy the nature of birthday celebrations and parties, but how often do we use this point to review and contemplate the actualisation of our solar potential, or commit ourselves to greater future endeavours? As each year passes, certain opportunities decrease; yet each of us has only a limited span of time to live in this world, and most of us waste much of our lives through lacking direction and purpose, eventually stirring in middle age to wonder where has the time gone, what have I done with my life, and why do I feel so dissatisfied? Evoking a solar contact will ensure that such feelings will not arise, except as a prompt for action and the commencement of the quest.

The transit through each house and the contacting of each planet serves as a solar renewal, with the potential for an annual transformation of any stagnant or static personality patterns that are inhibiting any creative expression. We can work with this solar cycle as a path through the houses of life.

There are two ways of considering this movement, the first being to plot the Sun's movement across the quarters or quadrants (across the angles of Ascendant, Descendant, Mid heaven and Nadir, or the axis of Horizon and Meridian).

The quadrant solar transit has correspondences to the four seasons, with the Ascendant considered as the birth of the solar child at the Winter Solstice, the Nadir corresponding to the Spring Equinox, the Descendant to the Summer Solstice and the Midheaven to the Autumn Equinox.

Solar transits through houses 1, 2 and 3 are the winter quadrant, associated with Intuition, and an inner subjectivity of a new impulse that is still latent but starting to announce its presence within the psyche/world. This involves the assimilation of the experiences and results of the previous three months of the cycle with the intent of gaining clarification of the nature of self and individual purpose. We can receive an intuitive glimpse of our solar destiny during this phase.

Transits through houses 4, 5 and 6 are the spring quadrant associated with Feeling, and a recognition of the objective signs of the new life within us. This can be through discovering more effective ways of using our solar potential, qualities and talents as a springboard for self-exploration and life direction. We may adapt our lifestyles and channels of expression accordingly to make space for this new impulse to make a mark on our world by expansionary growth.

Transits through houses 7, 8 and 9 are the summer quadrant and associated with Sensation, when the challenge is to apply our flowering talents and qualities in ways which benefit the collective, by effective action and externalisation within our society. We are asked to manifest our solar function by our inner light blazing forth in harmony with our solar pattern. By the arrival at the Midheaven, the apex should be reached in our solar year.

Transits through houses 10, 11, 12 are the autumn quadrant of harvesting and associated with Thinking, where the seeds sown during this annual cycle are to be reaped, and the consequences shown of our actions and efforts. This involves the social recognition of our solar manifestation, which could be negligible or considerable; this forms the seed impulse for the renewal of the cycle and the next phase of opportunity. As the transiting Sun crosses the Ascendant, a point of 'judgement' may occur, as an inner process or outer experience when we are faced with either new positive options or a repeating of unresolved patterns.

The alternative cyclic working of this is literally to take each house and its correspondences, and to contemplate their monthly meaning within your life and psyche, looking deeply into your attitudes, values and beliefs associated with the house, evaluating how these either help or hinder your solar purpose, and then decide if changes or modifications are necessary. This cycle of inner enquiry can be commenced at the Sun's entrance into the 1st house, or from the Sun's transit into its natal house, and could become an annual pattern of renewal. This may appear easy, but in fact can be a most powerful exercise if seriously applied, stimulating a personal revolution.

The essential point to be recognised is that both the Sun and Moon offer paths for us to penetrate inwards to discover wholeness, and that by working with them the dualities of opposites can be resolved into unity.

MIDPOINTS

Considering a natal chart through the perspective of midpoints can be a useful adjunct for those who are seriously applying astrological theory and insight as a foundation for self-exploration and path of development.

Midpoints are points in space calculated from the relative positions of two planets, which ideally are in natal aspect. The midpoint can be visualised as the apex of a triangle created by the base-line of relationship drawn between the two planets. In this sense, the midpoint becomes a resolving factor, a position of potential harmony or dynamic release for the planetary energies involved.

For instance, Mars at 17 degrees Taurus (6th house) is in square to Uranus at 17 degrees Leo (9th house), forming a midpoint at 2 degrees Cancer in the 8th house. This can suggest that personal action and expression of will through the house of work and service is being inwardly affected by the need of Uranus for novelty and mental stimulation in the 9th house, thus creating an unsatisfactory and disturbed employment situation, a lack of clear direction or practical, tangible results. Yet by taking the midpoint into account, as the indicator of where those energies which are engaged in inner friction can be more successfully released, the implication is that by looking in the direction of Cancer in the 8th house, a suitable release could be achieved which diminishes that inner friction and tension.

Here, releasing emotional frustrations and pressures arising from a lack of work satisfaction are redirected into activities that transform these energies into constructive and positive channels, becoming regenerative and rebalancing. The potential of working in closer co-operation with people is noted, perhaps founded on mutually compatible emotional responses to life (Cancer), which ideally include a progressive and inspiring new mental vision of life (Uranus) absorbing the vitality of life (Mars) by attempting to manifest in real life. The themes of work, service, new experiences and mental stimulation could be fulfilled by a co-operative group endeavour to enrich the quality of society by creating tangible improvements, a task which could be emotionally fulfilling too.

The degree, sign and house of the midpoint symbolically suggests the channel through which the energies of the aspectual planetary relationship can be released in the most dynamic and externally focused manner. If another planet is located within 2 degrees of such a midpoint, then consider that planet to be especially important in releasing or directing the energy.

Opposite to the midpoint position is an inverse point. Referring to the above example, the inverse position of 2 degrees Cancer is at 2 degrees Capricorn. In distinction to the realisation and practical use of the planetary energies through Cancer, this Capricorn position represents more of an inner significance and insight into the nature of those planets, an intuition of their role in integrating the personality and in the inner evolutionary development. Noting the relevant Sabian symbols for these zodiacal degrees can be suggestive, and add an extra dimension to personal exploration (see Chapter 8 for further references to the Sabian symbols).

Planetary midpoints involving sextiles and trines can point to releasing the constructive energies of the planets involved, but squares and oppositions in particular can benefit by the application of the midpoint theory, as offering directions to resolve those inner and outer frustrations and conflicts. Conjunction midpoints are either identical or extremely close to the aspect position, so are probably not worth considering unless the midpoint moves into an adjacent sign or house; then it could be significant in indicating an alternate direction for expression, especially if the conjunction's planetary relationship is a less harmonious combination of energies.

Sun–Moon midpoints suggest the sphere of externalising individual purpose through a practical realisation and expression of personal abilities; a way of fusing self-acceptance and nurturing to provide a firm foundation for solar development and individual assertion through following the light of the personal 'star'. The midpoints formed from square or opposition aspects can suggest ways to resolve inner divergences between messages of the instincts and feelings of the individual purpose; the pull between patterns of the past and the future self attempting to be born, and the reactions of others and the environment.

As the only major aspect that can be formed by the Sun with Mercury or Venus is the conjunction, midpoints here are less relevant. In a loose conjunction the midpoint reflects the issues of the conjunction.

Sun–Mars midpoints suggest ways to unify will and purpose with action, so that determination and focus are clarified, and a single-minded approach can be taken to achieve aims. Square and opposition midpoints indicate directions which may offer channels of expression which can release inner tensions and external relationship frictions in a less abrasive manner, through the dimensions of life implied by the midpoint's house and sign position.

Sun–Jupiter trine and sextile midpoints offer a direction to expand towards, where trust and faith in the abundance and beneficence of the universe can be felt. The midpoints of the challenging aspects point to a sphere where resolution of doubts and mistrust of life and people could be achieved, a source of a new vision of life which enables expansion to occur as a change of mind.

Sun–Saturn suggests an area where the individual can positively apply themselves within their existing limits and restrictions, making the best use of 'being here now'. The square and opposition midpoints can indicate an alternate direction to resolve self-created difficulties through restrictive attitudes, values and beliefs, which can negatively affect relationships.

Sun–Uranus trine and sextile midpoints indicate a possible area of constructive focus for any agitating inner need for stimulation, change and novelty, through consciously directing that impulse. The square and opposition midpoint offers a redirection of those pressures to break free from all restrictions, by pointing to a more positive channel of expression, instead of allowing a potentially destructive style of release which can shatter whole lifestyles and relationships.

Sun–Neptune midpoints are concerned with the direction of creative and imaginative tendencies within the personality, focusing them into specific areas and forms of creativity. The rising of spirituality and compassionate service can also be associated with this midpoint. The square and opposition midpoint can point to a releasing of blocked creative and imaginative abilities, the gaining of a new perception less influenced by glamour and illusion projected onto self and others.

Sun–Pluto midpoints refer to the potential of rebirth, new channels for regenerated and transformative energies to undermine inner limitations. The square and opposition midpoint is concerned with the releasing of repressed and self-contained energies, so that a healing, purification and liberation of energies can occur to be used for a future positive application.

The Sun and Physiology

In the human body, the Sun is associated with the heart and its function of circulating the blood, pumping it out via the arteries and capillaries, and then receiving it back from the veins. This is the human version of the Sun's vitalising energy transmitted through the body organism, although the human form is a self-contained system where recycling of energies occurs.

The role of the heart's motion is to distribute vitality, nutrients, and oxygen through the bloodstream by means of a muscular, rhythmic contraction and relaxation process, which also deals with the movement of waste materials for later excretion. By this activity, which commences independently at birth and continues until death, the heart has a most important function in controlling the well-being of the whole body, and the effects of its circulatory system through the network of veins can determine physical health.

As the position of the heart is in the centre of the torso, its function of maintaining equilibrium is implied, integrating the whole body system. Esoteric teachings concerning the heart and blood are considerable, and confirm their importance to the evolutionary development of humanity. The heart's valve action of perpetuating a constant flow of energies out to the body and then back for recycling can be reflected by the universal life process and the interplay of spirit–matter, where force and form are in a complementary relationship. The Qabalistic sphere of Tiphareth (see Chapter 8) is concerned with this function of equilibrium and transmittal of energies.

For the individual, the heart is of supreme importance. If asked, 'How long is your life?', the answer can be 'As long as my next heartbeat.' While modern medicine and surgery has entered the era of transplanting organs, heart disease is still a major contributor to ill health and death. Our physical heart can be intimately connected to our emotional and spiritual well-being, and many a heart has been 'broken' through unfulfilled romances and failed love affairs. On the spiritual path, opening the heart is an early and vital stage to achieve, as it is the foundation for all later progress. This consideration moves the enquiry into less physical dimensions, and a personal balanced flow of energies within emotional and spiritual levels may be as important in maintaining the right physical heart activity. As we now recognise, excess stress and tensions can lead to heart attacks and strokes, so the linkage between life experiences and responses is clearly made to the personal state of health. To aid personal equilibrium, it is beneficial to reduce tensions through meditation, relaxation techniques, and reasonable exercise to enhance circulation. Creating a suitable lifestyle, and living from our own 'heart centre' is also necessary in moving towards our personal solar path. In doing so, our health may be improved, but certainly we will enjoy and appreciate life more, and our vitality will increase.

The gland which has been associated with the Sun is the thymus, which is one of the ductless endocrine glands, positioned near the base of the neck. There is some uncertainty regarding its specific role in the human physiology. What appears to be definite is a function during childhood where the natural processes of growth rhythms are regulated, harmonising and co-ordinating the many profound changes that sequentially occur throughout the child's passage to maturity. Again, a role of synthesis and organisation is indicated within the body, a director of various physical processes coming into their timed schedule of activity. Previously, the thymus was supposed to diminish its function once childhood was completed, yet it has now been established that this gland is influential over the immunological aspects of the body, especially connected to the contents and quality of the blood and our specific body chemistry and biological reactions.

One of the productions of the thymus gland is the lymphocytes and the T-4 'helper cells', which are white blood cells which aid the body's immune system in recognising previous exposures to 'intruders' and fight against infection. It has been observed in AIDS and other diseases of the immune system that the quantity of these supportive white T-cells has been greatly diminished and that the cells have been damaged.

Speculatively, it may be implied that in working more closely with the personal solar path, better health may be achieved, as a corresponding vitalisation of this centre may be stimulated by a solar resonance, thus enhancing the whole immune system. The Aesculapian healers favoured the solar potency above all in their therapeutic work, and many find today that exposure to sunlight and warmth has a rejuvenating effect on physical and spiritual vitality and enjoyment of life. Currently, experimentation in some progressive alternative therapies is looking at the potential for meditation and creative visualisation to be directed at activating the thymus gland to improve the quality of individual immune systems, and this can be helpful in decreasing the speed at which AIDS and similar illnesses attack the body. For adherents of the 'energy follows thought' meditation paths, the use of directed visualisation to help balance specific malfunctioning glands offers opportunities for experimentation and potential healing, instead of or in co-operation with drug prescriptions.

CHAPTER 4

The Sun and Planetary Aspects

ASPECTS MADE BY THE SUN indicate planets that are especially significant in terms of unfolding the individual solar purpose and path, either by suggesting an easier expression of potential through the sextiles, trines and certain conjunctions, or by noting those with challenging aspects of square and opposition which imply the need for inner resolution of personality conflicts. Any aspected planet receives an energised infusion from the vitalising solar force, and so becomes more prominent through its influence within the psyche.

Routes for the release of solar power are suggested by the nature of the planet aspected, either by the free-flowing of the Sun's vitality or where that energy is being blocked and frustrated by the challenging aspects. Additional attention must be directed towards the square or opposition, because success in liberating these energies aids greater integration and deepens the contact to the solar self.

The challenging aspects reveal areas of the individual life where difficulties are often experienced in satisfying aims, ambitions and needs; the square indicates inner tensions, where the application of will and potential is restricted, often by choices derived from personal attitudes, values and beliefs about reality. The square suggests that the answer lies within the personality, and that by deliberate and conscious effort change can be more easily achieved. As beliefs and attitudes often attract corresponding life experiences – especially when these are painful or unsatisfactory – looking within to gain greater self-knowledge can be the solution, so that through inner modification, wiser choices and decisions can be made. With the opposition, the emphasis apparently changes to external resistances, with the choices of others diminishing individual freedom and options. Yet it is often by transforming the individual perspective that any unconscious projection which is being reflected by 'outer opposition' from people or circumstances can be dissolved and reintegrated safely. Everyone projects on to the outer world; gaining insight into how our Shadow-self generates many of our experiences and shapes our relationships is crucial, and is often a key to taking control of our lives again.

These harder aspects of square and opposition can imply certain compulsive pressures or unconscious personality patterns that in some cases dominate individual lives, depending on the planets concerned. The transpersonal Uranus, Neptune and Pluto can be highly activated in many people, even when their presence is within the unconscious mind. One consequence of their activity is a debilitation of vital energies, where the solar force is redirected or blocked by their distorting inner presence. The results are frustration, a lack of self-confidence, a sapping of the will and application leading to indecision, and a surrender to the status quo even when the lifestyle is unsatisfying. Or else inner pressures reach a peak and have to be explosively released, often shattering existing personality or family structures. Challenges related to personal expression and assertion will occur, and these will create insecurities within the psyche and intimate relationships. Yet these are the challenges that can also stimulate the search for self understanding and the resolution of inner pain, and if rightly approached, can be the source for a powerful self-renewal and liberation of solar energy. Dealing with the obstacles of the squares and oppositions forms a major part of the heroic journey, and everyone has their own share of hindrances to overcome; they become 'character-forming', and every step taken to cleanse the inner darkness becomes an increase in inner light.

Another dimension of challenging aspects can involve childhood and parental relationships, and the emergence of the individual self from the protection of parental and social conditioning. Analysing a chart from this perspective opens out insights into the formation of self image based on childhood experiences, and the internalisation of parental attitudes and beliefs, or even the quality of the parental love and concern for the child.

The flowing, harmonious aspects of the Sun to any planet (sextile, trine and some conjunctions) reveal where natural talents, abilities and ease of expression can occur without struggle. These become innate qualities that should be fluently expressed, and through which the solar vitality can move to manifest potential and individual life-paths. These can be considered as innate assets, be they a Venusian charm and attractiveness, an attunement with the Uranian higher mind, or the artistic creative imagination of Neptune; the presence of such assets can help form the personal direction, purpose and meaning in life. For everyone, the main issue is ensuring this latent potential is actually released, and all of us have a greater potential than we succeed in using. It can be a worthwhile and interesting exercise to evaluate our aspectual patterns, not just those of the Sun, although that is very important, but all of our sextiles, trines and conjunctions, and to analyse how effectively we are using these positive and constructive gifts, and then study any challenging aspects, to focus on our inhibited energies and to resolve means to transform them within our lives, to heal stresses and to stretch out and grow.

MOON–SUN CONJUNCTION

All Moon–Sun contacts indicate the relative degree of individual integration between instincts, emotions and feelings which have been highly influenced and conditioned by earlier childhood experiences and relationships with parents, and that sense of unique identity and life direction, the essential tone underlying the personality characteristics.

The conjunction indicates the potential integrated personality, moving towards self-containment and self-sufficiency focused on a firm identity and a purposeful life direction. As there can be a fundamental inner harmony between your feelings and will, energy will not be diverted into dealing with inner conflicts and stresses, and this will enable you to concentrate on unfolding a life-path or career.

You will feel comfortable with your temperament and pursuing your aims absorbs most of your time and energy. Success is likely due to the consistent level of motivation and perseverance that you can apply, and the ability of making maximum use of personal and material resources to further your ambitions is a great asset. Wasting time or effort is not your style, as you feel that you are following a golden thread of destiny which offers meaning and continually urges you to follow its direction. If the spiritual dimension is your chosen route, then you may feel a 'mission' waiting for you to perform, some type of world service. This can be the presence of your solar centre making an impact on your consciousness, trying to guide your path of purpose.

Taking responsibility for directing your life is important, and you can display a self-assured independence of spirit, refusing to accept any unnecessary interference and being determined to follow your own light. You may find that working alone, or taking full responsibility for a self-employed business, is preferable to being an employee, so that you gain the full benefits of your efforts. While you may be able to act in a responsible position of authority, there may be a question mark against your style of relating. Through tendencies of self-absorption you may lack awareness of others, and this can result in authoritarian attitudes, creating barriers of communication and retaining a detached role denuded of any concern for how others are reacting to you. Relationships can be a weak point, except on basically superficial social levels, and people may receive the impression that you are not unduly interested in human contact and friendship. They may also note a certain inflexibility about you, which rarely dissolves unless it is for a matter which will actually benefit you; compromise for mutual harmony may be a casualty with this attitude, which could be described as an almost innocent self-centredness. Privacy and independence of thought and action remain high priorities for you.

Much of this stance is derived from a need for protectiveness, emanating from the Moon's influence. It is not that you feel threatened by others, but that you feel you should protect your vulnerable emotions. This side of you is often kept hidden, although you recognise how intense your feeling nature really is, and in many circumstances you are highly dominated and influenced by the Moon's promptings in choices and decisions. There is a fear that your emotions may be battered by experiences, so at times there can be an avoidance of certain relationships or contentious issues, because your sense of well-being is intimately connected to the feeling tone of your emotional nature. You can be emotionally impulsive, especially if the balance between the Sun and Moon is swinging to favour the Moon, as there can be an alternating pattern where one planet is more dominant than the other, before the balance rectifies itself again.

It is perhaps fortunate that you are able to trust the unity of feelings and will, applying it instinctively and spontaneously in chosen directions and expecting that it will lead you towards right results. This enables you to concentrate your energy into narrow channels of attention, and through the act of focusing make it more powerful and penetrating.

Being self-contained, you may lack the ability of self-reflection and have no objective perspective and appraisal of your actions and temperament; you may rarely try self-analysis. Your ambitions are often extremely personal in nature, and may not be easily understood by others. What you may need to guard against is an overemphasis of either Sun or Moon tendencies, perhaps through an excessive preoccupation with career developments which can amplify the Sun principle in your nature, or even through an absorption in the traditional lunar preoccupations of domestic life. An equal expression and balance is required, or there is the possibility that health problems may occur if one planet becomes consistently dominant. Your emotional and physical well-being can be affected by unbalanced activity, especially if the career/mission consciousness rises to ascendancy. To remedy this, you may need to withdraw into periodic inner communication, possibly through quiet retreats and meditation to recharge your batteries. You should also ensure that your emotional nature is regularly vitalised by intimate human contact and not left to atrophy through a temporary ignoring of its needs. Maintaining a flowing balance helps to achieve your goals as well as keeping that temperament healthy.

MOON–SUN SEXTILE

This indicates that you should feel at peace with your temperament, easily accepting your nature and experiencing good relationships and a fluency of communication with others. Your personality has a consistency which enables you to feel relatively tranquil in the midst of life, and which isn't affected by inner storms. You are comfortable with your feelings, transmitting a sense of enjoyment and goodwill. If necessary, adaptations to your social environment are made by concession or compromise, if you believe that relationships will be improved; you see such actions as sensible and beneficial, and that compromise is a quality of a mature adult rather than an action which diminishes individual expression.

Your relationships are characterised by tolerance, consideration and understanding, and these will be appreciated by any co-workers, friends and acquaintances. Your attitude is essentially 'do to others as you would have them do to you', and you recognise the frailties of being human and usually resist the temptations to express condemnatory attitudes. You are optimistic and hold a belief that through mutual understanding most disagreements between people can be resolved, and that equality of status and opportunity is a social path to encourage. This ease in communicating with others often places you in positions of being a confidante, as you help through the act of listening, and your sense of self-confidence and balanced attitudes offer an objective perspective for others to gain a reflected clarity about their problems. They can sense your genuine concern, and sometimes this alone provides a healing quality for people in need, when that sense of isolation becomes too much and problems seem to be growing ever larger.

You often perceive life as a lesson, an ongoing school of experience, and you try to discern whatever messages are contained within your experiences. You feel that learning the lesson now means that you will not need to pass through that experience again, and that it will provide a platform for future progress and success. The past does not unduly attract, except as a source of understanding, and you ensure freedom to move onwards. You will recognise what is needed to feel emotionally satisfied, and what can be done to achieve your desires, trying to organise your life in such a way as to maximise enjoyment, which after all is a sensible approach to take.

There is probably creative talent within you, generating ideas and schemes that can be attempted, although you may need some self-discipline in order to fully express such gifts. However, your emotions are harmonised with your will, so provided that there is an emotional resonance to your actions, there should be minimum inner conflict interrupting the achieving of aims. As your inner intention and energy drive are united, there is likely to be a corresponding reaction from the outer world, and people will often be present to co-operate with you in fulfilling those ambitions. Sometimes, though, awareness may be needed that your strong will and assertive focus is not becoming too dominant and unconsciously having a negative impact on the sensitivity of others.

You should find that intimate relationships are enjoyable and successful, and that marriage and family life permit the easy expression of your emotions and keep you attuned to their activity and needs. Your earlier childhood and relationship with parents was probably quite good, and you try to duplicate this in your own family home by forming deep and loving bonds, and by communicating to any children the benefits of your own philosophy of life. Your general level of health and vitality should be good, although this may rely on the maintenance of emotional well-being.

As your inner life is relatively centred, and emotions are well integrated into your nature, there may be a lack of stimulus to growth and change. You may prefer to remain with those comfortable and successful behaviour patterns, rather than risk any degree of disruption for yourself or your family. You may lack an objective mirror to look into, and can be advised to evaluate things periodically, not to destroy them but from a perspective of 'How can I improve this level of satisfaction?' Without stimulating a phase of discontent, there are still areas of your life that probably could be improved quite easily, so why not try to do so? Stretching out may also serve as a prompt to encourage you to make full use of all those latent talents; you have a firm base to work from, so accepting growth challenges should not be too threatening, and should evoke the strengths of your solar nature even more effectively.

MOON–SUN TRINE

This indicates that there can be a positive harmony of conscious will and your instinctual, emotional, and habitual response patterns to life; fewer inner conflicts between your feeling reactions and the application of your purpose should occur. You are likely to feel self-confident and optimistic about fulfilling your potential, aims and ambitions, and you may discover that doors open for you at the right times, or people offer support and help which enable you to move forward; luck may be a factor in your life.

Your early life experiences, parental relationships and childhood social conditioning are likely to have been generally favourable, and little negativity has made any deleterious mark on your development. There may be benefits from hereditary influences, possibly in natural talents and gifts, and some of your habitual pattern tendencies may be family traits, although the likelihood is that they are essentially positive and constructive. In your adult life, you will try to maintain good family relationships, both with your parents and with any family that you are responsible for creating. You tend to relate well with young children, who enjoy your sincere concern, care, understanding and attention.

You ensure that you learn from all experiences so that lessons do not need to be painfully repeated. One area where extra prompting may be needed is in application. As your basic temperament is relaxed and laid-back, generating sufficient momentum towards achieving aims can sometimes seem to be too much hard work to bother. You may be unwilling to stretch and really challenge yourself to develop, and thus may fail to realise the depth of latent potential that you actually possess. In fact, you should have considerable natural talents waiting to be exploited, and you should become alert to any opportunities that offer the prospect of growth and unfoldment, so that your creative drives and ability to unite feelings and will are successfully released in your environment.

Self-assertion may need a concentrated focus for you to progress in a career; although the potential is there for good advancement to be made, there may be a question mark against your level of commitment and desire actually to enter senior positions. Your sensitive good nature may be less of an asset in such positions, however, where harsh impersonal decisions may be required for business viability. Yet you could effectively serve in an authoritative role, especially in spheres of interpersonal contact and communication, where your assets of friendliness, sincerity, persuasiveness and understanding people's motivations can make you a very good mediator between levels of employees.

Feeling right with yourself is important, and you recognise that is a key to good personal health and enjoyment of life. The free-flowing nature of this Sun–Moon contact helps you to appreciate your strong physical vitality, stamina and ability to recover easily from any temporary illness.

In social situations, you tend to act as a 'bridge' between people, being able to understand and empathise with different types, and through that reconciling aspect of your nature can help people to join together more easily. You can be sexually attractive, and this can lead you into successful relationship experiences. The main issue is to use this aspect's positive and constructive nature as fully as possible, and not just allow that stable, tranquil and contented nature to cast a soporific spell over you. You need to awaken your solar nature and qualities, in addition to expressing your lunar qualities comfortably, because that will become your path of self development.

MOON–SUN SQUARE

This suggests the existence of considerable inner stress and tension within the personality, where solar will is in conflict with deep rooted feelings, emotions and instincts, and where the conscious and evolutionary self may be trying to move in a direction which is contrary to certain habit patterns, especially those connected with security and protection of self boundaries.

The ongoing struggle is in resolving contradictory inner messages, a psychological tendency which may have its roots deep within childhood perceptions of the parental relationship and your sense of emotional contact with your parents. As the Moon signifies the mother, and the Sun the father in this context, there is the implication that there was a crucial problem inherent in that parental relationship, perhaps incompatibility on some vital level, or a lack of communication which may have led to a marriage breakdown in some respect. This may not have been evident on the surface of that relationship, but existed as an underlying current within the domestic psychic atmosphere which you registered. There may have been a partial identification with one parent to the exclusion of the other, perhaps because one parent had little time to spend with you. Somehow the inner dynamics have been distorted, resulting in personal frustration and difficulties in joining will and feelings in co-operation together.

Unless steps are taken to achieve individual integration, you are liable to suffer from emotional insecurity founded on a resistance to fully accepting the nature of your habitual feeling responses. A probable action that you take is inner denial and repression, and this will have eventual consequences of intensifying those inner tensions and possible personality splits. Yet because these powerful emotions seem to burn within you, you try to control their release through expressing them in daily life, and because of the pressures that can accumulate you may display argumentative, provocative and belligerent tendencies in your relationships at times.

The danger is falling victim to your own powerful desire nature, and being perpetually frustrated through aiming high and losing an appreciation of what exists in the present. There can be a restless, searching quality to this aspect which results from the need to resolve deep inner conflicts; the problem is finding the way to achieve those desires. This need stimulates inner questioning, especially related to 'What's it all about?' and 'What is the meaning of life?' These become promptings from your inner Sun, encouraging you to start on your heroic quest to discover the solar centre and the spiritual dimension of life.

Yet you can often act as your own worst enemy, reacting in ways that diminish any likelihood of success. You may fail to see how you can utilise existing resources to deepen life enjoyment or reach aims; you may refuse to make necessary compromises; you may consciously devalue your potential and abilities, eroding away self-confidence; you may clash with others who could have been supportive to your efforts. These unconscious patterns of unresolved frustrations interfere between your conscious will and deeper needs, tending to negate satisfaction for either. Sometimes, as a result of this inner stress, all you feel like doing is being very destructive, liberating the repressed energies by either verbal or physical expressions of bad temper.

The problem facing you is the movement from 'here to there'. That abyss stares you in the face and will not go away, and apparently, try as you might, you still cannot cross over to the promised land. Being 'here' feels wrong, and you believe that you should be 'there' but how can it be achieved? The only way to gain your aims is through a radical transformation, so that the 'old you' remains on this side, and the 'new you' appears there to claim your ambition. This is the challenge confronting the hero at every stage of his quest, and each step forward on his path represents difficulties overcome on the journey towards the magnetic light that he senses and follows.

How may this be done? The honest answer has to be 'with difficulty'and with much hard work. Your promised land will not be gained without great perseverance and struggle, proving your capabilities, transcending any obstacles on the way and never accepting defeat. You may need to pursue additional training or study in order to qualify for a specialist skill, or to help unfold latent qualities and talents. You may need to apply self-discipline to maintain your efforts, and to display your intention to work until success happens.

Relationships may need improving through compromise to avoid unnecessary conflicts resulting from your frustrations. Lessons need to be learned from previous experiences, and applied in daily living. Clarity may be required between what you desire and what you are prepared to do to achieve it, and trying to ensure that your aims will actually be emotionally satisfying when achieved. Integration between your conscious will and those underlying emotions is vitally necessary, and the best way for this is to allow the emotions to rise to the surface of your mind, so that you can look at their nature and develop an understanding of their needs, and then attempt to fuse will and emotions via the medium of the intellectual mind, through imposing a more powerful light upon that emotional sea. Investing great effort should result in steps towards realising those desires. It is not an easy path, although viewing that inner stress as motivation is at least a positive perception of what personal frustration can provide as a transformative spur.

Otherwise, what options are left to you? Living with personal disharmony; experiencing lack of success and frustration of aims;

a restriction of personal potential; problems spilling over into your domestic life, career and social relationships; dissatisfaction in intimate affairs with the opposite sex; domestic responsibilities and duties limiting your freedom to reach your ambitions, and possible ill health (digestive problems) stimulated by emotional and psychosomatic tensions.

If you take the challenge to resolve the conflicts and contradictions of this square, then finding constructive outlets for your powerful energies may help to form your new path. Learning how to listen to those agitating feelings and managing to integrate them into your life instead of ignoring them, will help to restore a sense of balance and well-being.

Moon–Sun Opposition

This indicates that there are likely to be two main challenging areas in your life. One involves your relationship with social and intimate partnerships, and your ability to adjust to the demands of the external world; and the second is concerned with inner tensions associated with conflict and contradiction between your conscious egoic will and your unconscious mind, feelings and emotions. Studying the nature of the specific houses of this planetary opposition can offer valuable indications as to the spheres of life that are likely to be especially influenced.

You will probably feel internal division, with opposing messages and impulses rising from the differing Sun and Moon tendencies, and this creates stress and confusion regarding which inner voice you should follow. What may be experienced is one voice encouraging you to follow an adult path of career, vocation and progress (the Sun), and another more instinctual voice (the Moon) trying to make you pay more attention to your emotional needs for personal nourishment. Pulled in two directions, looking towards those individual future aims and desires, while also turning towards the secure and familiar past, you become unsure of what to do. The Moon's instinctive responses may reject the egoic ambitions of the Sun, and the Sun refuses to allow time and attention to satisfy the Moon's need for emotional nourishment as this does not conform to an adult self-image of independent maturity.

One consequence of this inner polarisation is a diminution of vitality and energy, which are burnt away by the friction caused by tension and internal fighting over supremacy. Diminishing both the expression of Sun and Moon reduces your opportunities for satisfaction in either sphere of life, ambitions may fail to be realised, and relationships fail to fulfil your emotional needs. Over time, there develops a pattern of oscillation as your inner balance between Sun and Moon tilts to favour either one or the other; if the balance is regularly in favour of one planet, then the qualities of the other planet are repressed into the unconscious mind. The tendency may be to repress the deeper energies of the Moon back into the unconscious due to their natural affinity there, but in elevating and listening only to the Sun many personal emotional needs are denied, and this will eventually stimulate later problems of integration and will burst through under pressure in later love relationships.

In opposition aspects, often part of the planetary polarity which is less expressed and integrated is projected externally on to the world and people, and it is likely that the existence of your inner conflict will be unconsciously transmitted to others, who then serve to mirror back your unintegrated aspect. Stress in the psyche is reflected by relationship difficulties, and this is likely to be an ongoing challenge for you to resolve, and may spill over into domestic, financial, romantic and marital situations. Continual tension may create ill health and deplete your vitality, and one sign of this may be experiences of restlessness, nervous agitation and psychosomatic illness. Changes of moods and emotional responses may occur, ranging from an exhilaration and sense of purpose, meaning and self-confidence to deep depressions, feelings of being unloved and loss of individual stability. These may be triggered by movement within your inner polarity of Sun–Moon, when the balance of energy flows erratically.

This unstable energy flow can be noted in times when you commence a new project or change direction with great enthusiasm and will, and then suddenly everything appears to be a waste of time and a mistake as your energy level wanes. Scattered and uncompleted schemes, projects and ideas may litter your life. Relationships too could follow a similar pattern, starting as 'the love of your life' and then collapsing into an unsatisfactory withdrawal as feelings change and disillusionment sets in.

Underlying your relationships lie those deep Moon needs and desires; fulfilling these are the root of relationship difficulties. You tend to hold an image of a loving partner being able to satisfy all your needs, even needs that you often deny or choose not to even acknowledge to your self, someone in whom you can almost become lost and rely on totally. These are probably reflections of previous childhood patterns where your parents proved unable to fully satisfy your childhood needs; now you search for another adult to do so. For you, a partner has to be a lover, friend and companion, sustaining you, healing your conflicts, tending to your needs, and offering clear directions in life. There are dependency needs entangled in this pattern, needs of belonging which temporary short-lived affairs will fail to satisfy. You hope to find someone who either takes charge of things, or helps you to develop your own potential; somehow you feel inadequate to do this on your own.

Your difficulty lies in a tendency to project your inner stresses on to your close relationships, with phases of dissention, confrontation and argument occurring as a means of releasing energies. Compromise may need more development, and learning how to give rather than just take is essential. Balance and moderation is one approach to consider, instead of reacting to contradictory feelings and responding only to the temporary dominating voice. Take time to determine what are your most consistent aims in life, make a realistic appraisal of your qualities, talents and potentials, and try to discover how the voices of Sun and Moon can be united and integrated into a common message to follow. Break out of that subjective prison, unfold a sense of objectivity, and refuse to blame the environment or people for the obstacles that stand in the way of your progress.

While part of this personality pattern may have developed during childhood, with you perceiving your parents as offering you two sets of opposing messages, or perhaps losing one of them due to divorce or death, it is your adult responsibility to transcend this difficulty rather than perpetuate it again. Integrating the principles of Sun and Moon in your psyche may not be easy, and a careful balance of listening and honouring both voices needs to be achieved, but discovering a way to do this may be essential to your well-being, emerging after a period of losing life meaning and purpose. A change in consciousness and integration of those deeper and ignored Moon needs can be achieved, if you generate the will to do so. Pursuing humanistic self-therapy techniques designed to liberate repressed feelings and individual desires/needs may be appropriate at such a stage, and looking towards psychosynthesis, gestalt, encounter and co-counselling groups may be beneficial. These can all help to stimulate the integrative quality of both lunar and solar centres, leading to inner balance and freedom of expression.

MERCURY–SUN CONJUNCTION

Only the conjunction and semi-sextile aspects are astronomically possible between the Sun and Mercury, as the maximum distance between them is 28 degrees.

Your self-image and identity will be closely connected to your mental expression and activity, and it is likely that you will be an effective and articulate communicator, enjoying impressing others by your intelligence and verbal acuity. Yet there may be 'blind spots' in your relationships, or in your ability for self-reflection, and becoming aware of such tendencies may prove to be beneficial.

Being so closely identified with your thoughts, beliefs, attitudes, values and opinions, you often fail to listen properly to differing views or treat them with due respect and consideration. This is because any challenge to your perceptions is equated with a challenge to yourself, and as you assume a more egocentric stance this is rarely welcomed. While you enjoy vigorously expressing your thoughts, you also feel it necessary to be dominant in company and through sheer force of communication may attempt to pressurise others into agreeing with you. Some may react against your style, especially if you are obviously disregarding alternative points of view. Your tendency to be overly preoccupied with your thoughts and personal concerns can restrict real communication, and others may gain the impression that their concerns are too easily dismissed or that your apparent interest in them is not genuine.

Due to a mental agility and verbal skills, you should be able to project yourself well within company or employment situations, and may rise to senior positions. You enjoy such roles as they enhance your self-image, supporting your belief in the correctness of your thoughts, which then adds extra force to them in expression. But, like everyone else, you are not right all of the time, and your instructions may be challenged. You find it hard to admit mistakes, as this is felt as a 'loss of face', and you may attempt to impose ideas and decisions by applying the power of your position or will, overriding any objections. Time will tell whether this is a wise course of action.

You have a quickness of thought which may not always work to your advantage, as you prefer to be active as soon as possible, and in some cases, you may be failing to evaluate relevant information or options sufficiently to make sensible decisions. Allowing that charged nervous energy to dominate will also increase your tendency for making unwise choices, and you may need to modify that compulsive activity from sending you along futile paths.

The actual quality of your thought processes may be variable too, depending on the distance Mercury is away from the Sun. If the conjunction orb is a maximum of 7 degrees, the most favourable is an exact conjunction where Mercury and Sun are aligned and in vibrational harmony, as this will improve the flow of mental communication and intellectual perception. If the orb is between 4 and 8 degrees, then the vibrational harmony may become periodically disjointed, erratic and prone to overloaded mental activity and nervous activity, which can result in distorted self-perception and illusions. Another tendency of this conjunction is the close fusion of the world view of the Sun sign and mental attitudes of Mercury being so similar that they form a filter over life experiences and understanding, conveying similar messages which exclude alternative ways of perceiving life. This creates a lack of sympathetic understanding and comprehension, and it could be more beneficial for Sun and Mercury to be in different signs, so that a greater breadth of vision is possible.

Once you ensure that you note the reactions of others to your style of expression, modifying this accordingly, or realise that you lack objectivity concerning your nature and then attempt to gain a clearer self-perception, you should be able to make more positive use of the abilities implied by this conjunction. These include the talent of generating 'ideas', which can be used by others more adept at developing and anchoring them in their right placing. You are excited by ideas, and can communicate this enthusiasm to others, stimulating their minds to wake to the possibilities that you are suggesting. Your ideas can be creative and inspired, and you may be able to use this talent in the field of education, perhaps as a lecturer or writer, although your verbal skills may be more developed.

In business, you may be valued for your contributions to 'brainstorming' sessions and new company directions, for sparking off new thoughts in others and sowing seeds that colleagues will take away for planting. Sometimes, though, you may meet resistance from those who believe that your ideas have not been thought through fully, or whose personal feelings have been dismissed by you in the past. The dimension of human relations is one that you should never ignore.

VENUS–SUN CONJUNCTION

Only the conjunction and semi-square aspects are astronomically possible between the Sun and Venus, as the maximum distance between these planets is 48 degrees.

This conveys an optimistic and cheerful spirit, where you will greatly enjoy social company and the pleasures of life, so that aesthetic and hedonistic activities are indulged to stimulate your sensual nature. Love and social relationships are highlighted, and you will be attracted to participate in the social whirl, circulating around your collection of friends, family and acquaintances.

You feel it important to be liked by others, and this need may make you act in certain ways which gain the approval of people, so care may be required to ensure that you do not overly compromise your own feelings and thoughts in order to remain socially acceptable. There can be a dramatic quality to your style of self-presentation, perhaps emerging out of an artistic and creative sensitivity, and this will be employed to gain the attention of people; you prefer to leave your mark and need to feel recognised.

While some may see you in a superficial light, this is not how you desire to be socially acknowledged. The recognition you are looking for is of your whole personality, your talents and qualities, and as you grow older you will prefer to enjoy the company of those who can appreciate you more fully. This may be through mutual interests in art, culture or the beauty of nature, because lying beneath any socialite veneer is your real appreciation of the harmony of life and nature which evokes that romantic and poetic spirit that inspires your perception of life and infuses a hidden desire for inner peace and integration. You enjoy quality in life, and will try to create a pleasing home environment which allows relaxation into domestic comforts and pleasures.

You will attract others to your potent magnetic personality, and you are likely to experience a variety of relationships as a consequence of your romantic attitudes. You open easily to demonstrations of love and affection, and your heart can quickly melt. As a lover of life, a certain intensity will be present, as will the tides of love's joys and pains, but never attempt to turn off your developed love nature, or you may find that life rapidly loses its lustre and become grey, mundane and lifeless. Part of your role is to spread life-appreciation, enlivening others so that they too can become sincere lovers of life, and isn't that a task well worth pursuing?

Some may find you 'too alive' or narcissistic, so you may need to be aware of others' reactions, and if they are correct in their evaluation of your self-centredness then some modification may be advised, so that you equally acknowledge their natures, qualities and personalities too. In conversations, the art of listening is as important as the art of communication, and your enthusiasms may require occasional toning down.

You can bring positive benefits to those who become intimately close, through sharing your vitality, love and affections, and even if your relationships do not persist, you hope that those involved with you do not regret the time that has been shared. Changes will come through the expression of your heart and life enjoyment, and these may reshape your conscious identity and self-image over time, so that more depth and insight begins to be unfolded. Others may turn to you for support and advice, wanting your flame to relight their own. Your path of solar development is through the unifying love energies of Venus, so let these radiate outwards into the world, touching and igniting the hearts of others.

MARS–SUN CONJUNCTION

This indicates the presence of an energy that is 'masculine' in essence, being highly vitalised, vigorous, forceful and assertive. The application and exploitation of your powerful will becomes a major impulse that demands expression, often resulting in a more self-centred level of preoccupation, focused on satisfying your desires and ambitions.

You may have an aggressive, combative temperament, which can respond quickly to any hint of a threat or potentially competitive situations, seeing these as an opportunity to display your force and innate abilities and talents. You will feel a need to prove yourself to the world through achieving, or at least rise to a higher social profile than the majority. You may tend to assume attitudes of superiority, which is often derived from a sense of self-confidence, and inwardly you hold a self-image as a leader in some capacity. An urge to battle lies near the surface of your personality, and you can approach life as if it is a challenge, almost provoking encounters by 'throwing down the gauntlet' as a testing of your strength and power.

To some, you may seem overly assertive, and your presence may threaten them by its forceful vibration. You may acquire several adversaries in the course of your journey through life, especially as you are liable to be insensitive to others' feelings. This may occur particularly within your employment or business life, where you are likely to contact other powerful individuals. You intensely enjoy applying your will-power, and may need to pay extra attention to your relationship manner and style of expression, as this could become a source of contention and downfall if it is misapplied. A liability to anger quickly may need some control too, or words spoken in haste may ruin relationships or friendships.

You react against limitations and restrictions, and find adherence to the status quo or repetitive routines anathema to your volatile spirit. You love action, and the adrenaline rush of physical or dangerous sports and activities is highly appealing. Your enthusiasms can be spontaneous and impulsive, and you prefer to leave space in your lifestyle for sudden decisions and changes of direction which can renew vitality and add a touch of freshness when life becomes jaded and familiar. You may be attracted to share this love of life and excess energy with others, stimulating them to break free of their self-imposed ruts and shake off their apathy. Some may not appreciate your endeavours though, and you may need to recognise when your efforts will fall on stony ground.

There is an opinionated streak in your character that can take offence if anyone challenges your attitudes, values, thoughts or beliefs, and you take this as a personal attack, rather than a sharing of differing points of view. You can adopt an attitude of 'I'm right, and you're wrong' in such encounters, and refuse to consider alternative perceptions; this can be a restriction of your openness to life's many wonders and infinite variety of perceptions.

In relationships, you do not easily compromise, as you tend to be self-centred and concerned about reaching for your desires; this could become a problem unless it is carefully modified, or you have an extremely passive and supportive partner. A strong sexual drive and inflamed passions are likely factors in your relationships, and you may be especially attracted to sudden love affairs, particularly if that theme of 'conquest' is paramount in your nature.

While you are likely to possess considerable creative abilities, you may have difficulties in focusing these constructively and consistently, and despite your high level of activity you may waste energy that could be more positively applied. Part of this is due to an impulsiveness that prefers action to forethought and planning, and this tendency may need tempering by better management of your resources and less haste in charging towards your objectives. Listen to the advice of others, or take professional suggestions; you may not always know best.

Your focus is power through action, and the main areas that this can be released through are the conjunction house, and the houses ruled by both Sun and Mars in your chart. Look at these, as they may offer additional opportunities for a successful use of your talents and energies, especially when you begin to handle them with greater self understanding.

MARS–SUN SEXTILE

The sextile can offer considerable energy that can be best applied through your mind and intellect, and this level may become the source of your life direction from which your main achievements may be derived.

You should have a gift for creative thinking which can be turned into building positive and constructive enterprises, and it is through developing these that your special talents will be displayed. Following your interests could open this dimension of your nature, creating channels to express your creative spirit. This creativity may flow through the houses and signs which are occupied and ruled by the Sun and Mars, and if your interests coincide with the associations of such planetary placings, then take a deeper look at their potential for exploitation. Additional opportunities may occur when transit or progression movements contact the natal sextile, restimulating the flow of inspired ideas.

The sextile energy is more balanced and capable of easier assimilation than the abrasive conjunction vibration, and while you will be a forceful personality with a powerful will, this is more controlled and less socially assertive. Your awareness of relationships is developed, and so you do not seem threatening or overly competitive to others. Your personality can be confident, secure and relatively stable, and others may acknowledge your integrity and interpersonal communication skills by turning to you for supportive aid. You will tend to express your views firmly enough, but are always willing to listen to what others are saying or suggesting, recognising that their contributions can be as useful as your own; you do not believe that you have a monopoly on being right.

You have an ability to initiate new projects and schemes, and can be an effective leader or co-ordinator capable of managing tasks requiring group co-operation. You will usually plan actions and make decisions carefully, resisting any impulse to launch into action until you feel totally satisfied about the feasibility of an enterprise. You recognise that you can make mistakes, and so try to minimise them.

Social interests are active in you, and following current world affairs will be a natural study area to pursue. The whole field of research, study and accumulation of information and knowledge will attract your curious mind, providing a constant source of mental stimulation and intelligent speculation. You may prefer a variety of 'different inputs' into your mental database, and it is likely that you will remain a 'student' all of your life, whether this is through improving skills and knowledge within formal educational courses or following your own independent research interests. These can link with areas of opportunity, especially within the spheres of writing, journalism, teaching, media and consultancy. You may be drawn towards working with the minds of the young, inspiring the future generation, or developing future directions for the benefit of the world, as you attempt to express social responsibility.

You have a highly developed sense of justice and fairness, and often view the world through this lens, possibly becoming involved in issues of civil rights and social matters. Even though you may be intellectually biased, you have the perception that everyone has their own gifts and talents, even if they are different to yours, and that all can contribute something valuable to the well-being of society.

In relationships, you prefer intelligent and cultured companions, those who acknowledge a sensitivity to life and appreciate its beauty. Partners could possess either a developed intellect or artistic awareness, and you will enjoy communicating on such topics. In love, you expect a high quality of partner, one who can match you on all levels, as well as being suitable for your energised physical nature. You will be careful making partnership choices, and finding a good relationship could be a key to discovering a deeper and more fulfilling life direction.

MARS–SUN TRINE

The trine enables you to turn theory into practical application, and this reconciling quality could become a source of your life direction, as your ability to apply your energy positively can generate ways to resolve problem situations. This may be one approach that utilises your energy in a creative and beneficial manner, and which poses challenges that you intend to overcome.

You will be self-confident and believe in your own abilities, setting goals and pursuing ambitions, emerging from your unique aims directed towards creating a suitable lifestyle, which may not always correspond to traditional paths and signs of success. You do not appreciate a volatile living or working environment, preferring a more tranquil atmosphere where you are free to follow your interests. While you enjoy new challenges, the cut and thrust of competition seems less appealing, and you see little value in exalting yourself if it requires another's detrimental fall.

Fairness, integrity and honesty are qualities that you respect and expect in your dealings with others, and ethical or moral considerations are taken into account in your life. These form your code of relationships, and you try to stay as true to these as possible, even if at times this may require you to forego some success or progress, as you are not usually willing to compromise for the sake of any advancement. You can adopt an individual chivalry and style of conduct. While you have leadership ability, you try to ensure that you deal correctly with others from any position of responsibility, and are willing to help others on their way, provided they do not attempt less scrupulous tactics to progress.

Organisational and managerial qualities are likely to be present, and you can take the strain of highly demanding tasks, proving to be a reliable, efficient and conscientious worker who can purposefully carry out and design successful plans of action.

Spheres that may attract include law, business management, education, media, personal creativity and physical endeavours. Opportunities may steer you towards deeper interpersonal contacts, and working in areas of counselling and guidance may be highlighted. One asset that you may possess for this work is a genuine tolerance for others, allowing each to hold their unique view of life, and having respect for their free nature. Many inwardly condemn people for failing to be like themselves, taking an attitude that everyone should conform to a picture that they have developed. Fortunately, the life process disagrees with that attitude, and displays an incredible abundance of variety.

You tend to form a realistic perception of life, so that your expectations are not too excessive and unreal, and you appreciate the gains that you do make through expressing your creative talents and powerful energies. A need for disciplined focus may be required at times, as you may be faced with various options and lack a clarity of purpose which diffuses your will power. Be wary against occasional acts of impulse; they may not always work to your advantage, and a careful and steady progression can prove more beneficial. Working in harmony with this trine energy can serve to open doors throughout your life; be alert to recognise when opportunities are being presented, so that you can take full advantage of the gifts of life.

MARS–SUN SQUARE

You may be confronted with frustrations and a lack of satisfaction with this aspect, partly as a consequence of your own attitudes and style of expression which often spoil your chances for success and fulfilment. You can feel a restless energy seeking release, and this inner agitation linked to strong desires can lead to an uneven and eventful life, resulting from the effects of impulsive and sometimes ill-considered actions. You easily become impatient, especially when results are slow in coming, feeling anger and frustration; your natural reaction then is to apply more force and will-power to attain your aims, but this does not necessarily create the effects you want. By tending to act without prior thought, you often sow the seeds of your future failures, undermining what might have been perfectly reasonable plans if they had been more carefully thought out.

You are a self-seeking individual, looking to impose your presence on society and make a mark on the world. Striving to prove your worth, you may find that by modifying your approach greater success occurs. You can have plenty of energy and enthusiasm, yet one problem can lie in your ability to direct and focus these along positive and constructive channels. It may be that certain lessons require learning before your path forward opens. More forethought and planning would be helpful, minimising wastage of energy and restrictive directions, enabling you to plan ahead and form contingency routes to surmount any predictable obstacles. Patience is necessary, so that temporary setbacks do not frustrate too much, and you are able to rely on ingenuity and faith in your abilities to persevere. Being able to maintain your directional focus is also important, as there is a tendency to lose confidence and change direction when you hit obstacles and disappointing results.

Changing your relationships may also be a key which benefits you, especially in consciously modifying any tendencies towards arguing, demanding attention, egocentricity and being temperamental. While you can be good company, your lack of tact and diplomacy is sometimes striking; ill-considered impulsive comments may not be appreciated nor any attempts to hijack conversations so that they focus just on you and your interests. You can react against any opposing points of view, often seeing them as a personal attack, rather than carefully listening to see if they offer new perspectives which can enrich your perception and understanding of life or a specific topic.

Sexuality will be a major focus of expression, and your passions will run strongly with this aspect, although there may also be frustrations and constraints facing you. These could range from a lack of a partner, to desiring someone who is unobtainable, to falling out of love with a partner. An ideal lover is one who suits your needs on every level, and careful choice needs to be taken in deciding to settle down with anyone, or else you may discover that freedom has been restricted through an impulsive action. Right choices depend on self-knowledge; deepening self-understanding will reveal the type of partner who can complement you. Be wary of allowing a contentious nature to interfere with your intimate relationships, or else they could degenerate into an emotional battlefield. If your sexual energies remain high, and there is little opportunity for a healthy release, then to avoid becoming increasingly irritable and unstable, a redirection into creative channels may be recommended. Allowing sexual preoccupations to become dominant in the personality is also unwise and rebalancing may be necessary for adjustment.

With several personality modifications, your future can look more promising, and you may direct energies into the spheres of writing, law, medicine, teaching, or military-type careers which could suit your temperament, although limitations on freedom may also occur. Freedom is important to you, so you may oppose any demands for commitment made of you, through work or partnership, and until that issue is resolved, you may feel unable to take full advantage of presented opportunities. If you are confronted with situations which may compromise your freedom, then you react by being less decisive, as you hate feeling imprisoned in any way. Finding employment that allows you scope for movement and independence, and a partner that recognises this need may be a step in the right direction. Your abilities are present, but may require further unlocking to become manifest, but once they begin to flow can be highly transformative.

Mars–Sun Opposition

You probably have a view that perceives life as a challenge, a fight between yourself and the world for supremacy, and you adopt this combative and assertive stance in an attempt to prove your self-worth. Underlying this attitude is a clashing of inner energies, which are projected out as shadow-adversaries in the external world, so that arguments, dissention and conflict almost seem to follow in your footsteps. There is little tranquillity in your world; it becomes more of a battlefield where you believe you can 'win your spurs' proving your capabilities. You are fired by the competitive spirit, intending to win and be number one, although the quality of your aggressive vibration tends to attract similar people into your life, and this can result in power struggles in working or domestic environments. Applying extra force may leave you in a position of superiority, yet can also increase the number of adversaries that you leave in your wake; your genuine friendships can be few if you act in this manner.

You have a powerful desire nature, and you easily become fixated on attaining these desires, whether they are lovers, positions of executive status, or whatever, even if your energies are focused only temporarily in such specific directions. These desires can reflect the themes of the houses and signs of Mars and the Sun, and often contain the issues that you feel most combative about. There can be an aura of 'danger' surrounding you, possibly with a sexual magnetism and aggressive power that some can find extremely attractive, although this energy can overflow through displays of irascible temper and potential violence if uncontrolled. You are very physically responsive, and will have a developed visual and sensual appreciation of life. You may have to ensure that your desires do not become compulsive or obsessive in nature.

In relationships, you may lack sensitivity to others' feelings and needs, and may need to transform expectations of a partner so that they conform more closely to a realistic appreciation, rather than providing fuel for later disillusionment. A wise choice of partner is required, otherwise your domestic life could become volatile and traumatic; a partner who evokes your higher nature and qualities is probably more ideal than one who just stimulates your passionate and vigorous nature. Finding a suitable companion, who is strong enough not to allow you to dominate, would probably help in modifying your attitude towards life. A danger can lie in a tendency to make impulsive decisions or actions, and then regret them later.

It may be that experience eventually influences you to make changes in your style of expression, and this may not occur until later in life, perhaps after the age of thirty and through developing maturity. Hopefully, there will come a point when you lessen that driving feeling of insecurity and lack of worth, so that you can recognise your real value and potential. Once that self-imposed pressure to challenge and compete has diminished, and acknowledgement of your performance has been achieved, then new life directions may open. When this occurs, take the opportunity to dismantle your combative attitudes, by broadening your world view beyond those limiting tendencies to perceive life in stark black-and-white distinctions. This could develop to include involvements with social causes and pressure groups, where your partisan approach and abundant energies could be put to positive use, providing that you maintain a balanced perspective on your beliefs and attitudes, and do not attempt a forceful proselytising or fanatical expression.

JUPITER–SUN CONJUNCTION

You will be naturally optimistic, enthusiastic and eager to explore the potential of life, looking to exploit your solar power and Jupiterian expansive tendency to enable you to taste life as deeply as possible. An image that fits this aspect is that of the *seeker*, believing that you are following a secret path towards a future destiny, reacting against and resisting any restrictive limitations that may occur as obstacles to your progress.

This can, however, be an ambivalent tendency. You may be correct in your intuition, discerning the signposts of your path; yet equally, this could become a path of evasion if you believe that it offers a justification for self-centred choices, or you assert personal freedom to the point where you wander through life with no sense of a clear direction.

One of your main assets is an innate self-confidence which generates a powerful faith in your ability to attain aims successfully. Through positive thinking you can attract 'good fortune' into your life, naturally expecting that all will work to your benefit. Usually, your positive attitudes will prove effective, yet there will be occasions when over-optimistic tendencies may stretch your actual capabilities too far, and you experience temporary setbacks to your plans. But even then, due to openness to new opportunities and directions, you'll succeed in discovering new roads to travel.

You may need to make more efficient use of your personal talents and resources, perhaps through greater self-discipline and focusing on your intentions. Forethought and planning may be skills which require additional development, and which can help to maximise future success. You will want to use your full potential, and searching for ways to do this may make you restless and unable to settle for very long. It is the expansionary quality of Jupiter that causes this agitation, and by recognising this activity you should ensure that routine work or lifestyles do not restrict or trap you, or else its intended positive contribution to your life could initially result in more disruptive effects.

Areas that may attract your interest include education, medicine, law, travel, philosophy, religion, social and humanitarian influence. You look for progress and scope for expansion wherever you become involved, especially when your contribution can be beneficial for others' welfare. There is the potential of merging your talents and interests with areas of social concern, so that your energy flows into the resolution of social issues, or you may become a spokesperson or representative of group ideals and social aims. Work involving the initial impulse for transformative social projects may particularly suit you, and offer ample scope for ongoing development. Linking your path with social needs could be an appropriate action and wise choice.

You enjoy expressing personal creativity and imagination, feeling that energy flowing into new forms and channels, sparking off new thoughts, directions and perceptions. Discovering a path which evokes self-motivation is very important, enabling that enthusiastic energy to be released. You like to be well-informed, and will be aware of most current social trends and world news.

Ongoing learning is especially enjoyed, as it provides a source for the renewal of interest in life and opens up new areas of fascination and experience. It is a fullness of life that you seek, a real enjoyment of yourself and the world, and this can lead you to be attracted towards more hedonistic explorations. Yet underlying this is a need to create your own unique perception, philosophy and worldview, which is a reflection of a spiritual need to discover your own meaning and purpose of life.

Your spiritual interests do not really fit within orthodox teachings and religious organisations, and mainly derive from the sense of inner guidance and trust in the beneficence of life. You will adopt a position of tolerance and freedom, especially valuing the unity of all life and the concept of universal human fellowship, so civil-rights issues may interest you, or ecological concerns.

In relationships, you prefer partners who are fundamentally in tune with your perception of life, fellow enthusiasts and positive thinkers who appreciate the subtler qualities of people and experiences, rather than being preoccupied with materialistic matters and the accumulation of money and social power. You will expect much from a partner, and can inadvertently place pressures on others to satisfy your needs, rather than being equally aware of their own feelings and desires. More awareness may be needed in intimate relationships. For example you may need to curb your tendency to over-indulge in pleasurable activities. Otherwise you may create imbalances in yourself that need adjustment through greater health care. Containing that restless spirit may also be necessary at times, and you may need to realise that if you always focus on the horizon then you can lose sight of what is around you, and so diminish your appreciation of what is currently present in your life.

JUPITER–SUN SEXTILE

You should find that you are able to keep focused on your aims and ambitions, and linking these with your innate optimism and self-confidence should ensure success. You may be especially attracted towards opportunities associated with the media and communication, or in the generation of ideas for schemes and projects which improve the quality of life in society.

You feel the need to develop a suitable personal lifestyle in which there are opportunities for freedom, growth, and creative development, enabling you to diminish those less enjoyable aspects of life, consciously replacing them by activities that evoke your strengths and talents. Seeking wealth may not engage your wholehearted participation, but the abundance and prosperity of a suitable lifestyle will attract your creative endeavours. This could be through creating a more simplified, natural lifestyle, provided it fulfils your need for enjoyment.

You may find many standard forms of employment restrictive, as they often prove to be inimical to creativity and the application of intelligence, through being repetitive and limiting the exploitation of natural talents and personal qualities. You may need to look for new employment avenues, or move into your self-directed path for real satisfaction and greater opportunities.

Your communicative skills could be usefully employed, and this opens areas of education, teaching, public relations, consultancy, law, media and theatre work for possible consideration. As your focus is probably on your mental level engaged in intellectual activity, you can easily manage to study and learn, and over time this increases your inner storehouse of knowledge and information, giving you a 'well-stocked' mind. Applying this can create opportunities for your persuasive skills, convincing arguments and displays of logic; associating these with a taste for dramatic expression could turn you into a 'character' capable of personality projection through media channels. Verbal articulacy is a valuable skill to possess, and if you feel comfortable with this skill, then look for suitable opportunities for expression.

You feel an inner resonance with the problems and pain of social issues, both nationally and globally, and your temperament is naturally sympathetic and caring. You prefer to act and live in ways which are beneficial to everyone, and underlying this is a philosophical or religious nature which forms your own worldview. While you may be directed towards attaining your personal aims, you do not choose to achieve by taking advantage of others, and your tendency is to look for the path by which constructive co-operation can be achieved to resolve difficulties, rather than attempt to manipulate for your own gains. This quality could offer paths of conflict resolution, where by applying your creative thinking abilities, differences can be healed through mutual contact and adjustments.

Integrity and ethical issues may become important, and you will carefully choose your intimate partners and friends according to certain guidelines and methods of evaluation. Acquaintances will be many, but the select circle will be more exclusively chosen, and will be composed of similarly confident and self-actualising individuals. Doors open for you, and you may feel that your life is guided and protected by an invisible guardian angel, helping you to take the opportunities that enter your life. Travel may become important too, or contact with other nationalities, as you open to the richness of the world and its varying rainbow colours of different cultures. Periods of contemplation and temporary withdrawal from the whirl of life may be worthwhile, as they enable you to gain a renewed perspective and recharge those inner batteries by reconnecting to your deeper self, especially if your lifestyle requires considerable contact with other people or 'personality projection'.

Your basic attitude is to put a lot of energy into living because life will return that amplified, increasing your appreciation and enjoyment. Providing you can create a suitable lifestyle, then you will recognise that your life has been blessed, and that even your earlier childhood had helped to sow the seeds for your future benefit.

Jupiter–Sun Trine

There is the indication that your life is 'protected and guided' and that 'luck' can lead you on the path to good fortune. However, the challenge is that you must fully use your qualities, talents and natural gifts as the means to activate this 'inner blessing'. While the trine offers a reconciliation of these planetary energies, the result may be an inclination to relax into a comfortable lifestyle, coasting along modestly and reasonably, failing really to apply and exert yourself. Growth and self-development does not necessarily occur naturally through life experience, and to some degree requires a conscious search and deliberate effort to stimulate the process.

Do you recognise your assets, your potential creativity and qualities or talents that could be positively used? Do you know what you really want to do, what your aims or ambitions are? Are such goals meaningful to you? Or are you content to pass through life without making much effort or exertion, failing to manifest your latent potential? Only you can answer such questions, and only you can choose how to live your life. Yet considering some of the astrological indications of this aspect may help you view yourself from an alternative perspective.

You are likely to be optimistic, enthusiastic, self-confident and to hold a positive, constructive and altruistic attitude to life and people. You can be very generous and supportive to others, finding social contacts easy to make and enjoying company. Your attitude is relaxed and easy-going, and you refuse to feel pressurised to conform to others' expectations. Freedom and personal indulgence appeal more, and apart from creating that comfortable lifestyle, you may evade more demanding endeavours. You may fall into the category of 'under-achiever' often applied by schools. Yet you also develop your own philosophy, founded by ideals, honesty, morals or religious teachings which underpin your life actions and choices.

The issue which may require confronting is that of application and use of resources. You are intelligent and reasonably articulate, but how far do you intend to actually apply that intelligence, and in what directions? Are there ways to exert yourself more that offer greater life fulfilment, but do not compromise either your philosophical ideals or demand that you enter a competitive rat-race situation? Are there opportunities within areas that may interest you – like medicine, law, writing, education, study, the community, communication – through which you could grow, expanding your potential without constraining your freedom too much? How could your enjoyment of study, knowledge and inner contemplation be used to create a compatible career? Or could this be linked to an ability to see future trends, perhaps as a 'future analyst' and a predictive social commentator in some capacity? Discovering alternative ways to perceive the uses of talents, qualities and interests can be crucial in forming uniquely individual life paths, and yet often there is a lack of social encouragement to learn the means and techniques of achieving these. You have the responsibility to determine your own degree of ambition and effort, but look first to see if an alternative path could open for you by a shift of perception and self-evaluation.

Your social relationships can be quite varied, and your level of tolerance is high, preferring to open to people, accepting them as they are, and not imposing expectations on them to conform to any inwardly preconceived impressions. You can enjoy the vitality and fresh minds of children, and skills in this direction could be usefully applied, providing you are not seeking to evade challenges and growth in other areas. You prefer simplicity in life, and may not be too attracted to people who offer greater intellectual challenges and complexity. It isn't that you cannot cope with them, but it's the effort that you may resist.

You will look for a high-quality partner, one who also has their own moral standards in life and possesses a compatible philosophy to your own. Practical abilities will be prized, as will stability of personality and genuine tolerance and understanding; your partner will be someone with whom you can easily relax and enjoy life, and ideally one who will also stimulate you rather than stultify you.

JUPITER–SUN SQUARE

This implies confronting frustrations which have their roots in your nature and attitudes, and which can only be resolved through changes and modifications within yourself. The Jupiterian quality of expansiveness is very potent, stimulating excess expansion in your actions and attitudes, tempting you consistently to overreach your actual capabilities. You may lack patience, planning abilities, self-discipline and persistence, and these will work against your ambitions succeeding, even though attaining your aims may be highly motivating.

It is not that you are incapable of success, but that your approach sows seeds of future failure as you pass. If this has happened in your life, then acknowledge it, and realise that future progress can be made if certain inner changes are taken. The first step is to ensure that you determine your intentions and aims, and how you can proceed to accomplishment. As your desires and dreams can be varied and multiple, focusing your path may prove difficult, and you may need to pursue a thorough re-evaluation of your priorities and major needs in order to gain clarity of purpose. Moving too quickly can often lead to failure due to ill-considered plans, so you may need to stop and think more deeply before jumping into action, or pay more attention to the advice of others. A careful assessment of your current capabilities is required, so that they match the level needed for your goals; working with talents tends to expand latent potential, but a requisite level of skills is initially necessary. A more realistic appreciation of time is essential, or else you will feel your frustrations rising if success does not happen quickly. Excessive optimism and enthusiasm may need to be warily reined back, as do restless tendencies for changes in life, which can become more disruptive than helpful unless properly understood.

The areas of life especially affected are the houses and signs which are ruled and occupied by the Sun and Jupiter, and it is through those spheres that you may over-expand or seek fulfilment within. If you sincerely wish to transform any pattern of frustration in your life, then becoming more realistic, mature and self-controlled will begin to show benefits, especially if you are systematically disciplined to overcome obstacles as they arise. Accepting that failure need never be permanent, or that success is never final or guaranteed, can offer you a more balanced perspective to view your progress. Modifying your attitudes towards life challenges so that they become opportunities for development and growth, instead of perpetuating attitudes of adversarial conflict imposed by a universe intent on thwarting your dreams, will ensure that every experience can bring something of potential value to use as a foundation for your eventual success.

Balance and moderation may need to be consciously developed in your nature and lifestyle, and extravagance or ostentatious tendencies may need to be controlled due to that pattern of excessive consumption that could be adopted as a compensation for other areas of personal failure. Learning to use your energies and time carefully is important, as you may waste them by futile pursuits. Unlocking latent creative potential may be difficult, yet if you can do so, this may open several new doors of opportunity, liberating both blocked inner energies and providing the key to future success.

In relationships, you may need to guard against tendencies to manipulate people, as this will rarely work to your ultimate advantage; there will always be some other puppet master capable of pulling your strings. Similarly, attempts to distort information for your own aims will equally be turned back against you by others also adroit at such tactics. Treating people honestly and directly is the best approach, and you should possess good communication skills which could be applied to transform blockages and obstacles. You will find that if you rely solely on your 'luck', then progress may be restricted; but if you begin to change those problematic attitude areas and approaches then 'luck' will begin to flow again in your favour.

You have high expectations in intimate relationships, especially centred around the fulfilment of your needs and desires; remember that it takes two to make partnership and marriage, and that there is no law that asserts that your needs are paramount. Real love involves mutual sharing and co-operation, each helping to make the other happy, fulfilled and capable of reaching their highest potential; it should not be a one-way traffic. Co-operation and interdependence may need developing, through a diminution of the insistent demands of your ego, otherwise excessive self-indulgence can stimulate problems of health and corresponding illness. Make sure that your expectations and demands of a partner are equal to your own contribution, and to the degree of commitment and effort that you are applying to make the relationship work.

Changes can be made to improve the quality and fulfilment in your life; but only if you are willing to start the process and then persist towards 'completion'. This may not always be easy to do, but all positive steps that you take will bring benefits into your life, and the option to take that path is yours to choose.

Jupiter–Sun Opposition

This indicates that there may be struggles and difficulties facing you from the external world that require overcoming, before you can move on to or along the path of your solar purpose and Jupiterian expansion. These are external obstacles which may obstruct or test your mettle, confronting you with situations that pose dilemmas and evoke your character strengths.

You should have many opportunities in life, possessing sufficient energy, vitality, creativity and intelligence which can lead you into several different directions. As you enjoy variety, and have a restless nature, you can be torn by feelings of periodic dissatisfaction and desires for radical change. This can create mental or physical 'journeys' and phases of lifestyle disruption, as new directions, distractions, jobs and people enter your life. There's a wandering element mixed into this pattern, activated whenever your priorities change, although as years go by, you may begin to discern an underlying meaningful pattern to the changes that you have undergone, and the broad variety of experiences lived through. Even the wandering river will eventually return to the sea.

One vital principle that hopefully you will realise as soon as possible, is that you create your own life, and that 'luck' or 'good fortune' is often what you make it. Taking responsibility for choices turns you into the captain of the ship. Then the onus is on you to make full use of your potential, and be less reliant on the decisions and impacts of external influences. This is the path to evoke your solar power, and the way by which expansion and life appreciation will deepen for you.

Once you begin to be more direct, straightening your lifestyle into harmony with your purpose and ambitions, by living from your centre, then your life will be rearranged into the new pattern that has been inwardly created in your dreams and intentions. Releasing that inner creativity is important, because through that the solar power can become effective. Careful planning and forethought will prove invaluable, and can minimise any over-optimism or excessive expansion that could cause imbalances. Make sure that you keep your feet on the ground, and that practical concerns are not forgotten.

Relationships with others may need to have an impersonal dimension to them, and points of possible contention may remain through your life, as frustrations caused by the external world are always liable to challenge your aims and progress. You can be a confident, forceful personality, liking to share your views with others, but there may be tendencies to be overbearing and too self-assured for some tastes, especially as you like to convert or persuade others to agree with your own ideas. Expressing religious or philosophical teachings can fall easily into the Jupiter category, and more subtlety, care and tolerance may need to be employed by you or others could find you too unbending and fixed in your attitudes. In addition, you will face the public challenge of acting and making choices in the light of your values, statements, opinions and attitudes; or else people may believe that you only give 'lip-service' to your philosophy, and fail to live it in the real world.

In intimate relationships, your expectations of a partner are high and can be a little self-centred, as you assume a position of number one almost without thinking. It may take some time and experience before you finally settle down to partnership commitments; making a wise choice is the key to this success. You tend to dictate, wanting everything your way, and this may need modification to balance out a mutually successful relationship more effectively. If you choose an equally powerful partner, then there may be power struggles until contentious issues are resolved. Your feelings may fluctuate at times, especially when you believe that the world is against you, but perhaps entering into such an ill-conceived challenge is the wrong approach; what is needed is the unlocking of the door to your potential. Areas of medicine, education, media, business, mental/physical journeys can attract and be suitable channels for expressing your talents and qualities. Ensure that any promises you make are kept as much as possible, otherwise you slowly erode the power of your word and integrity. Also, the tendency towards making the dramatic grand gesture or leaping into expansive schemes may need controlling, or else mistakes may easily be made under the influence of excessive optimism.

Reorientating your focus from challenging 'out there' to furthering the release and application of your potential may be the key to fulfilment, and help to discharge the pressures of frustrated expectations. You will discover more meaning and purpose as you tap your potential and your path slowly forms before you.

SATURN–SUN CONJUNCTION

Your potential success is dependent on personal qualities of perseverance, self-discipline, organisation and your ability to maximise the effectiveness of all your available resources. Ambition is likely to be a powerful motivating force within your personality, and once your aims have been clarified, careful planning and application can help you to achieve them. Persistence and hard work may be the keys to later success, and it is unlikely that progress will be swift or aims realised at an early age. As Saturn implies limitations and barriers, it is probable that even when following your solar path there will be obstacles and frustrations confronting you, and there may be periods when you begin to feel the inhibitions of your nature and path acutely.

You can lack sufficient confidence, adopting a self-deprecating attitude as justifying any lack of progress. Temperamentally, you are serious and reserved, often taciturn in expression, controlled and disciplined and viewing life with an uneasy attitude. To you, life demands effort and application, and nothing comes easy or free. So you believe that to become materially comfortable you may have to deny certain feelings or needs in order to concentrate and focus on your aims. Unfortunately, through self-denial and austere attitudes, you may repress self-expression, creating inner imbalances which have later negative side-effects. These could become more predominant if you enter a phase of frustrations, where disappointments generate tensions, stresses, angry thoughts and emotional attitudes. Disorders of the digestive system may be associated with this, and you may need to increase relaxation in your life, perhaps by consciously dismantling any fixity of lifestyle and daily habit patterns that may be unconsciously erected around yourself as a form of protective barrier.

The house position of the conjunction is a sphere of opportunity and of limitation for you, depending on the inner changes that you can consciously make. Success can result from applying your strengths, which are likely to be in areas of organisation, self-reliance, discipline, persistence and determined application. The theme of consolidation and building is associated with this aspect, where existing resources are used in ways which take greater advantage of their potential, expanding from a secure foundation but not overly risky or speculative. Careers in management, politics, law, scientific research, teaching, local government may be attractive, especially if you are able to use an ability to assume responsibility within your employment.

Your earlier childhood development will have been influenced by the relationship to your father. Look at the attitudes towards life that your parents expressed, and see if these have become your dominating attitudes and values too. You may have received a highly ordered and strict parental discipline, encouraging conformity to parental desires and codes of conduct; moralistic or religious attitudes may have conditioned your worldview. There may have been a lack of parental approval or response to your unique childhood nature, perhaps a lack of emotional affinity (perceived or actual) which made you feel more isolated and independent; certainly you would have experienced an early inner maturation process. Have you become what your parents wanted you to be? And is this in accordance with your desires and dreams? You may need to break free from these earlier psychological programmes that are still operating in you, so that you can move in new directions or transcend those restrictions in life that are acting as barriers to fulfilment and success.

You have much of value to share with the world, but this may need greater releasing. For instance, you may feel that everyone makes their own destiny (and certainly, to some degree this is correct), but this should not stop you being generous if you have financial abundance in your life; you could help others to help themselves. There may be a belief that there is a lesson or message within every life experience, but this should never stop feelings of love and friendliness flowing out naturally from you to others. Acknowledging others in a different way may be necessary, so that you are more aware of their needs and qualities, and this can divert you from your self-preoccupations. Certainly you will require a compatible intimate partner who recognises your need for achievement, and who is willing to support your endeavours; but equally, you should not forget that your partner also has their own life path to follow, and you should not forget their needs either. Mutual aid is the ideal approach. Loosen the chains of your self-imposed limitations, and you may be surprised by how your life can favourably change.

SATURN–SUN SEXTILE

This indicates that you will have a conservative attitude to life, preferring order and discipline linked to traditional values and social life paths. You will naturally follow a mainstream course through life, which also offers established routes towards achieving 'success'.

The sextile is especially effective within your mental nature, helping you to deepen your understanding and extend your communicative skills. Your thought processes are likely to have a natural logic, organisation, clarity and perception that can be exploited through several careers. Mental precision is valued in management roles, scientific research, law, politics, teaching, business, and this backed by leadership ability and practical, methodical abilities should enable you to attain your ambitions.

Work can become extremely important, offering a purpose and life direction, as well as being the sphere where many of your major personal assets are applied. While success highly motivates you, there may be a distaste for assuming a 'high profile' that draws personal attention, as you prefer to remain quietly working in the background. You can feel uncomfortable at personality extroversion, and in some situations this can work to your detriment, and you are overlooked or misvalued. Opportunities could be lost and progress halted. If this does occur, then you are faced with two alternatives. You either adopt a higher personality profile, or you consider different routes to your ambitions, perhaps a change of job or career. Doors never close for ever, unless you refuse to open them; there are always alternatives and different options available to those who refuse to limit themselves.

Remember your qualities of competence, efficiency, honesty, application, reliability, responsibility and your ability to absorb knowledge and information by paying attention to new developments. All these attributes can be valuably applied in many situations, so ensure that you are not taken advantage of by less responsive superiors. This can happen, especially as you have a natural respect for authority, and you can easily be limited by a permanent role as a subordinate.

You may find your life path in the sphere of communication and teaching, mainly through your ability to explain and express your knowledge in an accessible and meaningful way. You realise the essentials of a subject and ensure that these are grasped, so that a good foundation of knowledge is transmitted. Social concerns may become more predominant in your life as you grow older, and political issues may attract your attention. You may become involved with community or social activities, or look for power and responsibility linked to political ambitions. While you favour traditional attitudes and values, you also acknowledge the need for development and progress, so you try to act as a 'bridge' between the past–present–future, carefully retaining the value of the past with an awareness of what is required tomorrow.

In social and intimate relationships, you prefer the company of like-minded individuals, those who have a similar or compatible perception, and whose attitudes do not openly challenge or disturb your implicit assumptions about life and yourself. Domestically, you will follow established social lifestyles, rarely considering any radical deviations, or choosing to step outside conventional patterns. While you are aware of your own limits – but less so those self-imposed ones – you may not always take advantage of your whole potential, and can create subtle demarcation lines of personal restrictions formed by your unconscious attitudes. Perhaps a greater tolerance of those who feel less need to conform may open you more to the potential and possibilities of life; not everyone has to follow the same road, and there are more ways open for you than have been consciously realised.

SATURN–SUN TRINE

The trine helps to reconcile these two planetary energies more successfully, and there is less evidence of any underlying Saturnian tendency to restrict and limit. The positive qualities and abilities of Sun–Saturn contacts are present; responsibility, self-discipline, practicality, patience, organisation, reliability, concentration, determination, persistence and honesty. These can all be used to further your ambitions, although you may need to be wary of innate Saturn tendencies towards caution which may prevent you taking advantage of all opportunities.

Determining your solar purpose and tapping into that power

will be most important in applying these energies and qualities, and gaining insight into your life direction may be a necessary first step to achieve before this trine can be used positively. As you can move through life smoothly without facing obstructive challenges, you may not always feel the need to draw upon your full potential. You are attracted towards having a 'comfortable life', and with your self-confidence and creativity expect that this will naturally come to pass.

You should be able to use personal qualities and resources effectively, especially to produce an intended practical result, and you probably have a sense of appropriate timing which ensures that your actions are successful. This can be used in a variety of employments and careers, especially management, law, politics, conservation, financial services and organisational posts. You will enjoy assuming any positions of responsibility, but you may experience inner resistances in any environment that is undergoing rapid change due to social or technological progress, as this can clash with your innate conservatism and preference for the familiar.

Your lifestyle is likely to reflect mainstream social attitudes, and you will try to develop it in a moderate and balanced manner, looking to create solid foundations and financial security. You prefer life to feel stable and almost predictable, and will take each step onwards with a patient attitude, usually rejecting any chances that may lead to speedier progress yet which also may lead to failure. A personal philosophy and value system will be established, and once you feel comfortable with your unique worldview, you may evade situations which offer valid alternatives to your chosen perspective. In this context, the Saturnian rigidity may act as a limitation, but as your conformity is grounded within established social values, this should not work against you in achieving your ambitions.

Choosing a right partner is important, as they need to be similar in nature to yourself, either wholeheartedly supporting your aims, or alternatively pursuing their own ambitions. Career and social involvement is the probable sphere of mutual endeavour, and personal honesty and integrity are qualities that are expected, as is stability and responsibility in your partnership. Balance and moderation are two keynotes that will apply across your whole nature and lifestyle, and this will be reflected in your good health and sense of well-being. Feeling respected and loved by others, and acknowledging your own talents will amplify your self-worth so that you can move confidently onwards on your solar path.

SATURN–SUN SQUARE

The square indicates that restrictions and limitations derived from your own inner psychological attitudes, values, beliefs and self-image are likely to confront you, and that these often emerge from a lack of self-esteem and personal insecurities.

The power of your solar energy is being held in check – almost imprisoned – by Saturn until you succeed in 'learning certain lessons', 'recognising inner messages' and manage to transform those constraining attitudes that can cause the failure of your dreams through attracting obstacles along the path.

Part of this may have been influenced by your early childhood environment, where conflicts with parents (especially your father) or with authority figures have left you feeling defeated and psychologically wounded. Possibly attempts at being childishly self-assertive were unsympathetically crushed and rejected by strict and disciplinarian adults, or your efforts at self-expression and communication of feelings were dismissed and ignored. Whatever circumstances were experienced, the result was a diminution of a developing personality and loss of confidence and self-esteem.

You are likely to hold psychologically defensive attitudes towards life, not able to trust in the beneficence of the universe or people around you, often expecting that rejection and failure will be the only results that come to you. With such expectations, the mirroring by the universe will bring such results. A transformation in your worldview is required to alter this pattern.

The operative effects of such a pattern are as follows: a fear of 'superiors' and authority figures, and the forming of negative comparisons between yourself and others; an underestimation of or failure to recognise your latent potential, qualities and strengths; a lack of personal assertion, and a tendency to be passive, fatalistic, pessimistic, rigid and insecure; a lack of self-confidence, and a belief that you are unlovable and will never taste success; health may be affected, with a loss of physical vitality and vigour, or psychosomatic ailments may periodically erupt. Looking out at life, you may imagine a constant frustration of your efforts, a life of hard toil for little result, and a scattering around you of unrealised dreams.

But if this is the case, then it is within you to transform the inner attitudes that generate such a reality; your life can always be changed for the better. This is the challenge and test facing you, to rise beyond those apparent inner limitations and restrictions that to some degree you are choosing to impose on yourself. Specific areas of oppression may be those associated with the sign and house positions of Sun and Saturn, and resolving the lessons implied in those spheres may hold a key to open the rest of your life to a more favourable future.

In failure and rejection lie the seeds of possible success, providing that you recognise the lessons and messages that are contained within such experiences. A new approach to self-evaluation is required, one that is not depreciating and negative in prior assumption, but values your strengths and qualities and sees them as assets that can be successfully employed. You may need to review all those traditional attitudes and worldviews that you have acquired in life, and see if they are restrictive or can positively serve you. When life presents obstacles in your path, you have two fundamental choices; defeat or discover a way of moving beyond. The first is a path of self-limitation and stagnation, the second is the path of self-development and evolutionary growth, and that is the assertion of the solar power and of a higher self. This second path is the one that beckons to you.

While success may never be easy, and you have to work hard for every step forward, changing your conditioning attitudes is the transformative key. Your character can be strengthened and amplified by attitudes of optimism and positive cheerfulness; begin to trust in the universe and yourself, and you will succeed in restoring your self-image to a positive perception. The aim is to re-empower yourself. One of the most effective ways to do this is through techniques of creative visualisation, which can aid in the psychological reprogramming of all inner attitudes, replacing them by beliefs and worldviews that become positively attractive to the good experience of life. Take the time to explore such techniques.

Relationships could be similarly transformed. If you have been holding a negative self-image, it is always difficult to believe that anyone could love or be interested in you, so relationships may have been unsatisfactory, uneasy and lacking development. If you transform any unsuitable self-images, then relationships can assume a new light and vitality. Partners may appear who understand and value you for what you are, and have a faith and trust in your latent potential being actualised. Love is a great transforming power, and you will develop under such a gaze from another. Through consolidating and recognising your power, your solar will can be applied to attain your ambitions. Through sharing with a partner, you can gain a renewed perspective, healing and resolving conflicts which may have been previously detrimental. This square's tendency for negativity is not inviolable; it can be the spur to change, provided you choose to take the future into your hands, and to recreate it into a positive pattern. This is the Saturn lesson and test that is really confronting you; a demand to assert your unique solar power.

SATURN–SUN OPPOSITION

The opposition reflects an inner conflict externalised into the outer environment and relationships. The issue of self-esteem and worth is highlighted, and you may experience a degree of hidden insecurity and fears of full involvement in life.

You may feel that your success is being frustrated by the world, which appears to confront you by obstacles on your way. Much depends on your reactions to such experiences, and your inner attitudes will determine how you deal with them. At times, you can seem almost over-assertive or aggressive, and this can diminish opportunities for co-operative endeavours to develop, especially when you fail to notice your effect on others, or inadvertently ignore their feelings and sensitivities. Often this is just an overreaction to your fears in relating to people, and instead of relaxing more, your tightness can project an overdominant energy that others can find uncomfortable. Alternatively, you could retreat back into a surrendered posture of passivity to life's challenges, defeated before you start. Certainly learning how to live with any restrictions imposed by Saturn may be a necessary form of adjustment, although this should not imply a resignation to them, but merely a conscious modification to circumstances and a consequent step to transcend them later. The choice is yours to reshape your lifestyle patterns into a way that is more suitable and open to development.

Self-expression and creativity may feel restricted, although this is often dependent on your confidence in your abilities and self-image, rather than on any lack of talents and qualities. Being able to perceive yourself in a positive light may become a key to your success, because that would also alter your relationships with others. There may be an emotional reserve and lack of warmth in your social contacts, so that you feel uncomfortable in bridging social divides and entering deeper relationships. Co-operation may need further development, and that air of formality and strictness may have to be relaxed so that friendships or partnerships can be more easily formed.

The need for relaxation is present in both your outer and inner relationships. You may be unable to see your nature and direction clearly and this creates an insecurity which destabilises your self-esteem. You try to protect this by establishing defensive barriers from the world, and probably by denying inner insecurities, with needs and potential being 'locked away'. You may choose to hide behind responsibilities, your work or career, family or parents, and these become an excuse for restricting options and failing to exert your power towards success. Personal tightness and control may need to be relinquished, and greater self-relaxation would be highly beneficial, especially in changing certain attitudes and increasing your physical vitality which periodically can become low as the energy is diverted towards restraints. Becoming looser, more tolerant, accepting and understanding would act as a great liberator, or you may begin to bow under the strain of those self-imposed restrictions, especially as your enjoyment of life progressively diminishes.

A new inner balance and self-image is necessary. As this is achieved, any outer frustrations will correspondingly start to dissolve in equal measures to the increase in your self-confidence and clarified inner perspective. While initially it may appear as if the outer world and people are opposing you, it is this same source which can offer great opportunities as your changes proceed.

Through the interplay of your nature and the environment, many inner crises and tensions can be healed and resolved, releasing latent qualities, talents and potentials in their renewal of blocked energies. Look especially towards the houses and signs of the Sun–Saturn opposition for areas which could be especially revitalised, or where your talents could be effectively applied.

Similarly, intimate relationships with partners or parents could be equally transformed, as old patterns derived from childhood frictions with authority figures or strict parents are replaced by more adult ones suited to your developed personality. Discovering a sincere loving partner could be very important, as a lover will revivify your self-image reflecting your qualities back, and this can convince you that you are worthy of being loved. Your inner question mark over this urgently needs resolving. A partner can also be a source of advice and confidence, and working co-operatively will open many new areas of potential, providing you relax sufficiently to be open about your feelings and fears, and to acknowledge the emotional vulnerability of others too. Through greater sensitivity you can enter a different type of social relationship, as those barriers will have been dismantled, and your controlling nature reduced. Taking such a step may initially feel uncomfortable and unsettling, but doing so will transform the nature of your universe and liberate many repressed energies, recreating your future and enabling the following of your solar purpose.

URANUS–SUN CONJUNCTION

You are likely to experience ongoing clashes and discord with others and society. This is due to your essential tendency to be highly individualistic and non-conformist, and this will inevitably bring you into conflict with the social traditions and lifestyle patterns of your country, by your determination to follow your unique path through life. You will not have a passive nature, or acquiesce easily in what is required of you by parents, school, religion or the state-approved ways of social living; but you will be a passionate rebellious spirit rejecting, questioning, or opposing those pressures with which you either disagree or believe are intending to hinder your freedom.

This 'passion' however, is not really emotionally rooted, but is your way of releasing a build-up of energy within your nature which has to find some means of release, similar to the boiling of water which transforms into steam to escape from a container. The slightest threat or fear of 'imprisonment' and you will begin looking for the escape route.

This need for freedom – in whichever and however many ways you define 'freedom' – will be a dominant factor influencing your life. The urgent need to express this tendency will create an unsettling impact upon your adult choices and life direction, and will probably interfere with focusing on your solar path. As a result of experiencing this inner pressure for change, you are likely to observe the elements of unpredictability flowing into your established life patterns. In some ways this could be beneficial, but an energy acting in uncontrolled unconscious ways can severely disrupt a relatively harmonious lifestyle or family, because someone under its influence begins to act in a potentially destructive manner. Just 'throwing the energy away', attempting to reduce the inner pressure, is not constructive or sensible. This inner process indicates that change is needed, that this will usually be associated with a particular sphere of life (indicated by this natal house conjunction or by planetary transits activating this aspect), and that a conscious attentive focus is required to tune into the messages being internally triggered so that the energy can be directed into suitable channels of expression.

You will have to acknowledge and confront the implications of any innate hatred of restrictions, as life will invariably impose them through family, employment, and type of social environment. You may struggle against restrictions all of your life, wanting to be 'free', but free to do what? And free to live in what way, and where? Probably you'll lack real answers, but a search to find a satisfying direction is crucial for you, and will reflect your quest for your higher solar path; otherwise in gaining your freedom you'll discover that through cutting the binding ties you have become lost or have destroyed those foundations that are now recognised as being important and meaningful for you.

In your intimate relationships, you will have to be aware of a tendency to invest your needs with supreme value and importance, where you insist upon individual rights and freedom to express your own nature without compromising, yet often fail to offer the same to your partner. You can have a problem of impatience tinged with intolerance, which can create friction, as can your attraction towards areas of experience that some may consider to be unorthodox or deviant from any socially acceptable norm. Not that such reactions unduly concern you; in fact you may feel tempted to flaunt any such preferences in the face of others.

Probably you will be attracted towards entering sudden, intense, exciting, physical and emotional relationships, especially spontaneous ones that can occur without too much consideration of any future implications. You prefer 'newness', through exploring the unknown and may often shy away from commitment and responsibility, partly based on fear and on your inability to often consider your partner's needs as highly as you do your own. The problem is how to balance your need for novelty and new experiences, the hatred of restrictions and desire for individual freedom with the demands of living with people in society.

You need to become more mature in relationships, to become more aware of the value of mutual sharing, to care as much for your partner as you do for yourself, and by helping them to express their own totality and not subduing their personal development by the dominating insistence of your needs, learn to walk side by side into freedom and fulfilment.

Recognising these tendencies is the first step to begin taking conscious control to use innate energies, so that your life begins to work better, and becomes more meaningful and satisfying by gaining a greater solar cohesion through integrating these planetary energies.

One direction that may help in this self-renewal and personal reorientation lies in expressing your urge for exploration, to investigate new horizons and interests; try not to live this out in a purely self-centred way, but attempt to redirect any benefits towards the well-being of others too, especially through improving the quality of relationships.

Your mind may have an attunement to the Uranian 'higher mind' or 'Universal Mind'. This implies that there can be mental power, perhaps by your mind taking sudden logic leaps and making connections which can offer new insights or ways of looking at life. While sometimes this can be too erratic and undisciplined to be utilised fully, the natural direction that it moves towards is futuristic. This is both a reaction against the restrictions of predictable staid and static social traditions, and can also be a tool to be used in the visualisation and formation of possible future societies. Combining your natural tendencies to permissiveness and creative expression, you may develop in terms of progressive futurist philosophies and attitudes, associating with like-minded groups and individuals to help build the Aquarian New Humanity. Embodying new lifestyle patterns and more open attitudes can offer a new world for you to explore and one which can benefit others too. Here lies freedom with less restriction, allowing you to express a rebellious nature against social limitations while helping to build a more understanding and free world for everyone to share. Taking such a direction can enable you to dissolve previous self-preoccupations into participation in group endeavours. This fusion of your Uranian tendencies with a projected heroic path can build a lighted way in your life, where the positive contributions of both Sun and Uranus can be released for individual and collective benefits.

Uranus–Sun Sextile

The more radical use of the conjunction energies are potentially easier to express in both the sextile and the trine. Whereas an important shift may need to occur in the individual with the conjunction aspect – in order to renew and redirect any overflowing, insistent Uranian energy through the unifying Sun centre – these other two dynamic, harmonious aspects are ripe for exploitation and unfoldment.

You should have a progressive outlook, and a sense of social affinity which is directed towards affirming its positive side and potential for future improvements in the quality of life. The assertive and possibly aggressive rebellious stance is already transformed within you into a reformist tendency. 'Change from within' is more your keynote, rather than a direct destructive attack or negative attempts to withdraw from participation in society.

Your mind will be very active, searching, questioning, and

naturally explorative, allied with an intuitive creative need for self-expression. It will be important to be personally assertive, but undue eccentricity is not your style. Due to that positive solar relationship you will feel more centred, forming a stable inner character and extending an ability to direct your life and make wiser choices. Tolerance and understanding of others will be more evident, especially an intellectually derived tolerance based on your innate humanitarian instincts, although often your emotional affinity with others can be a little cold or withdrawn. You do not feel at one with the world, yet intellectually your mind is; perhaps more empathy is required.

You are likely to contribute to groups which support social reform, and have an attitude of 'changing the world to be a better place for everyone to live in'. Probably you could rise to important positions in such groups, transmitting your enthusiasms and positivity by becoming a spokesperson for their visions and ideals. Your opinions are usually forthright, and you try to stay true and committed to your beliefs. Honesty and straightforwardness are high on your list of essential values, and you have little tolerance for lies and deceits and those who perpetrate them. This can easily lead you towards opposing a national government or establishment groups who are 'economical with the truth' on orders from their 'superiors'. Equally, it could lead you to break away from groups that you are associated with, if they – in your opinion – fall to such low levels or compromise and fail to live up to the high ideals which they may offer to the public.

You believe that life has an inner meaning of great value, and continually search for the threads of this throughout your life, trusting in the belief that life is good, often despite appearances. This is part of your quest for the spiritual dimension of your solar centre, and will draw you increasingly closer to that integrative heart of your nature. However, you are aware of the darker sides of existence, and feel inspired to try to improve the quality of life for those who suffer or for the following generations. At times, especially perhaps after any disappointments on your path, you may coolly withdraw from relationships or social involvement. See this only as a temporary phase for re-evaluation. You need to communicate with like minds, sharing experiences, insight and knowledge. This may easily develop over time into forms of teaching where through sharing you can contribute towards progress for others, and this could become a fulfilling route for you to follow to embody a higher solar purpose.

Uranus–Sun Trine

Similar to the sextile, the energy emanating from the trine aspect is harmonious in direction and able to be positively assimilated. Most of the characteristics of the sextile are repeated with the trine.

The natural attunement with the 'Universal Mind' should help you to receive valid insights and intuitions, especially at times when the trine is reactivated by transit or progression movements, which offer opportunities for greater creativity and usable ideas. Such periods may also stimulate a heightened awareness of your solar path and purpose, and should be carefully noted so that you can hold your mind in a meditative and receptive mode of operation, in order for insights and promptings to be consciously registered and then acted upon.

The future orientation preferred by Uranus will be present, but it is likely that with the trine such ideas are founded on a more immediately practical basis, possibly as a result of an attitude which is more rooted within a scientific, logical and objective perspective.

You should find it relatively easy to exploit your creativity, as this aspect releases a large quantity of potentially productive ideas into those areas of life for which you require inspiration. Study the house positions and signs of both Sun and Uranus for areas that may be specifically influenced by this trine. Aided by perseverance and the application of a focused will, you should have no real obstacles confronting your efforts to manifest creative ideas. These can take a myriad of forms, from experimentation aimed at developing new projects, to more adequate modifications of existing products.

There is likely to be an inner detachment to your searches and creativity, a perpetual quest of enquiry and fascination, with a form of creativity which works through the creator, and is never perceived in any egotistical perspective. This can help you to become quite productive and varied in your chosen sphere, as you look around to find ways which are suitable to stretch your wings and explore new horizons.

Your reformist, idealistic and humanitarian tendencies can find success through communication and sharing with others, and this can be important to your sense of well-being, as you do need to feel that you are of some use to others. Your sense of commitment, enthusiasm and positivity can be most helpful in supporting others, or through transmitting these energies to help motivate group endeavours. Your relationships can also benefit from this outpouring of optimism, positivity and sense of mutual sharing, helping to develop those strands of intrinsic meaning and purpose in both your and others' lives.

URANUS–SUN SQUARE

The energy of the square aspect can feel highly frustrated and in some cases turn towards a more aggressive and potentially violent form of expression, if there is not a suitable channel for it to be released through. Discovering adequate forms is important to anchor the Uranian energy successfully, so evoking that Sun centre cohesiveness is essential in dealing with the highly charged Uranian energy and is common to all these aspects made to natal Uranus. This is a perpetual Sun–Uranian task.

You can be erratic, individualistic, restless and nervously agitated, desiring independence and freedom from all social restrictions. You may be a natural dissenter, a social troublemaker, preferring to support your own minority view; it is even likely that your tendency to dissent can lead you to become isolated and alienated from others or radical groups with whom you are in basic agreement. If unmodified, and released indiscriminately, this energy is quite capable of 'causing trouble in an empty house'! Being the devil's advocate is a function that can often lead to confusion and loss of self, as eventually you either erode or lose sight of your own attitudes, beliefs or ideals, and this displaces you from strengthening your solar centre. Even if the majority hold a certain opinion or belief then that alone can require you to reject it and to oppose its validity. From a more inclusive perspective there can be some truth in such a standpoint, as the majority viewpoint is often that of 'the lowest common denominator' and can reflect the most separative beliefs and opinions.

It must be remembered that such an attitude is really the intrinsic tone of the excitable, highly charged and volatile Uranian energy, but taken to a more personally destructive extreme. The exaltation of the unique individuality has to be achieved in a correct and wise manner, by attuning to the deeper solar centre of the individuality, otherwise the negative and separative destructive tendencies can emerge into action.

You can be undisciplined, hating those predictable routines of life and work, often finding it hard to act responsibly and with full commitment. You react against conforming to social rules, feeling that they constrain your freedom, and you often follow your choices, irrespective of the repercussions and costs of doing so. You will probably fail to listen to well-meaning advice, and a stubborn need for self-assertion can lead you towards those very experiences and problems that you were being warned against. If you look honestly at your life, you will observe those times where you misjudged, making foolish decisions and choices often through sheer contrariness and by asserting your 'free individuality'. Without awareness no one is ever free, but is merely a prisoner to their own unconscious tendencies, a prey to them, like playthings of the inner gods. It is only through your solar centre that the planetary influences can be controlled and balanced, so that the positive characteristics can shine through, illuminating your life and creative expression.

At times you may become a little paranoid, especially when your choices have been unwise, influenced by less conscious and unintegrated factors in your psyche. It does not have to be like that. You can choose to take a more direct conscious role in your life, and not be a victim of your own ignorance. Those 'enemies' that you can project out into the external world are often your own unresolved inner demons that are slowly consuming you from within.

The square can be an aspect of frustrated blocked transformation and renewal; the inner personal revolution that both Sun and Uranus would like to bring is being blocked. These inner tensions can become potentially violent, and need to be redirected into constructive positive channels. You need to release any tendencies towards impracticality, antisocial attitudes and hidden urges for personal power, to stop being antagonistic purely for the sake of performing the adversarial role, and use the freed energies to renew your own life. Compromise and balance within your nature, and allowing an inner transformation to strengthen your focus on your solar centre, is the key to a more satisfying relationship with the greater community, and for you to enter into more beneficial and harmonious intimate relationships.

As is probably recognised, you like others to be submissive to you, yet tend to lose respect for their individuality when they fall into that pattern of behaviour. You need to learn how to respect and elevate their uniqueness because that is the corollary of your 'trip' and 'philosophy'. Emotional depths need to be stirred more, letting those poisons of frustration and emotional conflicts rise to the surface to be encountered and understood, releasing and transmuting them by accepting them as a shadow part of yourself which should be acknowledged and never denied. Doing so will harmonise your energies more, offer greater inner peace and tranquillity (as far as Uranus will allow!), and clear those festering poisons out of you. This will enable your unique individuality to flower in freedom. Your life can change from acting as a frustrated opponent, and becoming more what you really are and what you truly stand for, moving away from a negative stance into one of positivity. Your choice is to do this, and the benefits will be yours to enjoy as the aims of your solar nature begin to reshape your life.

URANUS–SUN OPPOSITION

Both square and opposition aspects have a peculiar quality which is similar to an 'on–off switch' energy flow pattern. Internal and external erratic behaviour may be expected, which can lead to those dramatic and often drastic changes of behaviour and lifestyle.

Within your hidden inner life, you are likely to feel undercurrents of restless activity, which while peaking and troughing, are an ever-present participant in your nature. This can lead to nervous tensions and irritability, an edgy tone to your energy which is often psychically communicated or received by others and experienced as an intangible sense of unease. Your emotional and mental moods are erratic, unpredictable and temperamental, creating sudden confusing changes in attitudes and relationships, or even contradicting statements that you may have just made. Sometimes you may fail to be aware of this lack of continuity that you exhibit.

Individuality and independence will be emphasised with insistence upon your own needs and freedom from all restrictions. This can manifest as a compulsion to display a rebellious anti-social attitude, mainly as a reactionary explosion of energy rather than any considered response which could also offer some viable alternative ways to follow. Your reactions are likely to be more negative in quality and content, and may need a conscious degree of self-moderation to avoid an instinctive 'knee-jerk' response. You may find that you obtain pleasure from seeing others react to your iconoclasm, as it can add some excitement to life, but it is unlikely to be inherently creative or positive action as you often fail to have anything of value which could replace whatever it is you are opposing.

In many ways you are insecure, feeling lost and frustrated with both the world and yourself. Your inner energy flow is uneven; sometimes you are highly charged and have difficulties dealing with that, other times the energy seems to be switched off, and life goes flat and colourless. You probably lack a stable cohesive centre, missing the positivity of an adjusted planetary relationship to your Sun, and you may need to struggle towards establishing a firm, secure point of balance within your identity.

You can be hypersensitive, but may tend to deny this aspect through feeling uncomfortable with your emotional nature and its ebb and flow, as this does not fit into that intellectualised self-image that you have developed. This can be quite delusory, but is also a prop for you to centre your identity around. These images can include considering yourself 'before your time', an unrecognised genius or artist, a cultural bohemian, a radical revolutionary, an important social adversary. Glamorous images emerge from that high opinion of yourself and those peculiar insights and ideas that you attempt to communicate to others. There are likely to be some nuggets of gold scattered around, but more often than not you fail to deliver, wisps of intentions dematerialising into the air. Your evaluations are often impractical, and due to either diversions towards new glamorous ideas, or through an unfocused will, you often fail to develop fully any natural gifts.

While you tend to insist that your will is paramount, you really need to learn effective forms of social compromise, realising your misapprehension of being the all-important centre of the universe, which is symptomatic of an imbalanced Sun. Just learning to listen seriously to other points of view and perceptions on life can teach you much, in distinction to one of your behaviour patterns which sees such contact and communication as a form of competitive challenge, mentally pitting yourself as an adversarial opponent of another point of view.

You may need to stop tilting against windmills. Your heroic quest should not be externally directed, but internalised in an attempt to achieve an inner transformation. This is not to imply that the windmills are not there – they probably are – but you need an effort to redirect and rediscipline your nature and energies so that your solar centre becomes more powerful and integrative. A redefinition of rebellious spirit needs to be made by you, a re-channelling of your scattered energies.

Learning forms of relaxation or meditative techniques could become very important to your well-being, and may help in this re-centering process of evoking the solar power. Highly strung nervous states are not beneficial to health. Relationships can also be fraught with problems, as your erratic hot and cold contributions are not always made in apt timing for your partner's behaviour patterns. You may need to be wary of making excessive emotional demands, especially as you may not be so balanced in your emotional nature, and you probably have a lack of understanding of that level. In many ways, it is likely to be an immature aspect of your nature, and may require conscious development and further exploration.

Attempts to restrict the freedom of others should also be guarded against, as should undue attractions towards promiscuity, unless you are personally liberated from any emotional reactions against such freedoms also being expressed by your partners.

NEPTUNE–SUN CONJUNCTION

Any Neptune aspect to the Sun is likely to have a distinct impact on the individual expression of personal power, identity and life direction, so it becomes important to create a positive approach to the Neptunian energy and especially so with the more influential aspects of the conjunction, square and opposition. The difficulty with an unintegrated or repressed Neptune is that its influence often appears to be negative, and with the conjunction aspect it is imperative to discover a way of joining this energy to the natural form of expression that the Sun sign indicates.

You will probably experience an ongoing challenge of self-confidence and of establishing a suitable and satisfying lifestyle and sense of purpose. The nebulous influence of Neptune's sea mists tends to confuse you, dissolving many of your intentions away, and making your sense of individual identity almost transparent at times as that personality centre seems to ebb and flow in tune with an inner tidal rhythm. Because of an inner experience associated with insubstantiality, you can lack the strength of a firm and fixed individuality, and this has the effect of diminishing confidence regarding your actual capabilities and will to achieve any objectives. You can find it hard to be consistent and to persevere through self-discipline and application for long periods of time. Your identity can appear to be periodically submerged by the powerful Neptune energy, dissolving plans and ambitions, and then leaving you washed ashore in another inner place wondering what to do next even before you have completed the last project.

That ethereal Neptunian music will invade your conscious mind, acting as a diverting distraction, and in some cases can influence the listener to become lost in the swirlings of their own hyperactive imagination leading to self-delusions. Confronting the stark realities of life is not always easy with a prominent Neptune. There is a tendency to build a private reality, one which excludes the dark sides of self and the world, establishing a veiled and limiting perspective of life which only generates activity by additional repression into the unconscious mind. Personal responsibility is avoided if possible, and all experiences are filtered through this restrictive veil, a state that if prolonged leads to inner and outer alienation.

Often these forms of self-delusion emanate from personal desires, emotions and sensitive feelings, as Neptune is associated with the plastic and pliable astral level. You may develop unusual desires and needs which are subtle, intangible yet peculiarly insistent, and you may feel inwardly driven to experience or actualise them in some way. For many, such hard-to-define feelings and yearnings create more confusion and self-deception, especially when attached to idealistic images of perfection and unrealistic expectations which can only bring disillusionment and disappointment in their wake. For the few, Neptune may bring genuine inspiration, although even in such cases, this may become mixed with desires of self-elevation and ambitions, especially in the sphere of the conjunction's house.

One of the hardest lessons for anyone with a close Neptune aspect is facing the realities of life. Neptune finds such confrontations almost inimical to its sensitivities, preferring to slide away instead of looking. You may have noticed such evasiveness in your life, manifesting in a variety of disguises through the years: the evasion of problems – the ostrich syndrome; the evasion of decision-making; the evasion of self-assertion; and the evasion of the effort to unfold your inner potential. It can become difficult to ensure that your solar path is clear when the mists of Neptune descend, confusing directions and masking the signposts along the way.

The disguises of Neptune are legion, but their cumulative effect is considerable, gradually creating an unsatisfactory lifestyle and diminution of direction, meaning and purpose as the real self is lost under veils of escapism. We are all prone to this tendency, and it is this that keeps us spiritually asleep. 'Wake up' is the cry of the spirit, a waking up that gives us the experience of a direct unfiltered confrontation with life, a connection to our solar centre which is a light exposing all those shadowy corners. Facing the higher aspect of Neptune is not a self-deluding experience either, but a sobering one. An unintegrated Neptune may offer delusions and glamour, but integrating the Sun and Neptune is a path towards fusing the individual emotional level with the universal life, in a similar way as integrating Uranus–Sun fuses the mind through intuition with the universal mind.

Recognising the negative expression of Neptune is the first step; the next is to choose to integrate this power into your life so that the positive dimension opens. There have undoubtedly been times when you have felt in full control, confident in yourself and your ability to achieve ambitions, only to pass into another phase when this confidence seeps away, dissolving as quickly as you try to hold on to it. This occurs when Neptune and the Sun are at odds with each other, where a fusion has not yet happened.

While this aspect can become a gateway to an inward turning, an entering of the inner worlds and mystical devotion, it is more useful to consider how an external expression of the energy can stimulate greater integration.

Neptune offers a variety of gifts that can be applied as creative expression, gifts which emanate from the inner seas and which are simultaneously a channel or path back into conscious contact with Neptune's realm and towards the higher solar centre. These include art, music, poetry, drama, literature, psychism, mysticism. The potential is to reveal inspiration through such channels for the benefit of all who are capable of receiving the transmission. Unlocking inner doors so that creativity flows is extremely enriching, and shifts the level of consciousness; there can be dangers in unlocking the flood gates, as so many creative individuals have discovered, but in many ways it is a sacred task to reveal the numinosity of the light behind the material appearance.

Adding or developing a creative and artistic dimension to your life will be a means of integrating this Neptunian energy, as it will begin to flow into those particular channels that you have opened. Allied to this it will begin to display its positive face, as greater meaning, purpose and life direction have more cohesiveness and substance, and your solar path will be strengthened, offering a more permanent direction instead of periodically dissolving. Even if such creativity is purely for your own satisfaction, enjoyment and need for self-expression, over time you will become aware of the benefits that it can bring to you. These talents may need deliberate training and development, but such time spent will be rewarding. Moving into this direction may require you to reconsider your whole lifestyle, as its influence will be profound, and understanding your individuality can be transformative.

Your type of employment may stand revealed as deeply unfulfilling and unsatisfactory, being restrictive rather than a positive factor; and this can pose the problem of an economic restructuring of your life. Finding a way of living that can satisfy those creative abilities may be difficult, but the alternative is even more damaging if you choose to turn your back on the seductive music of Neptune. Creativity or craftsmanship is the route that Neptune is indicating, or alternatively, working with people in community service to be of social benefit. Perhaps through teaching, medicine, social work, you can contribute to others' welfare. This is a heart response to the music, equally significant and satisfying that desire to be positive in the world.

Find a way which offers more freedom than traditional work structures, a way that encourages creativity or service to flow. In so doing, you unravel your Sun-path to travel along, and those times of confusion and indecision are relegated to memories. The potential of working with Neptune is considerable; this god can transform you if you are open to his promptings and messages. If he is rejected, then his waters will slowly erode away your dreams and desires, denuding you of power to achieve your aims, leaving you with an unfulfilled life; it is wiser to acknowledge his inner promptings and try to change in accord with them. The gods do not take kindly to being mocked through being ignored, and they make their presence felt.

NEPTUNE–SUN SEXTILE

Unlike the conjunction aspect which poses the problem of dealing with both the positive and negative influences of Neptune on the individual life, the sextile is an easier aspect to live with.

The themes of creativity through art, music, crafts, writing, and drama are highlighted, as are the inner paths of mysticism and psychic sensitivity as ways of co-operating with the Neptunian impulse and moving towards the solar centre. You are likely to be aware of your own creative potential, and inclined to allow this natural expression. One ability that you may possess is creating vivid mental images, which through the process of creative visualisation can be used either in the building of your own future path, or by offering these for the stimulation and enjoyment of others through music, art and literature. Manifesting these evocative images into a tangible form is a very important gift, and can be applied in a variety of ways, for self-aggrandisement, the accumulation of wealth and power or to help benefit others. This issue of selfish versus selfless actions is one which may confront you, influencing your decisions and motivations. The art of visualisation is a powerful merging of mind– will–imagination, and is the source of creation.

Your sensitivity to others and world pain will be strong, connected to a reasonably well-developed awareness of social responsibility, where by empathic feelings you believe that you should and could aid in the alleviation of human suffering. Yet this psychic absorption of pain can also make you turn away from actually doing anything about this social awareness, so you may register and acknowledge its existence yet attempt to deny your role in healing. It is unlikely that you will be capable of dealing with the causes of suffering, but may prefer to hold a soothing and healing balm to the symptoms of the pain. You hope that others who are stronger and perhaps less sensitive than yourself will deal with the negative causes in society.

You may be of value by communicating inspiration, perhaps through writing for publication or through the media. Linking your grasp of social responsibility with a good dramatic expression could bring aspects of society that need transforming to the attention of others; crusading journalism and TV documentaries are prime examples of such work. This is an asset that you could apply, and if you choose to develop this, then your imagination and inspiration will be rekindled. This need to maintain relationships with people which also involves a broader social sphere than that of just friendship, is a route which Neptune works through, leading you towards your solar purpose.

With most people, you experience a *laissez-faire* relationship, where tolerance and empathy dominate, and interpersonal pressures are not imposed. While your sensitivity is ever-present, you are not overly demanding or tied to impossible expectations of others, although you do prefer self-confident companions whose associations force you to firm up any tendency towards Neptunian nebulousness and indecision. You have a humanitarian spirit, relating freely and easily to a wide range of human types, seeing value in all and not just in those who are 'successful' in terms of social evaluation.

There is an element of a chameleon nature about you, a malleability enabling you to fit into a variety of situations and social scenes, an inner flexibility whereby your attitudes and expression mould themselves to any specific environment and take over from deeper personal preferences. This is a Neptunian water quality in your personality, where you 'take the shape of any container'. It can be advantageous, yet equally can lead to losing your distinct identity due to repeated chameleon transformations. This may therefore need to be carefully monitored or guarded against if your personality begins to fragment and dissolve, although if you are following a mystical path, dissolving into the 'ocean' becomes your aim, where the droplet of the separate self loses all boundaries and disappears into the universal ocean of life.

NEPTUNE–SUN TRINE

With the trine, there is the potential for a successful reconciliation and resolution of the Neptune–Sun energies, leading to a powerful positive blending of the individual Sun centre and the transpersonal outer planet.

Potential is present, but there may be question marks against your incentive, motivation and application in exploiting latent talents. This is the hurdle that can face you, especially when confronted with the nature of choice and decision over your life-direction. You may be multi-talented in a variety of artistic and creative ways – music, art, literature, dance, drama – yet find it hard to be focused and sufficiently disciplined to become a master and not a jack of all trades. Ideas spring forth easily and naturally, followed by an enthusiastic grasping of them, only for them to be put quickly aside, replaced by the next set of shooting-star ideas. Commitment and perseverance may be lacking, and the directed energy is fragmented by turning towards too many directions at the same time.

Associated with a perceptive mind, which is capable of good assimilation and understanding, should be an intuitive quality too, which you can use as a source of insight and knowledge. This intuitive or psychic faculty will mainly operate through the emotional nature as empathic identification, in distinction to the Uranian intuition which is more mental and impersonal in nature. This intuition often gives you insights into the nature and motivation of others around you, and environmental atmospheres can influence your state of mind and well-being.

There can be an ambivalency towards social involvement and responsibility. Much depends on the nature of your expression; if it is within creative and artistic spheres, then your focus of attention and energy is absorbed within the creative vision. You are not unresponsive to social concerns, but you feel that being a creative channel is your contribution to society. Or you may respond to the Neptunian vibration by opening your heart wider, feeling a channel for 'universal love' supporting and uplifting others. This path is one of service to the community of human beings, and medicine can be a favourite expression, or similar forms of physical, emotional and mental therapy and healing.

Becoming clear as to direction is the challenge; once determined you should be able to pour your energies and talents into achieving those aims, and in so doing walk your solar path of purpose. You have the capabilities to achieve your objectives, once definition and focus is made. There may be a need to be more practical, perhaps modified by evoking a strong Saturn or Mercury influence to ensure that material results occur, or you could waste those talents and end as a negative dreamer, chasing your flights of imagination but never containing them within objective form.

In relationships, emotional freedom and trust is highly valued as components of an ideal romantic love. You tend to be emotionally faithful, and give priority to the virtues of a close and loving family environment. Your empathic and sympathetic nature adds to those feelings of closeness with family and friends.

Neptune–Sun Square

This indicates tendencies of psychologically based inhibitions, restrictions and frustrations which pose considerable challenges that need overcoming before the more positive characteristics of Neptune and the Sun can emerge.

You tend to lack confidence in your identity and ability to achieve your ambitions. Part of this may have been derived from your parental relationships, especially with the father, as your developing nature may have experienced conflict through lack of understanding or perceived love; it may have been that by asserting your own individuality you clashed with the stronger parental will. The results are that your self-confidence has fragmented, and that your application of will is less focused and effective, and consequently you have developed psychological defences against others and from facing personal failure.

This is displayed in escapism, avoidance of responsibilities and of the need for self-discipline, unless a powerful Saturn in your chart can rebalance this tendency. Preferring to run away from confronting reality leads to distorted perceptions, which makes careful evaluation of options difficult as well as generating fears of making decisions which may prove to be unwise. At its worst, this can create inertia through fear of taking deliberate action. These inner images of failure tend to create external failures, and so emphasise a repetitive vicious circle. Yet by linking this pattern of failure within aims and ambitions that are probably beyond your current capabilities to achieve, you also succeed in evading the realisation that you are creating most failures in your life. This is exacerbated by the dreams of the unintegrated and unfulfilled Neptune, who may be noticed as a thread of guilt related to your lack of achievement, and as an ongoing sensation of discontent. Your solar power is being diverted and dissolved by the activity of an unintegrated Neptune, and unless you can begin to reassert this solar centre and face your Neptunian challenges, then this unsatisfactory condition may continue.

These challenges can be mitigated by a decision to make sufficient effort to connect to your hidden solar centre, to move beyond those superimposed images of guilt, failure and inferiority that have developed as a defensive response to emotional pain. Such a reorientation may not be easy to make, as you will be opposing established patterns of behaviour, yet the gains that can be made are likely to transform your life.

The first step is self-acceptance, to cease any self-judgement and condemnation. Then, if you really want it to happen, feel confident that change can occur. You have sufficient inner creativity, imagination and potential waiting to be released from imprisonment, although finding appropriate channels of expression may still take a little longer. However, you need to define any ambitions within a more realistic perspective than previously. Possibly some form of counselling may be effective in helping you gain more clarity regarding your self-potential, or workshops in self-assertion and decision-making/goal-setting. In effect, you are being asked to see yourself as a young child, ready to enter adulthood, and you are expected to recreate yourself into a new and more suitable identity. Take smaller and easily achievable steps in this process of recreation; acknowledge that occasional failures are inevitable, but try not to turn them into traumatic dramas, and realise that success will not happen without the parallel risk of failure side by side. Everybody is a failure at something, and that isn't an excuse to condemn yourself again.

As your self-confidence grows, your life will begin to take a more positive shape. It will not happen overnight, as transforming long-established behaviour patterns cannot be changed that quickly, but persevere and changes can happen. Perhaps using techniques like creative visualisation and affirmations, or subliminal programming encoded on self-development cassette tapes could strengthen this process. The essential realisation is that change is possible, and that you can achieve this in your own way; in hope lies the fountainhead of the waters of potential and transformation. Such improvements can benefit your intimate relationships too, as well as enhance your self-image, confidence and decision-making abilities.

Generally you are emotionally vulnerable, possibly exploited or abused by others, deceived or manipulated in various ways; but if these tendencies exist, then they are reflections of those dominating patterns within you. There can be unusual emotional needs and desires linked with romantic idealism that are expressed in physical sexuality; these may require healing and cleansing in some way. But the proposed transformation and refinement that is implied by resolving the conflict of the Sun and Neptune would simultaneously deal with that level too.

There can be an attraction towards occultism and mysticism, which if followed in the pre-transformation stage can lead to self-exaltation in contrast to an inferiority complex, becoming self-deluded as a voice of God or the Masters; although if the transformation has been made, then you could actually function in such a way as a purer channel. But some degree of caution and restraint may need making if you do explore such dimensions of life, as there can be an unconscious desire for self-aggrandisement operating through and motivating your actions. As the imagination aspect of Neptune is so strong, this can create inflated egotism and self-delusion where instead of finding the light, you become lost in the dazzle of glamour and illusion.

Neptune–Sun Opposition

The opposition between Neptune and the Sun can stimulate a distorted and self-deluding perspective of reality, which tends to create additional problems and obstacles in your life and decision-making. You may find it difficult to analyse and evaluate options and choices correctly, often focusing on self-created and imaginary issues rather than actual problems. Sometimes these can take the forms of voluntary suffering arising from inner guilt patterns associated with deep-lying desires, an expiation or atonement of 'sins', actual or imaginary. This can result in the sacrificial martyr attitude, and is often quite unnecessary, yet in a strange way provides a foundation to your life. A sacrifice may well be required, that of your imagined illusions, prior to attaining the deeper solar centre of balance, but such a sacrifice is often misunderstood and misapplied in daily life.

You tend to react strongly against any domination imposed by others, yet can easily submit if under the influence of a misplaced sacrificial trip. Your relationships can be characterised by degrees of confusion and misunderstandings, and through powerful emotions you are liable to overlay intimate relationships with fantasies and wishful thinking, forming a deceiving miasma which affects all involved. There can be a pattern operating through you that subverts clear, honest and direct communication, even though you may not fully accept or realise this. As you tend to be insecure and defensive in relationship attitudes, tensions can be generated by your style of expression which rarely accepts being wrong or any responsibility, yet does so in a manner which attempts to lay any blame on the shoulders of others. This creates confusion rather than clarity, and over time it may produce considerable friction. This nebulousness dominates your personality, turning you into a 'psychological chameleon', changing appearances and attitudes as distorted perceptions and personal biases intrude into reality.

You often avoid commitment and entering fully into emotional involvements through fears of being trapped or dominated, which allied to a suspicious nature does not auger well for stable relationships. As you are liable to fall under the negative Neptunian glamours regarding love and romance, this tendency may have developed from previous shattering disappointments. If this becomes a repetitive pattern in your life, then the cause is probably within yourself, and it is by exploration and inward journey to contact the solar light that you can discover and illumine your potential solution.

Coming to terms with such influential patterns concerning your identity and relationships requires considerable honesty and commitment. Beneficial change can be stimulated, but only if you really want it and are willing to put in the effort. The main problem with inner glamours and illusions is that they are so difficult to identify correctly, and obviously such distorting mirrors make it hard to perceive with clarity. The real effect of spiritual transformation shatters these mirrors. Being able to recognise and acknowledge that such problems exist is the first and most important step, followed by consistent action to discover the appropriate remedy.

Through insecurity, you are liable to doubt your capabilities and potential, fearing challenges as exposing failings and weaknesses. Retreat or defensive mechanisms may have been established as forms of protection. Essentially, you need to strip down your habitual perceptions of others and yourself, so that the reality can shine through more objectively. Facing the reality of avoidance patterns and observing the influence of your emotional biases and defensive mechanisms can be very revealing, as can noting how you distort relationship communication; consider all this without self-condemnation or judgement. In looking lies the seeds of transformation. Refinding your own solar self and centre beyond these ephemeral influences is the purpose of your journey, and establishing a strength in your own identity and resources will demonstrate a developing maturity, rather than any unhealthy reliance on others.

Discerning your aims in life, perhaps developing a programme towards achieving some of them, can give a directional focus, and allow you to express freely that blocked and frustrated creative potential which may have been previously inhibited. Taking such steps can renew yourself and relationships, protecting you from being negatively influenced by surrounding environmental influences entering your psyche. Once the changes are made, you can have much to offer people, where your sacrificial tendencies can be beneficial and reflect your higher solar path instead of an illusory Neptunian one. Working with types of meditation which deglamorise and strip away illusory veils of personality, or with relationship therapies, can be suitable approaches to cleanse yourself of the negative Neptunian tendencies, in order for the light of your co-ordinating Sun centre to shine through more powerfully.

PLUTO–SUN CONJUNCTION

Your ambitions and desires will be highly influenced by your natal Sun sign, and these can be achieved by applying the Pluto energy to amplify your solar will power. Potentially, this conjunction aspect can be very valuable in enabling you to reach your objectives, but to maximise chances of eventual success you may need to adjust certain attitudes.

Pluto offers the potential of regeneration and rebirth, which is also reflected in the pattern of solar myths, so you should be able to transform yourself and also to some degree your immediate environment to match your purpose. Once your direction is determined you will see what may require changing as a prerequisite to achievement, and then commence applying your will accordingly.

There can be attitudes of extremism, where your beliefs, ideas, and opinions are expressed with force and intensity. You will feel quite clear about your preferences in life, and often your attitudes could be polarised into 'black and white', with little space for 'grey' to be considered, or to be accepted as a viable alternative. Once your choices are made, it is as if you have written them on tablets of stone; even though you have the ability to change, you may not willingly do so, or you may alter fixed attitudes only when you feel there is no option. You find it difficult to be balanced, especially in tolerating and understanding the frailties of humanity. You probably adopt a fairly hard-line philosophy, having the opinion that people can change their lives and be self-sufficient if they want to, instead of being weak and relying upon others, although you tend to resist change yourself.

You may tend to be assertive and attracted towards power; those who appear to possess influence over others will serve as a magnet, at least in the sense that you would like to be in such positions of authority. Such an inner desire is likely to influence your direction in life, work and career, or even in the struggles of family life. You may use manipulation and psychological pressure tactics as levers to guarantee winning in the midst of any power struggles with others; your one-pointed ruthlessness can bring apparent success, but may also bring an increasing number of 'enemies' in its wake. You will have to learn that you are not 'the centre of the universe', and that others have rights and purposes too, and that they should never be sacrified or walked over just to achieve your desires. An adjustment to become more aware of others, by acknowledging that their feelings and unique outlooks on life are as valid as yours, would create a much more harmonious energy in your life and the fulfilment of successful personal relationships. Being willing sometimes to accept inevitable failures would be a positive step for you, so that tension could be diffused and break any compulsive search for 'success'; otherwise, you may become obsessed with achieving your goal and possibly be willing to damage people more, apart from allowing 'failure' to gnaw away by unhealthy brooding.

Much of your energy will carry a sexual potency, and irrespective of your physical sex, will have a penetrative quality to it and an aggressive masculine nature. Your physical needs are strong, and there can be a single-minded directness about your desires, as you pursue your 'prey' without deviation once your choice is made. Elements of victory, success, and manipulation will be present in your relationships and you will take any rejection hard as it negatively affects your self-image. However, your relationships will be very intense, and you will give a wholehearted commitment to them while they last, becoming very emotionally involved.

Emotional understanding is likely to be a weak spot until certain transformations have occurred within you which break down self-preoccupation. You may experience feelings of almost dissolving into passionate relationships, becoming lost in absorption with your lover, or possible obsessions with the affair. Such experiences could be the key to your transformation, or could fill you with so much fear for your sanity and chosen purpose that you begin to reject such intensity for more superficial physical relationships and energy release without the emotional dimension being evoked.

Almost paradoxically, you can also strongly react to social injustices, and may be attracted towards the alleviation of social problems. Movement in this direction is dependent upon the degree you become aware of the needs of others, and a corresponding diminution of your own need for power and success. The key issue is whether you are self-or other-orientated; this will determine your responses to others, either forming attitudes of 'they can change and help themselves' or 'I will change and use my power to help others to help themselves.' Such a step would involve a realignment with a higher inner ideal and purpose, and would represent your initiation into being a responsive member of humanity. This is a progression towards embodying your solar path's spiritual dimension, where the inner light begins to unify life and you feel the interrelationship with humanity and the world. Taking this approach can regenerate your life direction, and will lead you towards the experiences of the heroic quest, challenging your perseverance and application of focused will, and demanding considerable inner growth which can enable you to attain your objectives.

PLUTO–SUN SEXTILE

You should be able to use your Sun–Pluto energies in a positive resourceful and constructive manner, believing that with clear motivation, direction, and focused will you can attain your ambitions. There will be considerable powers of endurance, and this will help perseverance through tapping your inner resources.

You have several natural talents, which can be used for both your own benefit and for others. Communication is one talent, where you should be able to transmit your thoughts to others clearly, fluently and with style. It is likely that you will work closely with groups, possibly through mutual ideologies aimed towards resolving social problems, as you feel a responsibility to add your support towards social betterment. You particularly dislike those social aspects which reveal a lack of natural justice for the 'underdog', and where disorder and chaos rule; you prefer to approach such challenges by direct encounter, using will and perseverance and believing that eventually your intensity will win through.

You can evolve into a spokesperson for such a group endeavour, as you give inspiration to people who respond well to the aura of powerful energy that you emit, creating confidence in your integrity and abilities to further the cause. For your immediate associates, the energy has a harmonising and vitalising effect. You tend to use it as a personal guide to determine the right approach to take in situations, almost as a form of psychic intuition, taking the place of logic and analysis; you rely on this sense of directive feeling to make necessary decisions, although it can be difficult to express your reasons to others in a convincing way. This joining of your solar path with the social concerns for transformation which emanate from Pluto can be potentially dynamic, forming a life direction which fulfils and continues to stimulate, even though it may be highly challenging and results may seem slow in coming.

A natural understanding of the life process should be evident, accepting that progression eventually requires the releasing of any old restrictive patterns, which you are able to do without much trauma as part of your process of regeneration. You have a capacity for ongoing creative growth in your relationships, achieved without unnecessary drama or crisis, almost as a natural evolutionary expression of the sextile's energy operating through your personality. You may need to review your relationships and social activity periodically to ensure that directional clarity is still present, but this serves to satisfy the Plutonic impulse to transform when necessary, and is consciously absorbed into your solar path without undue force or pressure. By adopting this approach, you can ensure that your Sun and Pluto remain co-operative and mutually support your endeavours.

Pluto–Sun Trine

The relationship of the Sun–Pluto trine is potentially quite harmonious, and you should have the ability to concentrate and apply your willpower, coupled with the option of a regenerative transformation which may be necessary to achieve self-integration and your chosen aims.

There will be less influence by the undermining quality of the Pluto energy, provided that you utilise your natural gifts in socially acceptable ways. You are able to make maximum use of innate resources, turning them to your advantage to achieve your goals. You will display a social awareness, and will feel attracted to applying your talents towards improving the social environment. Your ability to have a natural insight into resolving problems in the most effective manner can lead to a possible career or vocation in challenging problem-solving areas. You will have certain financial skills and a logical and deductive mind, preferring to tackle projects where you can reclaim order from chaos. This gives a sense of satisfaction, as you dislike chaos and a lack of structure; you want to be in control and create an ordered harmony in your life and environment.

You have the potential to be a spokesperson or leader, where your vitality gives the impression of purposeful direction, and your optimistic and inspiring creative expression can attract support. This occurs naturally, without the usual Pluto desires for power and manipulative influencing of others; indeed, you have little compulsive desire to be an authoritative leader.

There can be an intuitive ability which offers you clear insights into situations, possibly even a degree of clairvoyance, which any exploration into yoga, meditation and ways of self-discovery could release and amplify. There may be a healing energy from you, possibly aiding others who can absorb excessive energy releases from you on an unconscious level, and you can be a reliable support to anyone who requires aid in resolving problems.

You may benefit from what appears to be 'luck' in your life; this can come from inheritances, or by the ill fortune of others. You have considerable creative potential, but to release this fully you may have to experience some inner transformation which dissolves any blocks which are initially frustrating your success. This involves learning how to use this aspect to full advantage. Assuming that you are able to channel this energy towards socially beneficent results, and ensuring that you do not try to evade facing and resolving any important personal problems that arise – within yourself or within a relationship – then you should experience few of the traditional difficulties associated with an unintegrated Pluto energy; which for many people, could be considered a blessing! Certainly, Pluto can be very co-operative with your solar aims, although much of this support may lie deeper in your unconscious mind and may not always be recognised. At least unresolved Plutonic patterns will not be subtly influencing and distorting your choices and experiences in an attempt to come to your attention.

PLUTO–SUN SQUARE

The energy and challenges indicated by this square can be difficult to deal with, as the unintegrated negative tendencies of Pluto can be fully present. Arriving at a clear understanding of such underlying aspects of your nature, by evoking the light and the cohesive nature of your Sun will serve to minimise the more negative and destructive effects of this abrasive Plutonic energy, allowing you to redirect it towards more positive channels which are associated with your solar path. However, you will have to remain aware of how you are expressing Pluto, as its peculiar quality will still be vitalised and cannot be nullified, only used in a wiser manner.

The Pluto tendencies of ambition, force, power, domination, aggression, and extremism can also stimulate similar tendencies in an assertive Sun, and will exist as motivating and compulsive factors in your character. Much may depend upon your Sun sign, especially if it is placed in either Earth or Fire elements, when those tendencies may be more present as an impulse for 'power over' others. If the Sun is in a Water or Air sign, then the emphasis may be placed on emotional or intellectual manipulation and domination.

You will tend to believe that your focused will power can act in a magical way, achieving desires and purposes by the wielding of a concentrated will; often, you will 'magically' succeed but there is usually some form of hidden cost to pay. Often applying your potent will, especially when your motives are self-centred, can lead to more negative and destructive results which oppose your initial intention; like the Scorpio energy, you are liable to sting yourself and others.

You may experience considerable inner tension as a result of this challenging planetary relationship, often finding it difficult to 'break through barriers' which appear to prohibit the attainment of your ambitions. This is Pluto attempting to force you towards an inner transformation, the need for which you will recognise whenever the pressures of frustrated intentions increase, until you find it hard to live with and in some way 'blow up' releasing the pressure. Some changes can occur as a result of powerful cathartic experiences, which will enable you either to move towards success, or create a new alternative route to follow.

Attitudes towards authority are ambivalent. While you have certain leadership qualities and management ability, you are often antagonistic towards authority, sceptical, subversive and iconoclastic in your speech and thoughts. Obviously, this will not lead to progress in many fields of society, but you are too independent and free-spirited to change and be subservient. It is likely that others will maintain a psychological distance from you, because your aura often suggests – in an unconscious manner – that you are 'dangerous'; that your way of looking at things is potentially challenging and transformative, and that a deeper involvement would bring about some unknown change in them. Others could find it a fascinating energy, and greatly enjoy your company; much depends upon their ability to handle it.

You are often looking to pit yourself against adversaries as a test and enjoyment, feeling like a fiery warrior at war. This can be expressed on all levels, physical, emotional and mental. You may not always express it in real tangible terms, often only entering into the adversarial state of mind, mentally enacting imaginary battles with an opponent in terms of ideological disagreement and inner dialogue, as you hate the thought of losing.

You will be hard to understand, appearing quite enigmatic to many, and may often have a resistance towards becoming emotionally involved with others. This is because you are aware of your emotional depths and strength of feelings, and this intensity can make you feel extremely uncomfortable, especially if you lose control when you have fallen in love. You have a fear of not being in full control, and will usually try to create a relationship context where you feel in command of the situation. While giving an impression of great self-control and balance, you often hide the evidence of inner turmoil, which can erupt as overreactions to trivial unimportant events in your life, or be forcefully released when someone 'presses your buttons' evoking a response.

You prefer stability, and are often resistant to change, especially when you have established a lifestyle which suits you. There can be a form of apprehension concerning actually achieving your purposes; sometimes you make good progress, only to run out of interest at the point when the final effort should be made, almost as if the subversive tendency of Pluto finally erodes your solar purpose. Until the inner friction between your Sun and Pluto is more resolved and integrated under solar control, then you may unconsciously act as your own worst enemy, defeating your own intentions. You should learn to acknowledge the aid of others in your life, and be open to all their suggestions, as they can often indicate the direction for you to take. Compromise and co-operation are two lessons which need to be learned as soon as possible, as well as more inner moderation. Once you achieve a balance between being receptive to others and your dominating tendencies wanting them to submit to you, then you should find that the quality of your relationships begins to improve in a creative and constructive manner.

Ideally, you should inwardly redirect Pluto's abrasive energy. This may not be easy, and can involve some personal suffering, but it can stimulate a radical transformation to occur, which offers considerable benefit and would make your life and relationships more fulfilling. This would also be the key to attaining your solar aims as you would be removing an inner barrier which is otherwise likely to prevent and frustrate many of your efforts.

Pluto–Sun Opposition

This suggests that most of your problems and challenges will arise in the area of interpersonal relationships, often created or stimulated by your own unconscious expression of this energy, which requires a deeper understanding and inner adjustment to be achieved before you can consistently benefit from its power.

Your temperament can be assertive, aggressive and extremist, tending to use your powerful will like a sledgehammer to achieve objectives. You prefer to force situations so that you are ready to take the advantage before anyone else can, or will act through impulse without fully considering the consequences of following your desires and aims. To others, your will and personality can seem a little overbearing, provocative and dominating, especially as you always prefer to be in control of all situations, and hate to feel unsure of your ground or realise there is nothing you can do to influence circumstances in your favour. This is why you desire to be in a position of authority, calling the tune and writing the rules, yet are so rebellious when roles are reversed; you then use your influence to be subversive and manipulate others to resist authority.

You will feel a desire to change the world into your image, reflecting the way that you think it should be. As virtually everyone else is attempting the same in small or large ways, inevitably you may experience conflict with others who do not agree with your panacea for the world's ills. If you attempt to dictate to people, by forceful expression, you may easily fail to get the right kind of support and co-operation, especially if it is made clear that you intend to be the kingpin and final arbiter. The problem with dominating and forceful personalities is that usually they insist on having their own way, and are rarely, if ever, wrong. This usually ends in relationship conflict which leads to their more creative supporters quitting, leaving behind 'mere followers' who remain with the 'leader' in sycophantic acquiescence.

Without proper awareness and understanding, these tendencies can become negatively expressed, eventually to your detriment. Yet equally they can become extremely positive qualities to be used in socially creative ways once excess self-interest is transcended, and you move towards the higher solar path of your individuality rather than just satisfying lower egoic needs and desires. You will need to undergo a period of self-regeneration, to acknowledge the needs of others to be themselves, not as mere adjuncts to your dictates, but people equally able and right to assert themselves. More harmonious and successful relationships are possible, especially when your need for self-assertion diminishes through self-understanding and confidence in your own worth. This can involve learning to be self-reliant in achieving your own aims, rather than having to manipulate others into unconsciously aiding your private intentions. Inner changes leading to a less aggressive attitude and less suspicion in working with others, more co-operation to achieve mutual goals plus a degree of compromise in your attitudes will certainly bring more benefit to you and others. Gaining an understanding of the elements present in your psychology which desires to become an authority and leader, can help to bring about an inner adjustment, and an ability to work with others can then emerge.

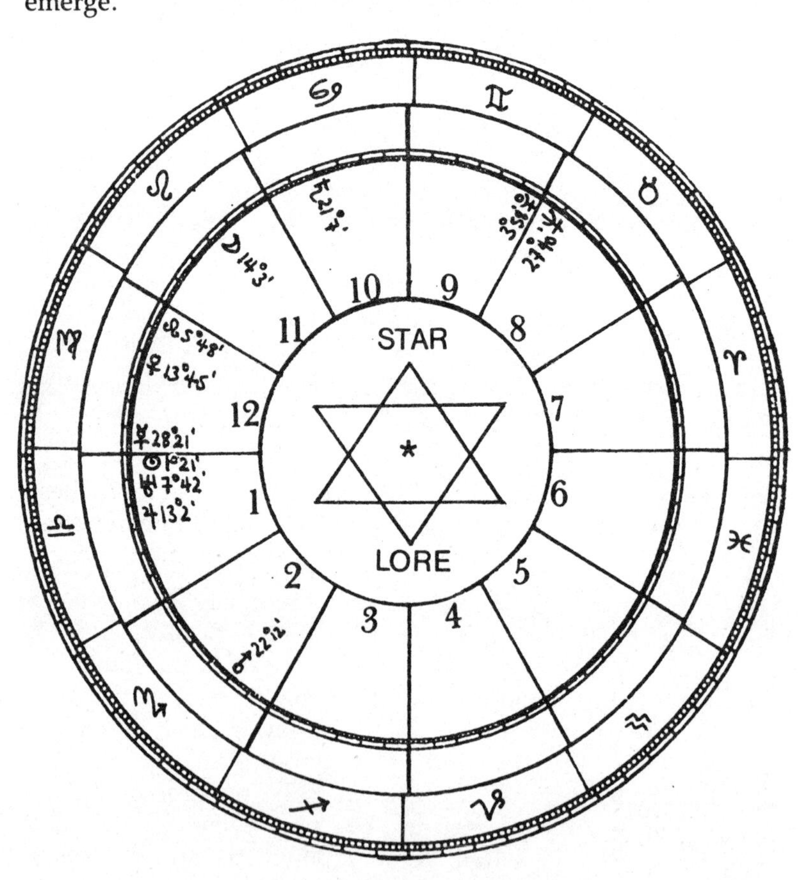

Dr. Edward Bach. Solar chart. Noon 24 September 1886. Moseley, Birmingham, England.

CHART EXAMPLES

Dr. Edward Bach

Sun in Libra. Sun conjunct Mercury, Uranus, trine Neptune, Pluto. Solar Chart, calculated for noon

Dr. Edward Bach discovered the Bach Flower Remedies, which have become an established and respected form of alternative health treatment, especially popular today with the increased public interest in complementary medicine. Dr. Bach was a practising doctor and Harley Street consultant, bacteriologist and homoeopath, and was highly qualified, yet after over twenty years of lucrative practice changed his medical direction to explore the mysteries of plant energies which he believed could be used as a healing agent. In private practice he grew dissatisfied with orthodox medical approaches, and began to believe that the problem in modern medicine lay in the attitude of focusing on the disease (the symptoms) and ignoring the actual patient (the source of illness). His work was to bridge different schools of healing, the Allopathic, Homoeopathic and the Naturopathic, and during his childhood he had a premonition of his destiny to evolve new methods of healing.

Emphasised in his chart are the signs of Libra, with Sun, Jupiter, Uranus and Virgo containing Mercury, Venus and North Node. This suggests that a major pattern in his nature was related to the themes of balance, work, service and health; indeed, these became the preoccupations of his life. His Libra Sun reflected his need for social relationship, and the necessity of attaining a balanced mind, emotions and body for physical well-being, and this was expressed through his medical contribution to others and by his later discovery of the power of plant essences, fulfilling his Virgoan North Node, Mercury and Venus.

His conjunction of Sun-Mercury reveals that his self-image and identity forms around his mental expression and activity, and in Bach's case, this included his assumption of the role of healer. The vitalisation of his Mercurian mind by the Sun helped him to become an effective and articulate communicator, impressing others by his intelligence. His tendency to identify closely with his own thoughts, beliefs, attitudes and values may have meant that he was not always inclined to listen to any views contrary to his own, yet this also served to give him the strength to pursue his own independent path with determination. His outstanding characteristics were his strong will, intense concentration, highly tuned sensitivity, a deep love of nature and a great compassionate desire to help resolve all distress in the world. The idea of discovering new dimensions to the medicinal value of plants excited him, and following this direction with great enthusiasm and at some risk to his own professional status and reputation, he eventually formulated his system of flower remedies which he then disseminated through his writings, explaining his method of preparation and specific usage of certain plants for particular ailments.

The Remedies are described as 'the simple and natural method of establishing complete equilibrium and harmony through the personality by means of wild flowers', and 'the 38 Remedies cover every negative state of mind known to man' and are effective in dealing with the inner states of the personality so that a healing integration can occur. Their influence operates on subtle levels, on states of mind which often act as a primary source for ill health, draining the body of vitality. Each flower remedy serves to restore an inner peace and harmony to the body–emotions–mind interrelationship, 'closing the circuit as it were and allowing the Life Force to flow freely again, thus providing the body its chance to produce its own natural healing'.

He discovered that the plants with the most effective healing power were found during the time of year when the days are longest and the Sun streams forth in power and influence. He developed a technique called 'solarising', which was based on solar influences, for the process of extracting plant and flower potencies, by floating the flower-heads in a bowl of clear stream water exposed for several hours to the full light of the Sun. In a parallel to the astrological concept of elemental balance within the personality, his technique utilised 'the earth to nurture the plant, the air from which it feeds, the sun (fire) to enable it to impart its power, and water to collect and be enriched with its beneficent magnetic healing'. Bach's insight was that the basic cause of disease lay in any disharmony between the personality and the soul, and his remedies were aimed at restoring this healing unity.

Amplifying his mental sensitivity of the conjunction of Sun–Mercury, is another conjunction with Uranus. This implies the tendency of individualism and non-conformism, where an eventual conflict with traditional approaches can lead to the creation of a uniquely personal path. Feelings of imprisonment are implied, as the inner impulses look for freedom, and Bach may well have felt this after twenty years of medical consultancy. His search for a new direction gained focus in his flower distillations. The challenge of this Sun–Uranus aspect is to deal with the impulse for freedom, and is related to the forging of the solar path, as the restricted energy attempts to transform the existing lifestyle pattern. For Bach, this was the cessation of his mainstream medical practice in favour of his own unusual and eccentric studies. This satisfied his need for mental stimulation and newness, enabling him both to renew himself and exploit his talents through exploring new horizons and interests. His idealistic nature and motivation to serve were satisfied by his intention to redirect all benefits for the well-being of others, and one famous example is his saving of a fisherman's life in 1930 by the use of his 'Rescue Remedy'.

This Sun–Uranus aspect is noticeable for the implicit connection to the Uranian 'higher mind', where rapid mental activity and logic leaps can lead to connecting insights, almost like an intuitive penetration into the nature of reality. His understanding of the connectedness of all levels of the human being, and recognition of the fact that attitudes of mind have either positive or negative health effects, led to his application of transformative flower essences as a rebalancing and purifying stimulus. This healing work on subtler levels is a precursor to the opening of more energy-orientated alternative therapies that are being currently developed. By listening to his own inner promptings, and having the courage to follow his own light, Bach travelled his heroic path and through his personal contribution has left a healing approach that can benefit all.

The Sun trine with Neptune is especially active in Bach, indicating the presence of a perceptive, intuitive and psychic mind, which operates through empathic identification, creating insights into environmental atmospheres capable of influencing the state of mind and personal well-being.

> [Bach] developed great sensitivity both in mind and body. If he held his hand over a flowering plant, or the flower in the palm of his hand, he could sense in himself the properties of that flower. Before finding a particular flower, he would suffer in himself, and very acutely, the negative state of mind for which that flower was needed and, at the same time, he was privileged, as he said, to suffer from some physical complaint. Then he would wander about the fields and lanes until he was 'led' to find the flowers which would immediately restore his serenity and peace of mind, and within a few hours the physical complaint would also be healed.

This planetary aspect of Sun–Neptune helped Bach to 'open his heart' and to feel that he was a channel for the universe, to support and uplift others through his path of medicine and community service. Once he became clear as to his new direction, he was free to explore his solar path of purpose.

The Sun trine with Pluto completes his solar resonance with the influences of the transpersonal planets, and indicates the option facing the individual of a regenerative transformation, which is necessary in order to attain a deeper self-integration and life purpose. The emphasis here is on using resources to their fullest for both personal and social advantages, and this Bach appeared to achieve. In addition, faculties of intuition and possible clairvoyance are also potentials with this aspect, as is the releasing of a healing energy. The only inhibitions to these manifesting may be inner and outer blockages that need dissolving. The aim of these tendencies is the creation of order and harmony, which again reflects Bach's Libra and Virgo planetary emphasis, as well as the intention of the flower remedies. The important point to realise is how Dr. Edward Bach embodied the higher qualities of both his Sun and planetary contacts, using them in the development of his earlier career, and also in the unfolding of his heroic quest.

Colin Wilson

Sun in Cancer, 1st House. Sun conjunct Mercury, Ascendant (Gemini), sextile Mars, Neptune

Colin Wilson is a prolific English author, and since the publication of his first book, the best-selling *The Outsider* in 1956, has produced over eighty books. His main preoccupations include crime and murder, sexuality, psychology, paranormal experiences and the occult mysteries. He is also a fiction writer, exploring similar topics through storytelling. Over the years, his interests have veered towards a fascination with the nature of consciousness, and especially the provoking of 'peak experiences', and for an individual who is a confirmed – even obsessive – intellectual, he has great interest and affinity with the sensual, ecstatic dimensions of human life, and curiosity towards so-called taboo areas of sexuality and human violence. He looks towards the 'high' levels of human activity, and balances this concern by studying the 'lower' types of expression.

While his interests and studies are nominally intellectual and reflect the vitality of his Gemini Ascendant, what really

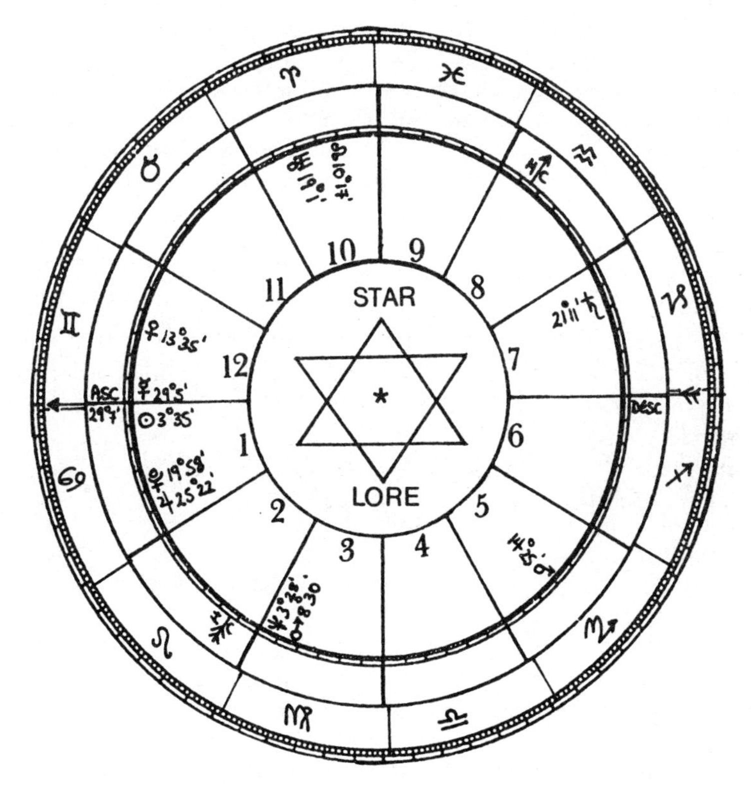

Colin Wilson. 3.30 GMT 26 June 1931. Leicester, England.

stimulates his quest is a search for the intensity of heightened feeling experiences which derive more from his Cancer Sun and Scorpio Moon. These reveal his underlying emotional depths and complexities, although they are also often veiled from public view by his Gemini Ascendant's detached rationality. In several ways, his preoccupation with research and writing enables him to withdraw from the world, in order to concentrate on his thematic obsessions, and this action evokes his own version of the Crab retreating into its shell, although in Wilson's case this is the absorption within the world of intellectual fascinations and ideas that stimulates his private enthusiasms.

He has recently stated that as he approaches the age of sixty, his life is increasingly focused on

> one basic obsession . . . that quite simply, in certain moments of great insight, great intensity we get a feeling that life is incredibly simple, and if only we could maintain this insight, no one would ever want to die. Because we can see in these moments that everything is absolutely superb, that in a certain sense, we are in heaven now (*Human Potential*, Winter 1989).

This is the foundation of the mystical quest for enlightenment, where the simplicity of life is experienced as universal unity and relationship, and where – as Wilson recognises – the complexity of intellectual analysis and investigation fades into relative insignificance when the experience of intense unity with life is actually felt. Certainly the experience of enlightenment is primarily the most intense feeling possible to man; after that diminishes from its peak, intellectual insight, understanding and attempts to explain its nature can then be formulated.

His 1st house Sun indicates his need for self-assertion, to make his mark on the world, by being 'someone' who is noticed, respected and acknowledged through his specific expression. The challenge of his life-path is to draw upon his latent talents, and this Wilson has consistently attempted to achieve, both from his school days when his academic nature was already present, to his emergence as one of the group of 'Angry young men' during the mid-1950s, and through his populist studies of the occult and paranormal. An early self-belief that he had something special to offer fuelled his ambitious desires for success, enabling him to focus and apply his will, so that he could manifest his dreams into real achievements. The essential tone of his nature is positive, forming an attractive if self-contained personality, although there is also an impulse of domination through the assertion of any positions of power and authority. Part of this tendency is reflected by his intellectual attraction to sexual and criminal sadism, the fascination with the murder impulse and the ultimate dominating power over others. Wilson has taken responsibility for his life, choosing his own path and following it determinedly. In order to clarify his understanding of his nature, he has needed to pursue paths of self-knowledge, taking a solitary and individualistic route as he responds to his inner messages.

The Sun–Mercury conjunction indicates that his self-image is more derived from his mental activity and expression, and that he probably prefers to identify himself consciously more with his Gemini Ascendant rather than his Cancer Sun. It is likely that, to some degree, he has distanced himself from the emotional fluctuations of Cancer by developing his intellectual objectivity, preferring to perceive himself through a mental filter. However, his emotional moodiness has been paralleled by his intellectual studies of existential angst and the loss of meaning and purpose in life; his study of *The Outsider* moves from the void of the meaningless of life to the mystic exaltation of the supreme meaning. Between these apparent opposites, Wilson's quest for understanding has ranged for thirty years. It could be suggested that he is now coming more to terms with his emotional depths, seeing them as a potential springboard for the intensity of experience for which he has been searching. He certainly embodies the characteristics of this conjunction through his impressive impact on others by his intelligence, articulacy and literary skills. In addition, he is personally involved with his own interests and fascinations, excited by his love affair with ideas and by his potential to share this with others through his writings. He is a disseminator of creative and inspired ideas, and uses his fiction as an alternative forum to expand key themes in an imaginative form, although his main interest is to use the novel as a medium of communication.

His Sun–Mars sextile reveals that his energy can be most aptly expressed through his mind and intellect, and that this will provide the source of his life direction and later achievements.

Evoking the power of his solar principle has certainly been Wilson's path-generator. The sextile offers a gift for creative thinking, and it is through developing this that personal talents will be displayed. In particular, following personal interests will be the specific way to open creative channels, and this Wilson has been doing since his emergence on the literary scene. The nature of his curious mind is suggested by this sextile, where the enjoyment of research, study and the accumulation of knowledge is mentally stimulating, as is the input of a variety of differing ideas which spark off speculative thoughts. He has remained a perpetual 'student', continually contemplating his personal interests, and expanding the parameters of his concerns through maintaining a relatively open mind to less tangible, subtle levels of human experience. In his own manner, he is contributing to what he sees to be the thrust of human evolution, the awakening of consciousness, and through his work is pointing to the development of future directions for individual and social growth.

While he has an intellectual bias, he also recognises that all have their own talents to contribute to society, and through his literary influence, he hopes to stimulate the minds of others to open to new potentials and possibilities.

The Sun–Neptune sextile also emphasises his talent for creativity and writing which can emerge from joining the Neptunian imaginative quality to his solar centre. This offers the ability to create vivid mental images, which are obviously a great advantage to any fiction writing, and these can be offered for the enjoyment of others. The power of images lies in the fact that they are more easily retained, and he recognises this, changing his intellectual style into an imaginative presentation of ideas.

It is interesting to note that his sensitivity to world pain and the suffering of others, reflected by this sextile and his Cancer Sun, is often evident in his portrayal and exploration of the psychology of fictional murderers; taking a humanitarian stance, his interest lies in investigating their human nature, probing to discern what has twisted and distorted them in ways different from the common man. One of his approaches is to reveal that it is through such actions that an intensity of feeling is attained, almost parallel to a mystical exaltation. This sextile also suggests that his personality has an innate mutability, a chameleon-type nature which changes according to circumstances. If this is what he has experienced, then it is likely that allied to his Gemini Ascendant dualism (the light and darkness in his fascinations), he has actualised a solar path which contains this tendency within a highly developed intellectual focus; that by preoccupation with ideas, their development and application within both individual and society, he has created a new personal centre from which he can guide and direct his life, and thus minimise the distracting effects of an emotional tidal nature by the power of self-discipline.

Salvador Dali

Sun in Taurus, 11th house. Sun conjunct Mercury, Mars, square Saturn, sextile MC (Pisces)

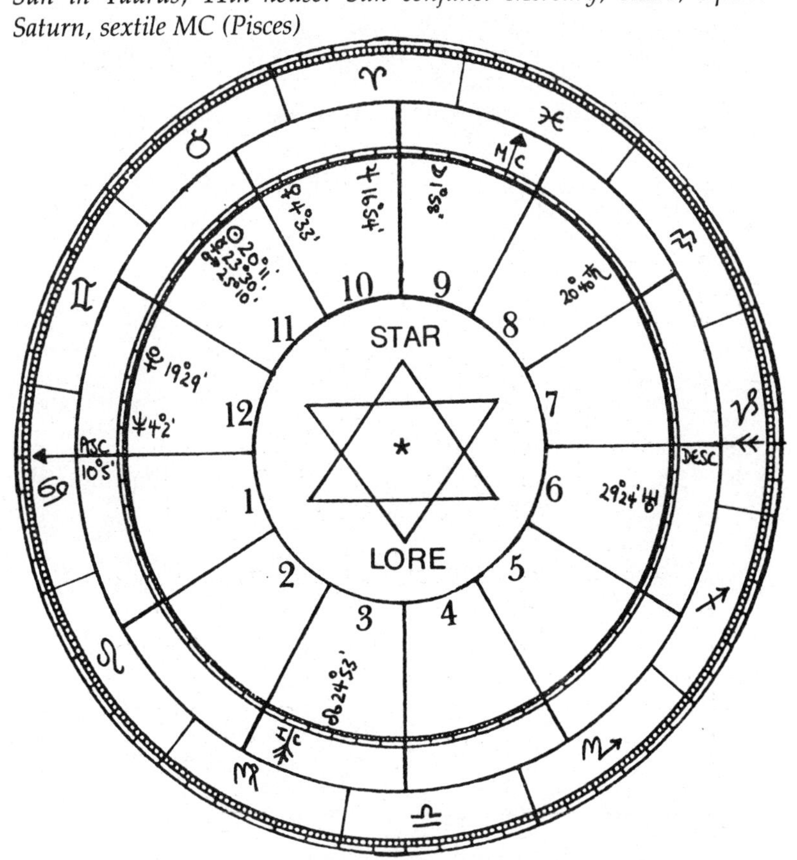

Salvador Dali. 8.45 a.m. 11 May 1904. Cadaques, Gerona, Spain.

Salvador Dali was a famous Spanish painter of the Surrealist movement, who attained international notoriety as a leading spokesman for that artistic approach, and for his own often eccentric and overtly egotistical behaviour. Surrealism is an art of the fantastic, the subconscious, dreams and allegory, developing from popular psychoanalytic thought at the time of its emergence with the First Surrealist Manifesto in 1924. The influence of Sigmund Freud with his emphasis on dreams, the subconscious and sexuality was especially significant in the intellectual formulation of the Surrealist concept.

Considering that Dali's Sun is in Taurus, which would normally be associated with favouring stability, security, and predictable behaviour patterns, his own artistic ideas led him in a most surprising direction. Surrealism evokes the irrational mind, creating unreal, unworldly and mysterious shapes and figures, posing an entirely new way of looking at the world and our own natures. In several ways, Surrealist art reflects the breaking down of twentieth-century certainties about the nature of reality, and preshadows our dawning insights into the quantum levels of existence, with shapes melting and merging into other forms and taking on disturbing and disquieting relationships to their immediate environment. Dali tried to embody a real process of thought beyond or beneath the conscious mind, which welled up in challenging images and which, in ordinary life, was often relegated to the imagination, dreams and psychological analysis. The Surrealists' intention was to shock their viewers into awareness and self-analysis; Dali's own personal technique was to allow his dreaming and imaginative mind full access into his life, and by opening up his psychological defensive barriers he shattered his more traditional Taurean traits, and re-created himself as an *artist*, a role that he assumed would justify much of his erratic behaviour.

It is particularly interesting to see how far beyond the characteristics of his Sun sign Dali travelled. Certainly he expressed the artistic side of Taurus, and the tendencies of stubbornness, sensuality, indulgence, persistence, vanity, but as the clocks in his paintings melted down, so did his personality controls until his inner cohesion anchored within the self-image of the artist.

This is evoked by his Sun–Mercury conjunction, where his

identity is centred on his mental expression and activities, although apart from the intellectual framework of Surrealism, his talents were mainly directed towards artistic articulacy of his ideas or subconscious manifestations of 'real thought'. Dali was especially true to his art movement, considering alternative approaches as not suitable for him or even worthy of attention; he was intent on imposing a Surrealist view upon the world, or intent on self-publicity, and over time the two become inextricably entangled by his egocentric posturing. Part of the Surrealist concept touches on a chaotic sphere of nature and the human being, and Dali became fascinated by exploring this shifting area of the psyche. It could be commented that he became the consequences of Surrealism, that his own psychological balance was irreparably shifted by the assumption of a non-consensus reality, especially as his artistic self flourished within an unintegrated personality.

His Sun in the 11th house indicates the importance of his impulse for group participation, which continued throughout his later life as an exponent of Surrealism. Part of this strand was a desire to see life anew, and linked to the belief in the value of psychoanalysis and the understanding of inner obsessions and compulsive patterns, offered an almost idealistic dream of a social and cultural progressive step. Through this 11th house, Dali became a living icon and channel for a new perceptive insight into an underlying half-hidden reality, and by disseminating this through paintings, film, literature, lifestyle and artistic happenings, he released a transformative potent energy into society for its renewal and revolution. The awareness of the relationship between the individual and the collective was present, and Dali often saw himself as a cultural hero, pointing the way to a better tomorrow for the liberated people. This was irrespective of an often negative and reactionary response by the common man to Surrealist art, which seemed incomprehensible and disturbing in its artistic implications.

It appears that this 11th house Sun position was more important to Dali than his actual Sun-sign, as his motivating thrust was towards the future, being less bound by any existing traditional attitudes of art or behaviour. Through his style of unique self-assertion, he often entered adversarial experiences with others who did not perceive him in the same light as he saw himself.

His radical attitudes were a direct challenge and disturbance to the status quo, and even the art world attempted to keep the Surrealist influence and artists at arm's length. He asserted his solar purpose through his group participation, and became recognised for his contribution to artistic innovations designed to regenerate society's view of itself. His own inner light was channelled through group activity, and this served to rekindle the artistic world.

His preoccupation with human sexuality, which was given an intellectual context by the Freudian influence on Surrealist concepts, is indicated by the Sun–Mars conjunction, where in his younger days his passions, curiosity and explorations ran strongly, although later his voyeuristic tendencies gained the ascendancy. As an expression of subconscious impulses, human sexuality was a ripe theme for investigation, and the use of overt sexuality was employed in Surrealist art, especially for its shock value to open and stimulate public discussion.

It is through this Sun–Mars conjunction that much of Dali's vitality and assertiveness flowed; his will and commitment to his cause rarely faded, and he had created an ideal forum for his self-preoccupation with his own desires and ambitions. He had an image of himself as a 'leader', and his need was to achieve visible success in order to prove himself to the world. The power of this conjunction also enabled him to liberate himself from many social and personal limits and restrictions, allowing him to indulge in impulsive, spontaneous actions and to encourage others to break free of their socially imposed chains. Compared to the rest of society, Dali lived in a uniquely free way, apparently immune to the pressures of social taboos and conditioning. However, one aspect to this was his insensitivity to others, caused by his self-absorption and assertion of freedom. His attraction towards the weird, the dangerous, the taboo, the feared and the unexpected led him to open doors that may have been safer closed; fascinated by the perverse, he moved further away from the human mainstream consciousness into his own Surrealist world.

The pressures that he placed on his own psychological balance are indicated by his Sun–Saturn square, which suggests a confrontation with his own limits and restrictions within his psyche, his self-image, attitudes, beliefs and values. This confrontation burst into the open early with his conversion to Surrealism, but also continued as he pressed onwards during his life. As Surrealist art is not a static and predictable form, Dali re-created himself in a similar style, he became malleable, an erratic changeling who once the barriers had been dissolved to his subconscious mind, often struggled against its potent invasion. Yet it was only by his success in transforming the initial conditioning attitudes of his early social upbringing, that his solar purpose could emerge. This metamorphosis of his worldview into the symbolism of Surrealism acted as the mechanism for the release of his old self, and the re-empowerment of the new Dali, the artist. His wife assumed the role of an artistic muse, who understood and valued him for what he was, and who trusted and retained faith in his potential. Her artistic contribution was of great importance to his stability and development.

CHAPTER 5

The Sun in the Natal Houses

THE SUN'S NATAL HOUSE POSITION is a sphere of potential transformation and consequent emergence of the unified higher Self, and will be highly influential in the individual life. As the Sun operates on two distinct levels within the human being, those of the separated egoic consciousness, the personal 'I', and the unified individuality, the universalised 'I' (lower and higher selves), then its natal house serves both as a testing ground for progress and as a specific sphere of individual expression and purpose.

The individual challenge of successfully dealing with these activities, which often assume priority and influence, are reflected by the areas of experience symbolised by the natal house position, forming a pivotal core on which life foundations and directions are established.

This requires qualities of self-assertion and clarity to be achieved, as a necessary development for walking the heroic path. The natal house indicates an area where we are asked to express our individual nature and creative power, and through applying a focused will make our unique mark on the world.

Yet to achieve this will demand inner changes and the strength to overcome whatever obstacles stand in our way, and we can approach this challenge from either a 'lower or higher' perspective, through a separative self-centredness aiming at personal exaltation, or as a path to contribute something of value to the world. The issues of the solar natal house are concerned with gaining consciousness and a purposeful release of personal power; it is a path towards our potential and centre of integration, and discovering how to align with our higher solar nature poses its own difficulties. Most people fail even to become aware of the existence of this level.

The Sun reflects an image of ourselves as an integrated, unified individual, expressing our life-purpose and reflecting the solar light into the world, so that through our influence a positive effect can be made in the world. This image magnetically attracts us towards the Sun's spiritual dimension, once we awaken sufficiently to search for understanding and meaning. The natal house becomes the sphere where we can focus solar energy more easily, releasing our deeper purpose and, in doing so, radiate the potency of our inner light and unique individuality.

It is through this natal channel that we can begin to take control of our lives, by making deliberate actions and choices to create an ideal lifestyle to suit our natures, assuming the role of 'Master-creator' of our lives instead of being passive and reacting against external influences. Evoking the solar power can be highly integrative, generating the ability to rearrange our personality and life-choices through perceiving new directions and alternatives to follow.

Taking this path will be difficult, and will provoke considerable personal transformation if we persist in our endeavours to attain the higher solar centre. Yet the benefits of all development and expansion in the Sun's natal house result in the emergence of a whole individual, a state of being that is both personally fulfilling and positive in the world. Consciousness becomes 'enlightened' on this individual journey, potentiality is manifested, and all areas of life are equally affected by the transformative solar emanation. Through the qualities of the Sun, all personality aspects can be rebalanced and harmonised until they work unitedly to fulfil your individual purpose. The radiance of the solar light illumines the whole natal chart, serving as the heart of the personal mandala of being, and all the personality/planetary aspects begin to dance to the solar harmony.

The challenge confronting each of us is this alignment to our solar higher nature. We have to become autonomous individuals, taking responsibility for our life directions and choices, prior to entering our higher universalised level of being. Our natal Sun asks us to step out from the collective mass mind, to stand alone and free, capable of following our unique path through life by releasing innate potential. The Sun becomes a transpersonal doorway, a source for insight, illumination and power to re-create our lives if we are courageous enough to take advantage of the opportunity.

SUN IN THE 1ST HOUSE

The Sun in the house of identity will encourage you to be self-assertive, intent on making your mark on the world. You will be attracted towards a 'search to become someone' noticed, respected and acknowledged by others, and by choosing such a life path you will have the opportunity to develop your latent talents and potential which can become the main channels for your unique self-expression. It is this desire and ambition for success that begins to focus your will and application into specific directions. The major challenge facing you is crossing the gap between your dreams or belief in being special and important and the real level of your actual achievements.

You are likely to have an eager, enthusiastic temperament, with abundant self-confidence and physical vitality, generally possessing an optimistic spirit which enables you to pass through times of adversity without allowing depression to occur. There is a positivity about your nature which helps to create an attractive personality capable of radiating a warm friendly atmosphere to others, and coupled with an enjoyment of life this can make you a stimulating and entertaining companion.

Underlying this, though, is an impulse which prefers to be dominating, attracted towards roles of authority and positions of power, which tends to reflect an attitude that to become influential in society you have to aspire towards leadership positions, perhaps through management or business endeavours. You dislike having to take any secondary and subservient roles as these fail to match your self image. This trait could be your Achilles' heel, if you assume the role of authoritative leader too strongly, and through the force of your self-assertion start to impinge on family members, fellow workers or employees. If an egocentric attitude becomes prominent, then your sensitivity to others may correspondingly diminish, and instead of being a bearer of a positive stimulating energy you may display characteristics which inhibit the self-expression of others, or which cause interpersonal conflict of wills.

It seems essential that you take the responsibility to unfold your life-path, through determining what you want from life and then pursuing this vision with persistence and determination. Without knowing your destination, which path will you take, and which signpost will you follow? Clarifying this route has to become a priority for you, and this can only be successfully achieved through knowing yourself, so that you can choose a path that has meaning, fulfilment and purpose, one that resonates within your being as right. Your way becomes an individualistic journey, where you learn to listen to those subtle messages and inner whispers so you do not lose your way. This can be a solitary path, even within a family environment, and while the opinions and contributions of others should never be dismissed and ignored, you need to give most focus to your inner promptings and take the initiative in following them. There may be a realisation that merely pursuing power and influence is not sufficient to satisfy, and that the real goal attracting you is the need to reflect an inner image of manifested potential, to become that special person by your state of being.

Aspects to the Sun (conjunction, sextile, trine) can indicate that your childhood was favourable to later development, and that your parents' contribution and early environment helped to form a stable identity. More challenging aspects (square, opposition) may indicate conflicts that require a deeper resolution, and attempts to impose yourself on the world may be frustrated until adjustments in attitude have been achieved. Much will depend on the influence of your father in the development of your identity centre, and certain keys to your ease of self-assertion may lie in the relationship with him.

SUN IN THE 2ND HOUSE

This involves the right use of resources and creating an attitude and spirit of abundance. The issue of materialism and possessions will be prominent, and you will tend to focus on material security and financial affluence as a means of defining your identity and as a channel for self-expression.

You may believe that all problems can be solved whenever sufficient money is available, and while this can minimise many of life's difficulties, a broader perspective may need to be gained. Resources are not just monetary or possessions, but also include *inner wealth* which can be reflected through personal qualities, talents and skills that are available for use too. Working consciously with these can help to develop your sense of unique individuality, and begin to transform that attraction towards material possessions into an appreciation of the wealth that is latent within your nature.

Displacing security needs into acquisitions is rarely fulfilling, and many resources can be misdirected into luxury-spending to maintain a consumer-driven society and to achieve ego gratification through conspicuous affluence as a visible symbol of success. While social status and prestige can be attained through the accumulation of money, this does not necessarily imply a corresponding quality of person. The most effective application of the Sun in this house is to unfold those personal qualities and talents through channels which can generate a satisfactory income, so that both inner and outer fulfilment can move in harmony. Applying monetary wealth in terms of dominance over others will prove unfulfilling, and should be avoided.

Effort may be needed to define your needs and values, so that through greater clarity you begin to feel less insecure. This involves 'taking stock' of your potential, aims and desires in life, setting targets and then using all resources to achieve them. Self-assertion is vital in this respect, and if you try to rely on the support of others then you are evading your development challenges. Will and application needs directing to this sphere of life so that inner wealth and power become actualised through your life.

More awareness may be required regarding *stewardship* of resources, so that you try to use everything in a positive and creative manner, maximising the constructive influence of your nature and possessions so that either enjoyment or value is consistently achieved. This may involve sensitivity to the potential social use of money, perhaps through supporting charity or groups dedicated towards social betterment or environmental protection. The transformative and positive use of money in society is a tremendous force that can be used for good if the imagination and will is present to do so. One area that may be especially responsive to developing this new attitude is the sphere of influence indicated by your Sun sign; application there will have great impact on unfolding your whole identity. The sign may also indicate the routes through which you tend to generate wealth and release it back into the community through choice of spending.

You should be quite skilled in managing your material life, possessions and wealth, and organisation is likely to be a talent allied to a determination and stability of purpose. Development will occur from careful and conscious use of resources, rather than any selfish approach or one which manipulates others' needs or is extravagantly wasteful; if you take that narrow path, then your energies will become dissipated and restrictive. Yet taking the higher path of stewardship will become expansive and satisfying, enriching your identity and life enjoyment.

SUN IN THE 3RD HOUSE

Your path to unfold life potential will lie in the cultivation of your mind, intellect and communicative abilities. This is an especially important area of experience for you, and will help to shape your identity, life direction and be the channel for your specific type of self-expression.

You will enjoy learning, and a spirit of curiosity encourages the examination and exploration of many varied and fascinating avenues of human knowledge. In such a rich world as ours, there is no real excuse ever to feel bored with life, as even the most active of individuals can only touch a miniscule fraction of its treasures. This curiosity may be strongest in those areas of life symbolised by your Sun-sign.

Your mind may be biased towards the external reality, exhibiting a more objective scientific attitude towards exploration, although the stimulus for this is often a less recognised need to understand the nature of the universal life process. As your mind tends to display a analytical tendency and intellectual clarity, life appreciation is often found in matters of mental interest, and it is important to continue stimulating this as it vitalises you.

However, if you elevate the accumulation of information and knowledge into a reason for life, then you may be making a mistake; it is understanding and synthesis that is the real key to applying knowledge. Intelligence is displayed through your whole life, not just in the reflection of a specialised area of knowledge, and also involves adaptation to your environment and the creation of a fulfilling lifestyle.

One of your major assets is that enquiring nature, and this can be directed towards an intellectual search in either the outer or inner worlds. You may find that a redirection of questioning inwards to explore yourself proves to be highly rewarding and illuminating. It is important to follow your light, having faith and trust in the validity of your beliefs, values, attitudes and feelings, rather than needing to rely on others to provide you with your worldview. Obviously social conditioning imposes its perspective on everybody while maturing towards adulthood – and many continue to reflect the mass mind all of their lives – but this is not inevitable, and you can break free to discover your own perspective if you are willing to make the effort to build a truly unique and personal view. If you can achieve this, then greater energy and vitality will begin to flow through your intellect, making deeper insights and revelations possible, as well as enhancing your sense of identity and self-esteem. Passive absorption of social attitudes, values, beliefs and traditions effectively diminishes individual identity, reducing it back into the mass mind and so restricting opportunities and freedom.

You will derive considerable enjoyment and stimulation from communicating with others, and the exchange of ideas and personal perspectives will prove to be highly valuable. This opens you to the multifaceted ways of looking at life and the world, pointing towards different areas of interest of which you had previously been unaware. A tolerance to other points of view can develop, but you may tend at times to become intellectually arrogant and too self-assured in the rightness of your views.

In relationships you may need to open to the variety of others' individual expressions, and to share whatever you feel might be of some use to them, such as your information, knowledge or understanding. This can minimise any tendency to force your worldview on people, or those projections of power and authority that can distort your relationships if mishandled and which derive from those needs to be assertive within your sphere of influence. Be wary of adopting an intellectually dilettantish approach, that of the 'accumulatory magpie', where information and knowledge is expressed in a style designed to gain admiration and social approval, and yet is inherently superficial and unintegrated. If aspects to your Sun are challenging (square, opposition), then you may have experienced some difficulty in absorbing information properly, perhaps an interrupted school life or an inability to know what to do with your knowledge or a struggle to convey this to others. More application on gaining intellectual clarity and articulacy may be necessary prior to your potential progress. The prospect is that your identity becomes defined and assured through deepened communication with others, and that by living from your light you are able to help others to develop their unique perception of the varied world in which we live.

SUN IN THE 4TH HOUSE

The search for the path of development lies in 'your roots', which can include family heritage, ancestral patterns, social traditions, the collective mind and your home life, both as a child and as an adult. These roots represent individual identity and security, and it appears as though part of you has been submerged and requires a conscious raising to the light through an inner investigation and integration of the creative roots that have been influential in forming your nature.

Look towards your early home life, childhood environment, social conditioning and relationship with parents, especially with your father. These may hold clues as to the later development of your personality tendencies. Try and evaluate if you have succeeded in asserting your identity by now, or do you still reflect childhood conditioning and live a life formed by powerful social traditions or family attitudes? Do your choices have to conform to parental or social pressures, or do you feel free (and guiltless) when you follow your path? Is your father figure a symbol of social authority, or a supporting parent who encourages the unfolding of your potential and identity, and who never condemns if you take wrong turnings? Can you stand free and alone from the shadow of your parent's presence? How do you perceive your father, as a source of strength and power, or as an absence in your inner life? What are your attitudes towards social traditions? Do you accept their validity, and conform accordingly to their directives; or do you challenge and question them, eventually creating your own response and way of living, irrespective of issues of conformity and social approval?

While you may look externally for roots, their real anchoring point is within your nature. Creating a beautiful, secure and safe home environment may be certainly an advantage, but unless those inner roots are secured will still remain unsatisfying. Family life will prove necessary for you, providing that you do not depend on it for your sense of life meaning and purpose. Otherwise changes in family composition and relationships will have great effects on your state of well-being, especially at times when children mature and leave home, or teenage friction with parents may be rife.

It may be during the later part of your life that you begin to shake off the influences of earlier conditioning, or find the path which redefines your sense of identity. Probably the earlier part of your adult life will be spent in following socially acceptable life-tracks with relatively little questioning. A reorientation towards inner unfoldment may be required, so that your attention is less focused on attaining security, stability and roots only in the outer world.

The point to be realised is that childhood foundations are present only to build the adult life upon successfully, so that individuality can flourish. Most adults fail to build upon their foundations, taking those patterns as boundaries and directions that they have to conform to for fear of losing parental approval, and so they fail to become free and independent. Through integrating those roots firmly in the ground of your being, you create the opportunity to grow and become self-assertive, confident in your nature, responsibilities and individual expression. As self-belief matures, a sense of inner security begins to form and a renewed degree of vitality flows, enriching your life again. You will feel that finally you have arrived home, and that your past is now fused and integrated correctly into your present.

SUN IN THE 5TH HOUSE

In this house, the natural tendency of the Sun is towards more egocentric, hedonistic pleasures in life, which may be associated with the releasing of a creative artistic spirit. It is a search for enjoyment that becomes a path of development, although care may be necessary to moderate any innate selfish traits that rise to the surface and demand satisfaction. An underlying attitude is likely to be a self-centred naïve innocence, which may sometimes fail to be consistently conscious of the reactions and feelings of others.

This can be displayed in attractions towards romances and love affairs which initially often appear so enticing and exciting, and yet can bring considerable confusion and emotional suffering in their wake when the spark of love or lust extinguishes itself. You may notice that while the flame of love burns brightly as passions are ignited, your intensity of feeling is more short-lived, and your interest wanes. Maintaining permanent relationships may prove problematic for you, and attractions to pleasure may sometimes prove detrimental. You will enjoy children, however, feeling great pride in your creative prowess, and will spend many happy hours playing with them or performing dramatic theatrical roles for their entertainment.

Your attitude is that life should be fun, and you intend to pursue this theory and prove that it is right. Your vitality is increased by spending as much time as possible devoted only to doing things which are genuinely enjoyable. Why waste time in activities that are not enjoyable? you wonder. Ideally, you want to transform your whole life into one of pleasure and interest, and it is through your endeavours to achieve this that your direction unfolds with a sense of purpose and meaning. The search for personal satisfaction motivates you, and if this diminishes in your life, then so does your level of vitality as the two are interwoven and affect both your psychological and physiological states of well-being. Expansive desires could become distractions for you, as you may feel that you have to chase every object, person or interest that activates your curiosity. You may express a childlike one-pointed focus of desire towards whatever promises you pleasure, and this could have compulsive aspects. You may be like a child standing in a toyshop, who looks round and says 'I want' to everything.

Developing your artistic creativity could prove important to release self-expression and a channel for some of your overflowing energies. Such creativity is likely to have a passionate emotional content, a dramatic or theatrical intensity and joy which adds increased colour to life, lifting it above the greys of mundane superficial existence. Perceiving yourself as a creative artist in some sphere offers an alternative self-image and a social role to perform to increase your influence in the world. You enjoy attracting attention, and this helps to vitalise your sense of identity, as you hope that you stand out from the crowd; being anonymous and invisible is not to your taste, and you prefer to be noticed and appreciated by others.

You may overproject yourself at times through sheer ebullience, and may need to keep a wary eye on any adoption of roles, so that you do not begin losing your full nature through the performance of selected aspects. You can be over-confident, taking unnecessary risks or adventures, or through unwise speculation may jeopardise your position or family security. Sometimes, a pause for reflection and thought may be appropriate before you leap into action.

Sun in the 6th House

Your life direction and sense of fulfilment can be discovered through involvement in the areas of work, health and service, and applying your attention to these spheres will help to define your sense of unique identity and offer channels for your path of development.

The organisation of life, both within domestic routines or through a working environment, is especially important and provides a focus for your abilities, efficiency and practical skills. Being capable of functioning well in the material world is probably one of your assets, especially if there are harmonious aspects made to your Sun, and this is also a source of competence that adds to your self-esteem.

You tend to develop regular routines or private 'habitual rituals' as an ordering pattern to your life, and providing that these do not become compulsive and you do not feel that these routines are inviolable, then they can serve as a positive structuring to your days. Retain some flexibility of action and choice within these routines. Associated with this habit-forming tendency is a willingness to accept the boundaries of your situation. This may be a pragmatic acquiescence to circumstances that you feel cannot be changed, or it can be a fear of actually stretching beyond your present limitations, in which case it can become restrictive. A point to be remembered is that if you choose, you can change anything in your life that fails to satisfy, once you decide to do so.

Part of your self-definition is derived from your work, and you are normally a hard-worker and concentrated on your tasks, hoping to achieve due recognition from your efforts, either from an employer or by the success of your own business. You feel that such acknowledgement is necessary, and can become disheartened whenever you fail to receive this for your wholehearted efforts. You may need to be wary of any tendencies to be a hard taskmaster as an employer, and need to recognise that not everyone has your capacity and dedication for work.

If your Sun has more challenging aspects (square, opposition) then you may discover hindrances within your working life, perhaps requiring additional education and training to open new paths for development, or there may be difficulties in settling into suitable employment. As your identity can be associated with your work, this can have a detrimental effect on your well-being, so you may need to ensure that self-esteem is disassociated from your working status or else it may become permanently diminished.

Health may become a focus of attention, especially the relationship between body–emotions–mind and psychosomatic links. Challenging aspects may imply physical weakness or liability to illness and lack of vitality, perhaps through a sensitivity to types of food and diet. Taking care of body needs and your level of physical vigour may be required, so listening to the promptings from your body is important, and exercise may also be necessary. The concept of body – mind wholeness may appeal, and you may choose to pursue studies in the complementary therapies or allopathic medicine. Herbalism and the medicinal use of plants may attract, especially once you have received benefits from any herbal remedies, or homoeopathy, aromatherapy, reflexology and the various types of body massage and energy alignment, such as Rolfing or polarity therapy. You should not forget the importance of your emotions and mental attitudes if you become involved in body preoccupations; the three are interwoven, affecting each level, and harmony and balance needs to exist between all of them.

This could become the sphere of service to a broader community for you, perhaps through helping to heal others or to show them ways to attain satisfactory health and well-being. You feel that it is important to be of value to the community and to contribute in some way for the benefit of society, and this could be a path that you eventually takc. The ideal of service is one that can inspire your energies, creating a focus and a dedication to your self-created tasks. Your skills of practical efficiency can be valuably employed wherever you choose, and seeing their results will help to heighten your sense of self-worth.

SUN IN THE 7TH HOUSE

The sphere of social relationships will assume a high priority and importance in your life, and your path of self-development will be interwoven with experiences within partnerships and relationships.

There is a need to reforge your identity so that you can follow the way indicated by your light, rather than acquiesce to paths imposed by social traditions, parental or peer-group pressures. By redefining your self-understanding and taking responsibility for your actions and choices, there will be a corresponding shift in social and intimate relationships. A new perception of the interaction between yourself and the outer world can begin to emerge, and a new type of relationship may be discovered.

Until this shift occurs, you may display dependency tendencies, allowing a reliance on others for a sense of security and life direction, lacking real confidence in your strengths and capabilities. Your solar power may have been projected into the world, so that others are perceived as expressing a quality of power which is actually latent within your own nature. Failing to acknowledge its presence within, you search for its reflection by others and become involved in a variety of relationships. This is not a power that should be dominating, but a power emanating from inner light and personality integration; yet through outer projection and reflection you misconceive its presence as only existing within others.

The dangers of such a projection is that you are left vulnerable to any tendencies of emotional manipulation and domination by others who may be less sympathetic or unscrupulous. If you allow a passivity to rise in your relationships, then partners may take advantage of you, until you begin to assert your own strengths.

Issues of domination are often associated with challenging aspects to the Sun in this house. An alternative expression of this Sun position is to be too assertive, lacking sensitivity to others, and adopting a more self-centred attitude which can ignore the needs and desires of partners. The lesson that requires understanding in this case is the development of a co-operative spirit which recognises the validity of differing styles of self-expression, and a corresponding diminution of that impulse to dominate. Sometimes there are needs to attain social prestige or community authority, so that a mark on society is made. The search for 'power' is again externalised into society, and evidence of personal potency is gained from the range of social influence, rather than unfolding the inner solar strength.

You will probably discover someone who serves as an inspirational role model to emulate, or you may observe qualities in associates that you would like to express. Part of your unfoldment will come through a process of personality modelling, although this should be only a preparatory phase to convince you of the mutability of the personality and the potential for a conscious reshaping. Later you can begin to work with the totality of your nature, revealing those innate strengths and qualities through your social interaction.

This stage may develop after experiences of relationship conflicts and disappointments have served to awaken you to your independent nature, transforming the nature of your social relationships. It is through participation with others that your new identity will be shaped, and you can discover a renewed sense of power, meaning and direction within your intimate relationships. As insight deepens, self-motivation expands and your life path becomes more illuminated. While external success may not form until after you have created a more successful partnership, inner changes will certainly compensate you for any earlier difficulties. There may be a potential to share your insights about the nature of relationships and the need for individual integration and partnership balance, through some sort of communication to others, perhaps through counselling or writing. But this is a later stage of your possible life path, and unless those earlier and necessary personal modifications are made, you may still be confronted by relationship challenges and disillusionments.

SUN IN THE 8TH HOUSE

One important tendency in the psyche is the deep impulse to move beyond existing boundaries, barriers, limitations and restrictions. It is an expansionary drive that seeks the experience of an intense union which dissolves the parameters and constraints of the separate self.

This impulse can be disconcerting and disruptive, agitating within your personality, manifesting as an undefined inner pressure striving for release, and often displaying its presence through compulsive fascinations, unconscious motivations and an ambivalent reaction to life; there can be a simultaneous desire to taste life as deeply as possible or to withdraw from external life involvement.

Underlying this is a need for reconnection, to touch a deeper centre of your nature that is magnetically attracting you. Your emotional and feeling nature is especially responsive, and due to inner conflict may become a battlefield that is opening you to experience greater life intensity. This may not be easy, as it is probably your relationships that become the source of contention, and as those inner pressures increase, they will strip away the veneers of control and self-image previously imposed upon these relationships. In the stark light of emotional anguish, you may become aware of unresolved areas of your nature, negative emotional patterns and unconscious tendencies that require cleansing, releasing and healing. Yet it is through such experiences that your lighted path can be discovered. By these unconscious patterns rising to the surface of your life and consciousness, you have the opportunity to use painful experiences in a positive and transformative manner, even though one result may be a phase of difficult relationships. If this has occurred, then the message is pointing you towards personal change, and such experiences are serving as catalysts for an expansion beyond your present limits.

You may become interested in deeper self-understanding, and through your need for this begin to search in the realms of psychology, religion and occultism and commence your spiritual quest to discover your holistic centre. This attraction to the mysteries of life is associated with the 8th house, and your solar path of development will lead towards such realms. Areas of social taboo can particularly fascinate and you may become interested in techniques that require the application of a focused will, such as magic or creative visualisation.

The exploration of your sexuality may assume a high profile, as that is one way to gain experiences of emotional and physical intensity. Much will depend on your reactions to the issue of life intensity, whether you wholeheartedly embrace its potential or whether you feel afraid of exalted and heightened feelings and senses. If fear dominates, through unease about moving beyond existing boundaries, then you may choose to resist deeper life intimacy and reject the potential transformation. However, if you persevere in daring to explore the scope of life, your inner experience can become enriched and those pressures dissolved through conscious self-expression. Relationships may then become less a battlefield and more a foundation for progressive growth and enjoyment of life, as you succeed in transforming your need for union into a positive life enhancement, instead of passively allowing yourself to be dominated by the consequences of inner storms.

Another sphere within this 8th house dimension is related to investments, legacies, law and resources. Your path may be helped or hindered by family relationships, especially through the potential of legacies and personal partnerships. If the Sun has challenging aspects (square, opposition), then there may be more difficulties occurring, which can frustrate and restrict you, so care may be needed in respect of marital and legal disputes. If the Sun has harmonious aspects (conjunction, sextile, trine), then you may have better fortunes if involved in family legacies, business, partnerships, financial transactions and speculation; but be cautious if you feel the impulse for greater expansion, and ensure that you carefully investigate and evaluate your plans and options to assess their viability. Fortune may arise from utilising your personal contacts, and through the sharing of resources in joint endeavours. Ideally, you could use any financial success to increase your potential for greater life intensity and inner abundance, rather than allowing money or possessions to act as a substitute for a life meaning and purpose.

SUN IN THE 9TH HOUSE

This indicates that your self-development path lies in the realm of the higher mind, which can include a spiritual search, creativity and imagination, philosophy, law, culture and foreign travel. This involves an impulse to move beyond existing boundaries through a broadening of life interests and experiences, so that your mental worldview gains an expanded perspective and the world is enriched by your intellectual curiosity and studies, becoming a perpetually interesting and stimulating environment for your exploration.

The motivation to pursue such a path may be present from birth, unfolding a natural curiosity, or may be awakened by an awareness of your life's lack of meaning or direction. You are likely to look for an underlying order to life, a structure that both explains and illuminates the questions about life that begin to preoccupy you. You may have an intuitive sense that a deeper meaning is present within life, and following such promptings you will begin to focus your explorations to discover this golden unifying thread. You want either actual knowledge or a suitable belief structure to create inner stability, and can be attracted to religious doctrines, moral and ethical philosophies, humanitarian principles or political ideologies, believing that these may hold the key that you seek.

It is the issue of relationship between the individual and society that perplexes you, and you need to arrive at an understanding of this interaction, which can form a dynamic and positive connection serving to inspire the creation of a more utopian vision of the world. It is a resolving and reconciliatory impulse acting within you, seeking to reconnect you to a deeper centre, that joins the individual in conscious relationship to the collective group, and begins to integrate the whole individual.

Through your ongoing exploration of varying approaches to this key issue in the world, you will eventually develop your own unique perspective and worldview which could be useful to others through shared communication. Your path could be highly influenced by foreign lands, people, culture and traditions, and this may imply a resonance and attraction towards the spiritual paths of the East at some stage.

You see your search as a lifelong quest, perpetually assembling new pieces of the cosmic jigsaw puzzle, recognising that there are many paths and viewpoints on the mystery of life, and that all could be valid and true from certain perspectives. A picture is assembled, a picture is disassembled; the mental search can be never-ending.

However, there may also be a tendency towards fixed attitudes, especially if your Sun is placed in a fixed sign. Under the influence of certain religious, moral and doctrinal teachings, the assumption of certitude may be made, especially as there can be an underlying pattern of desiring to be authoritative, and to assert or impose personal views as being the only correct ones. Ultimately taking such a stance proves to be restrictive and self-limiting, closing perceptions and options down to only those which are 'allowable', and thus distorting individual understanding and perspective. Taking moralistic attitudes often corresponds with assuming critical and judgemental positions, which only fuels the separation of people within society rather than connecting them more strongly. Take care not to fall into any trap of viewing others through moralistic filters; allow them freedom to live their lives in their way. Why should they conform to your precepts? Do you intend to conform to theirs? Moving towards a higher path always takes you closer towards inadvertently assuming condescending and hypocritical positions, and those who take that road need to remain on their guard against their own separative inner patterns reasserting their presence in more subtle ways.

By discovering the foundational patterns of life, your vision will expand due to the insights revealed by lighting your inner flame. Mental intuition will be amplified, and you may feel inspired to offer your direction to others who are still searching in their own darkness, those who are trying to discover their path. Whatever you have found useful can be shared, and hopefully will be of value to people too. The dissemination of knowledge, insight and information is probably one of your skills, and may be expressed through the spheres of teaching and writing as your vision becomes more widely influential in the world. The content of this is likely to include the themes of inspiration, relationships within society, the potential for individual development and integration and the visionary pointing towards future trends. For those who become channels for insight, one of the greatest tests is for them to embody the wisdom themselves, rather than just perform the role of offering it for the benefit of others.

SUN IN THE 10TH HOUSE

The focus of attention is towards the outer world and the assertion of your nature and qualities through social status and acknowledgement. Your motivation will come from a desire to become socially influential, aspiring towards public recognition and the satisfaction of needs for power and the attainment of your ambitions. This will attract you into striving for career or social progression, so that you can rise to positions of authority and responsibility, and others can easily recognise your success and achievements. You want to rise above the crowd through expressing your abilities, to become a leader directing others rather than be a passive follower.

This reflects a need for egoic assertion, and your experience of self-worth and esteem will be directly related to your degree of visible success in the community. Entering socially respected professions may be the direction you choose, and your self-image will be closely connected and modelled upon the ideals of your profession or type of employment, especially if you are at supervisory or management levels.

As success is so important in your chosen direction, you should have the ability to focus your will, consistently and powerfully applying it to amplify self-discipline and perseverance so that some degree of attainment is achieved. However, by rigidly pursuing this path you may simultaneously restrict your freedom and options in life, as certain ways may be considered to be unsuitable as they fail to fit into the idealised image that you are projecting. The danger may lie in the possibility that even if you do reach your aims, the apex fails to fulfil and you are confronted with the question of 'What next?'. At some point you will reach your apex, which can become a limiting plateau and may have a dispiriting effect on your well-being and identity.

While you have to strive for your ambitions to activate your path of development and purpose, try not to narrow those goals but instead expand them so that they become more inclusive, touching all areas of your life and nature. This will lead to a greater sense of satisfaction, and will unify disparate aspects of your life. Otherwise, by following the star of the glorious career to the exclusion of other spheres of life, you may be creating your downfall in your private and domestic life, having a negative effect on marriage or family relationships. Conflicts may rise between career and home, especially with any challenging aspects of square and opposition to your Sun, and a balance may need to be established for personal security and stability.

Your Sun's ideal is to help you become centred, expressing your strengths and qualities; this is what can make you impressive to others and a source of inspiration and influence, rather than the positions of prominence that may glitter as the summation of your dreams. Displacing your sense of identity into a professional community role or position of social status is often unwise, because at the end of a career (through retirement, ill health or redundancy, or perhaps through some career reversal or disagreement), there is always the possibility that some external agency can be destructive to both your aims and stability of identity. You may fall prey to temptations which surround positions of influence, and your morality and integrity can be challenged or impugned; few rise to the 'top' without having upset others along the way. If your Sun has challenging aspects (square, opposition) then you may display dictatorial traits, a love of power and tendencies to be less than scrupulous in chasing your aims, or fail to realise how power can 'turn the head' through an egocentric misapplication. Your need for personal and social power is likely to be directed through the Sun-sign associations.

It may be beneficial to consider parental influences upon your life path and career needs. The 10th house is associated with the importance of parental conditioning, particularly that of the mother, and evaluating their impact on your attitudes, values, motivations and aims may be illuminating. You may be striving to achieve so that they fully acknowledge your worth and abilities; you may have come from a high-achievement family, and so need to match an unspoken level of success; you may be living out parental desires, rather than fulfilling your needs, as they may have encouraged you to take a certain life path and you surrendered to their pressure.

A need to be seen by others as being an achiever can emanate from a hidden insecurity, but the right use of your Sun potency would heal any such tendency, giving you a stable, deeper centre to live your life from, transforming your style of personal assertiveness from any predisposition to exploit power over others into a co-operative attempt at mutual benefit for all.

SUN IN THE 11TH HOUSE

This indicates that your path of development is directed towards group participation in the ongoing search for social and cultural progress. Idealism and dreams of a better future are vitalising energies, and you may become a channel or for new perceptions, insights, knowledge and understanding of society, and a living example of how such abilities serve as a transformative potency which generates periodic social reform or revolution in varying ways.

You will probably have a developed group or social awareness, conscious of the interplay between the individual and the collective, and an awakened heart to the often unnecessary suffering that man often inflicts on his fellow men, animals and nature unknowingly. This will lead you eventually to become more active in joining with others to propose creative solutions to minimise group pain and discomfort through the creation of greater public awareness and alternative policies that can be applied to resolve conflict situations.

Such group endeavours can include those of the ecology and environmental causes, civil liberty and community welfare groups, or those dedicated to providing spiritual, religious or psychological techniques designed to integrate the individual and awaken them to their power within society. As you are more future-orientated, you will feel less bound by the weight of existing traditional attitudes, and may enter into adversarial or conflicting relationships with those who stand firmly behind older viewpoints. You may be considered to be radical in attitude, and this can always make those who prefer the maintenance of the status quo feel uncomfortable.

Following your sense of universal fellowship, you may become a staunch advocate of human rights and liberation, and through integration with the collective favour a vision of universal guiding principles. This can involve you with activities related to political and social humanitarian development, and provide you with an ideological foundation in life and a defined meaning and purpose. Enlivened by such group participation, you may need to be aware of the nature of your self-expression, so that you remain open to other points of view too and do not become blinkered by the particular focus and worldview of any particular group. The persuasive powers of a group cause and belief structure are often extremely powerful, and liable to overshadow individual attitudes; by choosing to remain a group participant, many lose the ability for free thinking due to having to conform to the dominant group perception, and they lose sight of everything except the group viewpoint. This is the main danger of the group potency and should be avoided through understanding.

Certainly the potential for your path of development lies within group activity, and increasingly your sense of identity will be associated with group affinities. If your Sun aspects are harmonious (conjunction, sextile, trine) then your relationships with groups should run relatively smoothly, positively and co-operatively; if they are challenging (square, opposition) then more friction and disputes may occur.

Through asserting your solar potency, you could rise to positions of spokesperson for such groups, and gain recognition for your social contributions and progressive innovations which help to regenerate and revitalise society. Public involvement and organisational abilities are likely, although you may need to ensure that your grand designs and schemes for social betterment are capable of being applied and are actually tested in the fires of daily life. It is through becoming a solar crusader for a better quality of world life that your identity is reformed into one of purpose and power. Releasing your inner light through affinitive group activity and kindling the collective light is the ideal direction for your Sun expression, and one to which you should pay the most attention.

Sun in the 12th House

This suggests an emphasis away from the outer world towards an inner direction, in an attempt to shine the Sun's light into those darker recesses of the emotions, mind and psyche. Your conscious identity needs to be redefined in a way which takes account of your whole nature, and has the healing quality of inclusiveness rather than tending towards a separatist exclusive bias which has consequences of inner alienation and personality splitting.

The 12th house has deep associations with the collective unconscious mind, the personal subconscious, and the past, and it is the psychic content of these that interferes with and influences your present life experience. Residues from the past and the constraints of 'unfinished business' may still litter your psyche, and you may need a phase of releasing energies and blocked emotions from your nature by experiencing a healing and liberating inner cleansing. If you suffer from feelings of guilt, irrational worries, sense of unease, then it is likely to be patterns agitating within your unconscious mind, which if left unresolved could begin to form neurotic complexes or inhibit your capacity to form satisfactory social relationships.

You may be highly self-aware and this can be restrictive, especially as you may register empathic vibrations from people around you which could become uncomfortable or even distressing, particularly if you fail to identify that you are being receptive to other's feelings and pain, and that they are not necessarily your own.

Your unconscious mind is demanding access into your life, and a confrontation with those inner ghosts is essential to begin resolving certain conflicts. These unlived or repressed aspects of your nature plus any absorbed psychic accretions from your environment have to emerge into the light, or else they will unbalance your identity and personality stability. You may sometimes feel as if you are struggling to maintain barriers, fearing that those inner dam walls will crack and those stormy waters will break through, tearing down all attempts at control and limitation. One of your strategies is often denial, but this is sowing seeds of later problems, as energies are repressed and personality splits amplified by such an approach; or you try to establish fixed habit patterns and worldviews which you hope will support security and stability in life, ignoring and disregarding anything that fails to fit the constrictive boundaries that you have established around yourself for protection.

Your path of development has to be two-fold: an inner healing is required which purifies and liberates any blockages, and offers a transformative attitude of self-acceptance as its foundation; and the next stage is then to begin opening the parameters of your self-circumscribed barriers against life, so that a new and more inclusive identity can slowly form and be more suited to deal with life.

This can involve a fusion of your conscious and unconscious mind, of your ego and higher self, and requires a greater flexibility of your personality than you have previously allowed or believed possible. This step may not be easy to take, and you may feel that everything is falling apart, but it is a phase of dissolution prior to a new reassembly of the psyche, and is a transformation of state similar to the phases of the new creation in the alchemist's crucible. A reunification of the separated components of your nature is required; this is your solar quest and task, and when achieved will open a whole new dimension for you to enjoy, as your inner life takes on a new vitality and cohesiveness.

It is unlikely that you will discover this path early in life, but may find it later once you have undergone certain experiences. You have to heal yourself, and may need periods of relative privacy or seclusion to generate the healing silence. You will probably feel uneasy about intimate relationships during youth and early adulthood, and may chose to withdraw from deeper human contacts. Transcending any feelings of inferiority and insecurity may take you several years of effort, but will be worth your attempts to change. Mundane life may seem to lack a vital spark with you, and you may not be at your best in dealing with the demands of everyday reality; it is not your favoured dimension, and you prefer the inner life, even when it is not so pleasant. Discovering a life purpose, meaning and direction is likely to be difficult until you reorientate your inner life.

There may be artistic and creative talents present, and these should be consciously developed as a medium for self-expression and as a channel to release blocked energies through. Dance, music and art may be specific areas, and there will be a latent psychic ability which could be exploited for both your own and other's benefit. Mediumistic tendencies may lie close to the surface of your nature, and through your sensitivity healing powers may also be contacted; but until you rebalance your nature and have healed your dilemmas and conflicts then it may be wiser to leave such types of expression alone. Similarly, prophecy and visionary tendencies may also be present, emanating from that close connection to the collective unconscious mind. Esoteric and occult work may appeal, especially the type of inner meditative service that invokes spiritual energies and potencies into fertilising, influencing and overshadowing the collective mind of humanity, and which inspires the global vision of interdependence. Participation in this service is an act that all can join.

Your potential is considerable, but it is imperative that you redefine your identity in more inclusive ways, so that you expand beyond the walls of your self-imprisonment, achieving this through an inner redemptive healing. Then your social contribution and desires for service can become more effective. Refusing to take such actions is liable to intensify your discomfort as inner pressures are amplified and become more insistent, breaking those dam walls which cannot remain intact for ever as the 'water level' rises. The preferable alternative is that through using healing and creative 'valves' the pressure can be regulated and directed into positive channels.

CHAPTER 6

The Sun in the Natal Signs

EACH OF THE ZODIAC'S TWELVE SIGNS symbolise the particular collective group that the individual reflects and resonates to during their life. Astrology indicates that these twelve groupings of psychological tendencies and characteristics are the formative patterns for the sphere of the collective human personality, and are located as the imprinting matrices within the collective unconscious mind. In Jungian terms, these become the archetypes of the zodiac, and individually we each reflect one of these particular patterns, as determined by our Sun-sign at birth.

In this sense, our Sun-sign is of less individual significance and is more a point of connection to a group embodiment of an archetypal pattern; which is why astrology can distinguish between the characteristics of each sign, and why each individual member of each sign has essentially similar tendencies to other group members across the world. The insight of astrology is that there are twelve psychological types of personality, twelve basic life attitudes, ways of expression, perceptions of the world, types of instinctive responses and reactions to experience; and that these can be interpreted through the medium of the specific sign qualities.

Individually, our Sun-sign connects us to our corresponding world group, and we will often display these tendencies during our lives without due awareness, as they build our personal psychology from their hidden roots in the darkness of our unconscious mind. Each sign embodies its own special gift and contribution to the world, and what is asked of us is to give our individual expression of this collective group function, as each of us embodies one of the twelve energy streams of the archetypal, universalised human being, Adam Kadmon in Qabalistic teachings. As with the natal house position, the Sun-sign position also displays two levels of resonance and expression: the mundane level of self-centred separative awareness, and the higher unified level of responsibility and group service.

Our particular Sun-sign symbolises our central tone of being, a foundational set of personality characteristics and the essential pattern of self that determines our type of expression, interests, strengths, weaknesses and motivations in life. While this is only one-twelfth of the range of the collective personality, it is sufficient to generate an inner cohesion and dominating mould within which all the disparate tendencies of the psyche (planets etc.) can be potentially integrated. Many people react against the astrological concept of psychological group types, but the real issue involves the development of the Sun in the natal chart (sign, house, aspects etc.) as a means of self-acceptance and acknowledging the individual role within the group endeavour. By attuning to our personal sign characteristics and function within the collective humanity, we can move forwards on our individual integrative path and transmit the gift of our sign to benefit evolution.

Within our unconscious mind lies also the potentiality of the other eleven signs, which will remain latent; it is not our task to manifest these, although the role of the astrologer is to become aware of their specific activities and interrelationships within life, as every sign is dealt with through individual clients. Even so, most astrologers would acknowledge that there are certain signs that they feel more attuned and comfortable with, and that these are reflected in their relationship experiences. In addition, most astrologers notice that they may attract more clients from certain signs or planetary placings, as if clients are attracted towards an astrologer who 'specialises' in working with particular zodiacal energies. For instance, I attract people who have a powerful Scorpio/Pluto in their charts, Sun-sign, Ascendant, or planetary positions/aspects, as one emphasis of my astrological approach is directed towards the issue of self-transformation, the regenerative task of personal rebirth.

Working with the Sun-sign is often the line of least resistance for the individual to pursue. Those characteristics are innate and natural, and energies flow smoothly along established channels, even though mixed results might follow in life. Evaluating the Sun-sign as it operates through the majority of people on the personality level can reveal these essential tendencies: the style of self-expression; the path to develop self-potential and fulfilment; the most effective way for self-assertion and focusing of will; the approach to shaping and influencing the environment; the releasing of personal power and energy; the type of creativity favoured and nature of its potential; the specific gifts and talents of the sign; the probable challenges and lessons facing that personality, derived from innate temperamental predispositions; the most effective ways to acquire and use wealth. Each of these spheres of expression indicate ways in which we can apply the energies of the inner Sun for personal advantage, growth and development. This becomes a lifetime task for anyone!

Aries Sun – Fire, Cardinal, Ruler: Mars

The Aries personality tends to be an initiator and pioneer, expressing self-assertion and direct energy into the world. You should have ample creative energy and enthusiasms that can be exploited, allowing you to start a variety of activities. One problem can be a failure to complete them, due to losing interest and becoming bored, and you tend to leave several loose ends of uncompleted projects in your life. There are strong motivations to prove yourself through energetic activity, to be enterprising and ambitious, making your presence noted in the world. You can be animated by a desire to be 'number one', becoming competitively minded, and this will influence your career and social expression. You could become an effective leader, as fame, authority and superiority suits you, or so you believe.

You can be quite impatient, impulsive and spontaneous in your actions and decisions, yet often you can fail to devote enough time and attention to actually listen to the advice of others, or to consider the consequences of your choices, and this can create several problems later. You may need to consider your options more carefully before you rush into action; if you can do this, then you will find greater success. Associated with this is the need to discover more effective relationships with others, to be more considerate and to think through the possible effects of any self-centred style of expression.

You will be attracted towards idealistic causes, seeing yourself as an opponent of social injustice. There can be a naive, innocent outlook on life at times, where you believe wholeheartedly in high ideals; while this can be battered by reality you are unlikely to become truly cynical, 'street-wise' or 'world-weary'. You try to speak the truth as much as possible, and can find it hard to lie, and even if you do try it is rarely convincing. You have a quick mind with distinct philosophical tendencies, and a sensitivity towards higher thought, morals and ethics. You need independence and freedom, so that you can indulge in your impulsive decisions to act.

You can be quite secretive regarding your personal life, feelings and emotional experiences, and are often reluctant to reveal your plans to others, especially as you can be deeply hurt. There is an attraction towards the past and traditional ways, which can be reflected in your home environment and attitudes, and you value domestic and relationship security more than you may be willing to acknowledge. This need evokes a sentimental response from you to family life, and you can be vulnerable in that area.

You need to share your life with a partner, although you tend to expect to be number one in the relationship. You want harmony at home, but you are unlikely to always find it, especially as your inner extremes and needs for assertion will tend to generate tensions, which spill over into everyday life. You may need to discover an inner equilibrium which counteracts personality divergences. At heart, you are a natural peacemaker, but as you have this powerful reservoir of emotional energy inside you, there can be difficulties in handling and using this energy successfully.

Although you have a strong will-power, you need to learn how to concentrate, focus and direct this, persisting long enough to achieve your aims. You have the ability to see the validity of different points of view, and this can sometimes create confusion in determining your own viewpoint; but it also implies that you do not rush to criticise others too quickly, and can be quite tolerant. You like to be noticed and admired by others, sometimes becoming a little too dominating in company, and you can be prone to over-dramatise your personality to impress others. In financial matters, you will usually be quite conservative, although in other attitudes and aspects of life you can be unorthodox.

TAURUS SUN – EARTH, FIXED; RULER: VENUS

The Taurus personality often displays stability, purpose, persistence, determination, self-reliance, reliability and sincerity. You will not usually take any risks affecting your material security, as your possessions and home environment are extremely important to you; in fact, you will be cautious in all aspects of your life. You tend to rely on a common-sense approach, quite pragmatic and practical, being efficient and often adroit at financial management and organisational requirements. You will take time to consider future courses of action, evaluating your options, and will need to feel as convinced and secure as possible regarding your choices before deciding to act; once your mind is set, you will see the choice through. You will apply yourself to the task of earning money and obtaining those material possessions which you believe are needed to build a secure lifestyle foundation.

Generally, your temperament is gentle and placid, and you try to live in ways which do not attract trouble towards you, but if provoked you can explode into a noisy display of temper. If others oppose you on issues on which you have already set your mind, then you can display a stubborn and obstinate resistence, failing to reconsider or listen to alternative opinions and advice.

You prefer a quiet, steady life, and can be secretive and reserved regarding disclosure of personal matters. Your sympathetic nature creates a sensitivity to natural beauty, as well as to art, music and literature. As sensual pleasures and comforts attract, you prefer to create a home which is pleasant and attractive with a relaxing atmosphere which can have a calming and beneficial effect on others. As your life can pivot around home, the quality of the domestic life is crucial to your peace of mind. Your health is often related to your success in creating a balanced and harmonious atmosphere around you. You tend to remain in touch with close relatives and friends, feeling secure in knowing that all is well with them.

You are rarely a 'romantic dreamer', who tends to distort relationships by an over-active imagination; usually you are quite straightforward and honest with any partners. You prefer to keep your emotions in their place as you are not always comfortable with them, and there can be a tendency towards repression, which can stimulate occasional outbursts of temper. Your relationships have a co-operative quality, and you can be tactful and diplomatic, even though you are often very direct in your communication with others.

Partners will be carefully and cautiously chosen, and despite your often laid-back and relaxed style, you can be a demanding marriage partner, expecting a high standard from others. The relationship being the main focus for your emotional intensity, you can be jealous and emotionally possessive. Satisfactory sexual relationships are important with your partner, and if your enjoyment of sexual passions fade, then the relationship becomes less stable and unfulfilling. A degree of intellectual compatibility is also required, as you tend to see intimate relationships as a source of mental stimulation in your life too, and a depth of communication is necessary to feel the intimacy of relationship connection. An element of 'best friends' is also included in satisfactory Taurean partnerships.

You tend to live by traditional moral standards and beliefs, and can be highly principled, and this often shows in your decision-making process and life choices. Your attitudes tend to be conservative and orthodox regarding questions of faith and religion, although possibly more fatalistic in tone, and less intellectualised or philosophical. You can become dogmatic and fixed in your attitudes and opinions, although an emotional involvement with causes can show you to be a tireless worker, sacrificing much for your ideals, especially in a supportive and practical context.

GEMINI SUN – AIR, MUTABLE; RULER: MERCURY

The Gemini personality is associated with intellect, mind and communication, and words are very important to you; you may possess literary ability and greatly enjoy reading and writing. You have an inquiring mind, being eager to accumulate knowledge and information through study, especially relating to factual and detailed topics. You tend to be curious about most things, and will search for intellectual security in the world. You need to be active and busy, loving change and variety which offers excitement to your life. You will be mainly focused in your mind, living in a world of fascinating ideas, although if over-familiarity occurs, then a lack of new stimulation can lead to a bored, restless mind beginning to look for the next interesting theme.

Gemini can be sympathetic and sensitive to others, having a quick perception and understanding of people, but this can be overshadowed by a self-centred attitude. Your temperament may be essentially idealistic, tending to solve world problems by producing theories, which may fail to be applied in practice. There may be some problems with self-discipline, but if you can overcome these, you can be quite creative in arts or business.

You are socially adaptable, being popular and easy company, and can be an interesting and entertaining conversationalist. You are effective at self-expression, and use you fluent communication both to persuade and gain respect from others. Friends are important to provide variety and mental stimulation, and you are likely to be attracted towards artistic and intellectual types. You do not like to be tied to anywhere, preferring changes of scenery and people in order to renew and revitalise your interest.

Your reactions to life can be a little erratic, varying according to your moods (Gemini Twins), and you can be quite highly strung if life is not working out for you, perhaps becoming depressed. You are not a naturally tranquil sort of person, needing to be almost compulsively active; there can be periods of experiencing anxiety, indecision, impatience and irritability.

You prefer tidiness, cleanliness and order, and may prefer to work from home where you attempt to create comfortable, peaceful surroundings, and to which you often need to retreat from the world for short periods of self-renewal. You may try to create a balance in your life between action, socialising and creativity, as you are suited towards application in several areas of life at once. The sort of work that may suit you includes research, investigation, and factual content, scientific or literary.

Your love life can be erratic, and you prefer to retain independence and freedom. You may marry more for mental compatibility than for physical attraction alone, and will require a partner to be able to handle the practical everyday obligations and also be mentally stimulating, leaving you relatively free. You also enjoy contact with children, especially the aspects of play and their enquiring minds.

You feel a need to maintain your individuality and separateness from others, and can resist any forms of imposition by others; you may rebel against the status quo and established attitudes, but as you grow older will realise the value of co-operation as vital in life to create harmony and peace. You apply logic and rationality to religious doctrines, which leads you towards non-conformist or agnostic attitudes. You enjoy sharing ideas and information with others, and are tolerant of alternative opinions and ideas, feeling little need to impose your view on others, but just to exchange them. It is essential to clarify your life direction, and you may experiment with several occupations and lifestyles, displaying your versatility and adaptability. You can enjoy travel, art, music and using your hands creatively.

CANCER SUN – WATER, CARDINAL; RULER: MOON

The Cancer personality is predominantly involved with emotions, feelings and sensitivity to life, which often stimulates changeable moods and fluctuating emotions. This can create situations where you often feel hurt by others – intentionally or not – and you feel extremely vulnerable and defensive. You will have a strong concern for family well-being, and will be very emotional and sentimental towards them, with a very private attachment to your mother. You often look back towards your childhood, feeling that it holds an important set of memories for you. You can be fearful of what the future holds, and usually you will avoid looking too hard in that direction.

You may tend to be quite talkative at times, despite tendencies towards a more retiring and reserved nature, and this can sometimes be a 'defence' from confronting yourself by joining in with others, rather than retreating into your own private world. You are a sympathetic listener, unless it coincides with a period in which there are problems with your own sensitivity, and then you are too preoccupied with your needs to be much use to others.

You have an active imagination, perhaps too active sometimes, as it can lead to brooding and worrying, and you tend to feel first and think last. This means that you can emotionally react quickly to situations, excessively so at times, whereas a more thoughtful response may have been more appropriate to avoid exacerbating any problems. You can tend to resist confronting problems, preferring to run away from pressures whenever possible. While you may give an impression of self-confidence and an ability to cope, you are only able to do so for a limited period, and then you need to retire into privacy and isolation to get yourself together again.

There can be a tendency to exaggerate personal problems – especially health – and this can cause illness through excessive worry. It is likely that you will become interested in health-giving foods and dietary concerns.

Home will be extremely important, both as a retreat from the world (your 'shell') and as your 'centre point' in life. You will try to maintain harmony and peace, hating any signs of discord. You prefer to live in style, and can become a knowledgeable collector of some type, enjoying the display of these interests in your home. You are fond of material possessions, and these often form your sense of material security. You enjoy and appreciate beauty in any form, and try to surround yourself with a pleasing environment, which can be enjoyed even more by opening your psychic sensitivity while at home. You need to feel that your family appreciates and thinks well of you, and will feel most uncomfortable if you think that you are being criticised or ridiculed.

You prefer traditional attitudes and values, despite any superficial appearance of contemporary style, and can sometimes find it hard to understand the complexity of the modern world. There may be an artistic talent present – perhaps a craftsperson in some way – but any artistic originality can be blocked by tendencies towards emotional repression, which is one of the major Cancer challenges to resolve. When feeling emotionally upset and imbalanced, your food intake will be affected, either eating to excess as 'compensation', or reducing food until the mood has passed.

You consider marriage is important, although you need to ensure a wise choice. Your emotional needs for love and nurturing may make you dependent on a strong partner, or attract a weaker personality to you, depending on whether your dominant pattern is for giving or receiving love. You can be highly supportive in helping a partner achieve their aims. You may become a day-dreamer, indulging in regrets or wishful thinking. Your inner life has an ebb-and-flow action like a rhythmic motion, emphasising your indrawn nature and then your instinctive outgoing social urge, leading often to moodiness and contradictions. The phases of the Moon may affect you more than you realise.

LEO SUN – FIRE, FIXED, RULER: SUN

The Leo personality is attracted towards power, influence and being in the spotlight, where people notice them and where they can perform. If you can achieve such positions, then self-confidence rapidly expands; you will be more successful when you act from positions of responsibility and authority. Yet underlying these needs are feelings of insecurity and uncertainty regarding your abilities, and these need transcending by attaining some success. You have the opportunity to inspire others towards greater achievements, unless you become too obsessed with exerting power and influence over others.

Once your direction and aims are determined, you can apply your powerful will to great personal advantage. You have a basic optimistic faith in the future and in your ability to meet life's challenges, and can have a secret conviction of performing some act of destiny in life, under the inspiration of unknown intangible forces which you believe are personally beneficial.

You can be quite highly strung, occasionally quick to anger, although tending to forgive people who you feel have wronged you. Your temperament is outgoing, expressing goodwill and geniality towards others, although you can also greatly enjoy those hours when you can be alone, quiet and with yourself. Problems that may arise are confronted and tackled with enough energy to dispose of them; you do not allow problems to persist or attempt to evade them.

You have a strong quality of pride, dignity, integrity, loyalty and generosity, and you try to stay true to your beliefs and values. You can be dominating in your social sphere, having an independent, outspoken and frank communicative style which can upset those who react against a direct, blunt approach. Sometimes you tend to play to the 'audience' and 'go over the top' in terms of what is acceptable, and so can lose friends or acquaintances through your comments. You can be an effective persuader, articulate and capable of communicating your ideas and enthusiasms. You are sincere in whatever you do, wanting only peace and harmony to exist around you. You tend to have extravagant tastes, but try to ensure that those spending habits remain prudent, and you hate to get into financial trouble, although you can be tempted to buy on spontaneous impulse.

You have a need to be dominant, at least at home, and this can cause some friction between personalities, especially if your partner is equally wilful and assertive. There is a strong need for freedom and independence, which, with a sometimes authoritarian attitude, can create partnership disputes. Dramatic artistic types can often attract you, but it is likely that once the passion wanes, personality clashes will later occur. You require an intelligent partner, and have a strong impulse to share, which can involve sacrifice by you, especially when it contradicts your natural urge to satisfy purely personal desires.

You rarely feel content with any achievements, always driving onwards, and you can be an inspiring teacher, helping others to fulfil their potential. You need mental stimulation, and this helps you avoid becoming fixed in attitudes and opinions. You may choose to associate with humanitarian groups, but can be too individualistic to stay, unless you are the leader. Sometimes you feel unappreciated, and become moody. You need a distinct purpose and life direction, and can serve selflessly, but you often look for the applause too.

VIRGO SUN – EARTH, MUTABLE; RULER: MERCURY

The Virgo personality is usually careful, efficient and methodical, deriving great pleasure in creating order from confusion and chaos. You will like to put things straight and tidy, to organise your environment and also any people that happen to be there . . . You have a high degree of common sense, and can be an active thinker who has to put thoughts into practice. You are efficient at handling and working with details in life, and are able to learn new things quickly and easily.

You may find it difficult to feel content with life, yet have difficulty distinguishing which aspects should be changed to improve it. There can be anxiety undercurrents, and through excessive worry your nervous system can be affected, creating ill health. You may need to be careful that excessive work does not place too much strain on your health, as you tend to be one of the consistent and reliable workers of the zodiac.

Your life-attitudes are fundamentally conservative and traditional, and you are cautious and protective regarding your interests. You tend to seek perfection in people and the world (which you will never find) and can tend to point out faults to others; sometimes these comments can be too sharp and upsetting, even if your perceptions are generally accurate. Yet when you consciously choose to be, you can reveal a tactful and diplomatic style of expression. You may not always judge yourself to quite the high degree that you expect from others though . . . Your attitudes, beliefs and opinions can become too fixed and inflexible, which can make change and development difficult to achieve, as well as leading to conflicts with others.

You can be an efficient financial manager and organiser of your domestic life, needing this to feel secure. You are very conscious of the value and importance of ensuring the family unit remains cohesive, and are willing to expend considerable effort in that direction. There will be a strong sense of morality – reflecting traditional values – and your life will probably move along socially acceptable routes; you prefer this as you are a bit restrained and choose to stay on secure 'well-trodden paths'.

You probably hold back your emotions, feeling less comfortable with them, because they represent elements of chaos and unpredictability which you feel you are opposing in the world. You will rarely be openly demonstrative about your feelings, which can lead to greater inner strains and tensions until they need to be periodically or explosively released. You need a partner who appreciates your efforts and sympathetically understands the challenges of your nature. You may display philosophic resignation and attempt to 'soldier on' when difficulties arise; you tend to subdue your desires in order to maintain a working relationship, but may have to beware of becoming resentful of your sacrifice and frustration of needs. There may be some inhibition with sexuality, perhaps a self-consciousness and unease with your sexual desires and feelings, until you can overcome deep fears of losing self-control to these powerful energies.

You are domestically orientated, enjoying home life, and are not too keen on travelling far unless it is with your family. You are orthodox and conventional regarding most things in life, but your main criteria and test is for practicality and applicability in life, and if so, then it is acceptable. You can serve as a valued adviser, organising behind the scenes, and be a performer of thankless tasks due to that self-sacrificial Virgo quality.

Libra Sun – Air, Cardinal; Ruler: Venus

The Libran personality seeks order, balance and harmony. You will be pleasant and an agreeable companion, looking for peace in life, but can often be emotionally quick to anger, especially within your intimate relationships. You will try to please everyone by using diplomatic skills, but can create situations where you are indecisive for fear of upsetting someone. Making decisions can be often difficult for Libra, and you would prefer to satisfy all options, not knowing what direction and decision to take. You are temperamentally more suited to waiting for things to happen to you, or decisions to be made for you, rather than initiating them yourself. However, this tendency can be modified by a strong wilful Ascendant.

You enjoy socialising, and your grace, charm and congeniality will be appreciated by others. Your favourite companions often display an artistic temperament which reflects your love of beauty, as found in nature, art, music and literature, as well as asserting free individuality and a dramatic presence which you would like to create as your self-image.

You can be idealistic and mentally adaptable, having an intuitive perception which should be used for life-guidance. However, you will also be very impressionable, and this can lead towards romantic fantasising, sometimes a distaste for actual reality, impracticality, plus a distinct changeability to your temperament.

Your social attitudes are humanitarian and sympathetic, although sometimes diminished by self-preoccupation, and you are often attracted towards the 'high-society' type of life with its elegance and money. You will be ambitious, but this is more directed towards creating a certain quality of life where harmonious balance is achieved.

It is quite important to you to keep your life ordered, controlled, efficient and organised. You are usually very patient and tolerant regarding house and family, and you require a sense of domestic security in a home of which you feel proud. You are especially sympathetic to the needs of children, and are usually good with them. You have an interest in tradition and previous expressions of style and culture, and this can be reflected in your home, where you create a homely atmosphere which attempts to reflect qualities of beauty and harmony for you. You may need to become periodically reclusive, so that you can restore your energy and 'social mask', and this can also be reflected in periodic changes in your choice of appearance.

In romance, you are often guided more by your head than your heart, as you lack total trust in your ability to be emotionally realistic, and can often be shocked at the power of your feelings which shake your inner balance too much. You can lose emotional control in love affairs which produce dramatic changes in you, and often your romances can become stormy. You are more able to apply your harmonising energies and talents for the benefit of others, than in your own passionate relationships. Often, while attempting to maintain your inner balance, by following idiosyncratic needs and desires, you succeed in stimulating imbalance and aggression in your partner who feels either ignored or dominated. You tend to have an idealistic and often unrealistic vision of the perfect relationship, so little wonder that your partners do not compare favourably. There is a dissatisfaction with unharmonious relationships which conflicts with your needs for harmony, stability, and the continuity of relationship; this is a sphere of your life that requires more clarity.

You can enjoy involvement with group endeavours, especially with those groups reflecting beneficial social aims and ideals, as you can become a natural fighter for the rights of others. As you mature, you tend to develop a personal philosophy which you try to apply in daily life, and can enjoy study and intellectual interests, being able to translate abstract ideas into more accessible forms for communication to others. Physical or mundane work rarely appeals to you.

Scorpio Sun – Water, Fixed; Ruler: Mars, Pluto

The Scorpio personality tends to mask its qualities, rarely revealing them too openly. You are likely to be extremely determined and resolute, possessing a very powerful will when you choose to use it. You will tend to be forceful when chasing your goals, often using subtle manipulation over others to achieve those aims.

You will have considerable self-pride, and will not take kindly to being embarrassed or humiliated in any way, and would certainly never forget who it was that placed you in such a position. Your sensitivity and feeling nature is a main source of contact with the world, and usually if someone offends you, causing an emotional reaction, then your perception and future response to that person will be affected from that point onwards. Generally, you are quite reserved, keeping others at a distance, trying to prevent them seeing into your inner life which can alternate between 'calm seas and boiling passions'; your inner life can be experienced as extremely 'raw' at times, and this can be difficult to handle.

You will seldom display deeper emotions and feelings, as they are too intimate to your real nature, and impulses may be repressed due to the passion and power that can flood through you and outwards. You are likely to be quite secretive and private, difficult to understand due to an inscrutable mask that you maintain giving the appearance of controlled intensity (except for the eyes which can reveal your inner state).

You can be direct, blunt, provocative and potentially confrontational in attitude and style of expression. Some may find this refreshing, others may not, and this can lead to broken friendships or enmity occurring. Your words will be controlled and deliberate; sometimes very diplomatic and cautious, sometimes very pointed and designed to make their mark. At times, your passionate energies will make you say things which perhaps you should not, but in the releasing of pent-up energy you are glad to have been honest. You can be cynical and sarcastic, and display sudden outbursts of rage and anger, especially if you have been repressing feelings for some time.

You are not easily impressed or influenced by others, and will usually tend to react against authority, even though in family life and personal expression you are authoritative yourself, and your attitudes, beliefs, values and opinions are clear and firm. You try to guide your life by relying on passion and commitment to those inner compulsions and motivating aims and purposes. You can be quite ambitious, especially when attracted to power and influence over others. You prefer to take control and initiative in all aspects of life, tending to be a natural leader who is prepared to take responsibility; but you do not make a good follower, often trying to undermine superiors by a very irreverent attitude.

You will be shrewd and enterprising, although you will only apply effort if you are genuinely interested in what you are doing. Research can attract, or any work involving investigations, mysteries or the occult. The energies of your inner passions can be used intellectually, probing the depths of mind/being, and your insights and understanding can become extremely profound and clear.

Your love life may be traumatic, with periodic crises or turning points, and can often be emotionally intense. Choosing a right partner is crucial in this sphere of your life, and you will have high ideals and expectations of any partner. You are likely to hold a traditional attitude to marriage, and can be very jealous. Essentially you are a 'loner' and even within marriage will walk a personal and solitary path.

SAGITTARIUS SUN – FIRE, MUTABLE; RULER: JUPITER

The Sagittarian personality is usually good-humoured, needs freedom and liberty to roam around, and does not respond well to the imposition of orders from others. Your temperament will be cheerful, optimistic and generous, being a consistent and reliable friend. You prefer to live as free as possible, and may need employment which offers considerable work variety and independence, so that you can organise your own endeavours while ensuring that the job is also completed. You may be attracted towards medicine, law and religion, and have skills to become an effective teacher, but you may need to avoid any authoritarian or patronising attitudes. You will be quite ambitious and usually quick to take advantage of opportunities; your attitude may be too optimistic at times, becoming overly enthusiastic about plans before you have had time to consider them fully.

You may need a clearer sense of direction and life purpose, which directs you towards suitable work, but once found this should enable you to strive one-pointedly to achieve your goals. You can be a conscientious worker, especially to ensure an income which is sufficient to indulge you need to spend on your particular interests. You may prefer earning a living by working for large organisations, feeling financially safe and secure within them, and they also offer potential progress towards positions of responsibility. Although you love freedom, security is also important, allowing relaxation so that you can enjoy your freedom. Wealth and possessions also attract, as you greatly enjoy spending and luxury possessions.

There is an innate sense of fair play and justice, and your manner is open and frank, possibly too direct, blunt and abrupt at times for some, but your comments and observations are usually quite accurate. You tend to make mental intuitive leaps, bypassing rationality and logic steps, but sometimes you are too quick jumping to conclusions about things, and then resist changing your viewpoint – even when it is incorrect. You may have an inventive mind, perhaps quite original in content through verbal or literary expression, and this will often closely reflect your moral values and beliefs. You can be an entertaining talker, and although you may not be too knowledgeable about all themes, your mind has an ability to piece together information fragments so that you sound quite informed.

Home and family evoke sentimental reactions, and you can have an image of self-sacrifice for their benefit, although you want appreciation for your actions. You can express fixed and assertive opinions at home, and while you attempt to create a free liberal atmosphere, this can lead to some conflicts, especially if your ideals or presentation of personal views tend to become a little extreme. You need mental stimulation and a variety of social company, and this can create a restless pattern of physical and mental activity. Your partner needs to understand your need for freedom, sharing your diverse interests and not attempting to limit or restrain you.

You may not always be fully honest with yourself, especially due to tendencies for emotional self-deception; self-enquiry may reveal two sides to your nature, one bright and amiable, the other broody and insecure. You can be an abstract thinker, idealist not realist, inclined towards stubborn, dogmatic and fixed ideas; in later years your interest can veer to philosophy and religious concerns. You have an 'interest in death', and often have intuitive feelings or prophetic insights which you note but may avoid trying to explain or understand, preferring to ignore them. The alternative approach is to pursue and explore your inner psychology and man's spiritual heritage to gain a deeper understanding.

Capricorn Sun – Earth, Cardinal; Ruler: Saturn

The Capricorn personality tends to be serious in nature, and you will display a cautious, thoughtful quality, being quite practical, prudent and economical in your affairs, as if you are on the defensive against the vagaries of life. You will usually consider all options before you act decisively. You prefer to express an individual dignity, often assuming a role of authority, as you highly value law and order in daily life and consider that these aspects are essential in both the individual and national life. You will be attracted towards positions of authority and social prestige, and will be ambitious to achieve them; this will attract and satisfy you more than just material possessions, although you may also 'use' them to enhance your status.

You will be capable of hard persistent work, designed to achieve your goals, and you should be an efficient organiser. You are usually very reliable at work, being quite conscientious, and are likely to possess the gift of a lucid and direct writing style which can prove to be an advantage.

You need to feel admired, respected and appreciated by others, in all your efforts at home and work. You are not especially emotionally or physically demonstrative, and although you are compassionate, you may find it difficult to display sympathy openly. You prefer to serve others through action, by physical aid in some way, rather than by emotional support, as you are less comfortable with that part of your nature. You prefer to judge others and be judged by them through actions rather than words; to you, words can be many, but few tend to back them up by action.

You may periodically suffer swings of mood, ranging between the extremes of optimism and pessimism, partly because you have difficulty in always maintaining faith in life. You can often be very reserved and private, keeping a distance between yourself and others, relaxing your guard only when you have known the person for some time, and feel safe and secure.

When you choose to apply it, you should have a powerful will, which can be used in a concentrated, persistent manner to achieve objectives.

You dislike wasting words, preferring precision and saying only what you want to say, or staying quiet, especially if you are afraid of being misunderstood; there may be some problem in communicating to others, particularly at times when you need to withdraw from excessive social contact. You often believe that you know best for all concerned, be they family, friends, relatives etc, and at times you may tend to be insistent that your ideas are the right ones to follow. This can lead to domestic or work conflicts as you enter into disagreements, especially if you express yourself dogmatically and authoritatively as you often do. You may need to learn more about the values of co-operation and joint decision-making at some time in your life.

Marriage evokes your sentimental nature, and you may prefer a partner who is either 'motherly or fatherly', looking for loyalty and reliability in partners and friends. Your view of life is realistic and pragmatic, preferring to establish a stolid pattern of familiar daily routines to offer a sense of security. You may tend to repress emotions from public expression, as you feel uneasy if they become dominating, and prefer always to feel in control. You may need to open your mind to higher things, to philosophies, fantasies, abstract thinking, as your approach may be too factual, critical, analytical and practical, and the danger is that this – unless modified – can make you too rigid, dogmatic and narrow-minded. In chasing your ambitions, you will have to ensure that any relative failure does not frustrate or embitter you through losing perspective on the totality of your life.

AQUARIUS SUN – AIR, FIXED: RULER: URANUS

The Aquarian personality displays a tendency towards humanitarian service designed to benefit others. You are likely to be friendly and sociable with a large circle of friends and acquaintances, although you also have an impersonal attitude towards them. You are sincere, or at least you think you are, and usually have quite distinct likes and dislikes in life.

Your mental outlook tends to be dispassionate, based on logic and reason, dealing well with facts, and you have a good retentive memory. You prefer your attention to be directed towards intellectually appealing topics. Your mind is very fertile, imaginative and quick-thinking, but you may need to stop sometimes and consider before speaking, as you can create problems by speaking out first without giving due thought to content or effect. You may be interested in artistic expression, and can display some ability too.

You are often motivated by strong ideals, which you try to use as a guiding force in your life. You believe in the values of a co-operative approach to life, but this can clash with your need for personal freedom. You often forcefully project your ideas and thoughts, and idealistic or practical disagreements with others can break down attempts at co-operation. Positively though, you are capable of applying great energy towards furthering any cause that you believe in, and are likely to tend towards unorthodoxy and unconventional behaviour, attitudes and ideas; sometimes you can be unpredictable, eccentric and attracted to anything unusual, at least through curiosity. There can be a conflict within you of introversion or extroversion, where a part of you wishes to be quiet and unobtrusive, and another aspect wants to be a centre of attention and a dramatic focal point.

You can be impractical with possessions, and may need to learn how to deal with money more efficiently, as well as adjusting any attachment to material possessions and the values given to them.

You usually overflow with ideas and talk about them at length, but there can be problems in application and seeing projects through; it is the mental world of ideas that fascinates and stimulates you, and you often lose interest when time comes for practical application. If you allow it, you can become obsessed and immersed in work, taking it very seriously, and this often leads to worry and nervous problems.

You do not fall deeply in love easily or often, as your mind remains detached from your emotions; when you do, however, you might have difficulty coming to terms with your emotional power and intensity. Generally you succeed in keeping emotions away from many aspects of your life, believing that they distort the joys of the intellect. You may be late settling down with a partner, and need to choose wisely by seeking an intellectually compatible personality. You wish to retain independence and do not like being dictated to or dominated.

This extends to common Aquarian beliefs in universal justice, peace, equality and radical change of anything that leads to suffering for humanity. Your views are strongly expressed and radical enough if you persist in them to disrupt groups or upset people. You may need to avoid a tendency to make 'speeches' calling for progress, liberation etc. and yet, when the time comes for action, be engaged elsewhere. You could be a visionary, but will need to learn the values of persistence and action to make those dreams a reality. Prestige and achievement is important for you, but be careful not to get a mentally inflated self image if it does occur.

PISCES SUN – WATER, MUTABLE: RULER: NEPTUNE AND JUPITER

The Pisces personality tends to be easy-going, sympathetic, trusting, kind, loving, charitable and modest, and not particularly interested in drawing attention to itself. You have a gift of understanding, although this may come about by using a psychic faculty which you can unconsciously rely upon to receive information. You tend to 'merge your mind' with another during communication, and information is transmitted, often bypassing the conscious mind.

Your approach to life and work will be orderly, although your inner states of mind–emotions–being will tend to be very changeable and fluid, reflecting the Piscean water affinity. You may be too impressionable, especially in your youth and early adulthood, and your life can be dominated in several ways by the power of your emotions and imaginative faculties. If you become committed towards supporting an idealistic cause, your involvement is likely to be an intense experience, partly because of the emotional attraction and energy expressed, and partly through the experience of disciplining your nature towards fulfilling any obligations and responsibilities that the 'cause' imposes upon you, and the inevitable inner struggle that usually occurs in such a context.

You may lack firm self-confidence, and are rarely keen to push yourself into situations of competition and aggression, preferring to make efforts to seek a harmonious resolution of problems and conflicts in any confrontational situation. Often, you may inwardly rely upon money and possessions to give you a sense of self-worth, to enhance your confidence in your abilities to succeed in the world.

Potentially, you can be quite creative if you succeed in finding appropriate channels of expression, and the most attractive areas for you will be music, literature and the arts, especially when responses from your feeling nature are evoked in addition to your mind. You tend to indulge in daydreams, partly as a form of evasion and escape from the demands of the real world, and you may have to be careful that you do not generate an inner climate of illusions, desires and wishes that prevent you from experiencing your actual reality or even make you blind as to what is actually occurring; inner unfulfilled dreams can make you lose appreciation of life.

You appear to be a flexible and malleable person, but there is a strong streak of stubbornness that can emerge when provoked, and you are not as open-minded as you can seem. Often you get 'stuck' on ideas, beliefs and attitudes from which you can almost refuse to move, and in a way, these tend to give you a sense of a personal centre amidst the ebbs and flows of your tidal feelings.

You will desire the 'ideal home and family', and chances for success depend upon the degrees of realism or illusion expressed by you in relationships, as your expectations may be too high and not easily attained. You are liable to be emotionally hurt and disappointed. Realistic perceptions of relationships may require previous disillusioning experiences. There is a tendency to initiate changes in relationships or environments which reflect a 'new start, new dreams to create and chase'. You will have a romantic attitude to your love affairs, and can be quite sentimental. Often you can be quite critical of your partner, projecting your feelings of self-doubt and supposed inadequacies or lack of certain qualities on to your partner, looking to them to provide you with these qualities that you lack. You need a reliable, methodical and efficient partner, and will work to make any marriage a success, but you may be tempted to evade confrontation and crises, pushing problems away. You may have difficulty at times making decisions, and can be psychologically dependent on others.

You need to discover an inner faith, finding a clear direction and purpose to your life, and forms of humanitarian service may be a suitable path to look towards.

CHAPTER 7

The Heroic Quest: Paths of Light

TWO MAJOR THEMES ASSOCIATED WITH the astrological Sun are the archetypal journeys of the hero's quest and the spiritual search for enlightenment, and these require a deeper consideration because anyone who is seriously attempting to evoke their solar power is likely to activate these patterns within their own psyche. The heroic quest is reflected throughout the world's myths and legends, occurring in similar story-patterns irrespective of cultural differences. The search for God and the spiritual impulse to attain enlightenment motivates the mystical quest to pursue the journey inwards to discover the non-separate reality of wholeness and unity.

These are the dimensions of life that an activated solar centre will begin to open within each individual, by moving deeper towards the level of the spiritual Sun, where the solar consciousness transcends the separate level of the human personality and expands to include the transpersonal reality. Both the heroic and mystical paths are interrelated, as indicated by the Arthurian legends, where the successful knights in the temporal world are then summoned to the spiritual search of the Grail quest. For those of us attempting to embody the New Age vision and new Aquarian consciousness, our paths through life will include aspects of both the heroic and mystical paths, and we are likely to touch several specific expressions of these paths of light through our own journeying. Being aware of these solar patterns can be useful in the context of a deeper integration of our divided self, and by enabling us to contract the archetypal matrices which form the root of the specific qualities embodied in each Sun-sign.

One image that has been suggested of the human personality is that we are like a shattered mirror, and because of receiving a multitude of self-images reflected by each splinter of self, we fail to realise the fact of our essential wholeness and unity. Mistakenly, we identify ourselves through roles and functions with fragments of our nature, and lose sight of the whole picture in the distorted reflection.

A parallel to this is astrology's approach to interpreting the natal chart, with all the factors of planetary position, signs and aspects reflecting fragments of the individual psyche, yet cumulatively creating that particular human nature. One role of the astrologer is to indicate the underlying unity of the individual, by pointing to the potential attainment of integration and wholeness, a stage which progressively reveals meaning, purpose and direction for the individual's quest of self-unfoldment.

By looking at areas of the psyche that may be unbalanced or antagonistic (challenging aspects, disaffinitive planet-sign positions etc), the astrologer may suggest ways or techniques that can lead to greater personal reconciliation, reassembling those fragments into a more recognisable unity. As this process continues to operate, the individual moves closer to becoming the 'Sun' of his psyche, the light of his own universe and reality, and he then becomes 'self-luminous', a 'living flame'. By the power of his quest, and his proximity to his living centre of Self, he becomes 'enlightened'. As Osho Rajneesh said, when the seeker approaches the Master, he comes closer to the fire, and all his illusions and separated consciousness will be consumed.

The house and sign position of our natal Sun is a testing ground for our potential; we are asked to follow our heroic and mystical paths from that sphere, and many are the challenges that will confront us. We may be faced by demons of our own making, our tendencies, strengths and weaknesses, our reactions and responses to life, the nature of our choices; each of these can either help us on our journey, or form impassable mountains which stop us in our tracks, making us wonder how we can proceed onwards. We spin out the path of light from within ourselves, and we create our own journey; recognising this fact is a major step forward, and discovering how we can create it to suit our intentions provides another key to progress. The heroic path is to fulfil a hidden destiny, to attain purpose and meaning in life; the mystic path is to attain revelatory light and greater consciousness; eventually the two paths become one. For the astrologer and their clients, working with the techniques of creative visualisation can become extremely important in the rearrangement of the fragmented self, and provide the means for a conscious creation of the personal path. One of the tasks of the hero is to accept self-responsibility, to assert that unique independent individuality, and this challenge confronts each of us and is one that we are unwise to evade.

The Heroic Quest

The heroic myths are stories of the adventure of life, reflections of inevitable trials and tribulations, of conflicts, pain, confusion, joy, and the exaltation of eventual success and attainment, the culmination of all efforts and the manifestation of latent potential. This is the discovery of the hidden treasure, the pot of gold at the end of the rainbow, the pearl of great price. For the triumphant hero or heroine the transformation is into becoming a *Son or Daughter of Light*, one of the divine archetypal images of Self, to which the evolutionary quest of life attempts to lead us back so we can discover our eternal nature. This Self is essentially androgynous and beyond separative polarities, where the individual archetypes of anima-animus have been reconciled within a unified mind, which is no longer split into conscious and unconscious levels.

The hero myth is often embodied in male heroes as the spiritual potency is connected more with the masculine polarity, and commences with the birth of a mysterious child of destiny, whose real parentage is rumoured to be either a king or a god. The hero-child remains in obscurity until maturity, with the light being dimmed or the hidden potential remaining latent. Then, as maturity dawns and purpose beckons, the child begins to awaken to a sense of destiny; as in the example of Christ being lost in the Temple of Jerusalem where he was discovered talking to the priests about the sacred Jewish teachings, or of Arthur innocently pulling out the sword of kingship from the stone.

Often these heroic myths unfold as specific forms of archetypal patterns, reflecting the individual urge for freedom, self-development and independence to follow their unique life-quest. The hero's early life is often threatened by the resistant forces of life, who try to prevent the future light-bearer reaching maturity. Herod attempted to destroy the infant Christ, and Joseph and Mary had to escape from Bethlehem and undergo a perilous journey to safer lands. The tribes of Israel entered the wilderness under the aegis of Moses, claiming liberation from Egyptian domination and searching for the promised land, following their inner lighted guidance. These children of destiny were often raised by guardians who were not their actual fathers, such as Christ by Joseph, Moses by the Pharaoh, or Arthur by Merlin and Ector.

The heroic adventure commences with breaking free from family bondage by asserting adult independence. For the male hero, this involves casting off the dominating mother archetype and his years of reliance upon parents, coupled with a determination to make his own way through life. The hero asserts 'I am what I am' and leaves the family home and protective embrace to explore his freedom of choice, taking the first step on his individual path.

This is an initiation of the threshold as he assumes the heroic persona, role and function, and is a stage that everyone can take during life when they step out from the collective to declare their individuality; later stages of this include the removal of the '10,000 heads' created by all parental, social, educational and religious influences in favour of the unified individual perspective when the path forms from the inner light.

Mythically, he crosses a demarcation line in his self-development, moves beyond a threshold and responds to the magnetic attraction of his 'destiny or fate'. Elements of this quest traditionally include the defeat of externalised shadow-projections, which may be faced in the forms of dragons and monsters; conflicts with the unintegrated feminine; or challenges by his dark twin brother and adversary. These shadows which stand in his way have to be consciously confronted, and he needs to reabsorb his projections back into his psyche, so that wholeness can be attained by the acceptance of his shadow and anima archetypes. His testing is through the many experiences of his journeys, which can take him across the seas, into unknown lands and cultures, meeting miraculous legendary creatures and guides, rescuing imprisoned damsels and succeeding in passing every ordeal.

On this path, he acquires friends and helpers, who can point to his future direction or offer wise advice as to his best course of action. He may have to attain the inner union of the sacred marriage, through transforming his masculine power by integrating his hidden feminine anima nature, so that a greater sensitivity can be born by a reconnection to the Goddess whom he had to deny in his mother in order to break free.

Many heroes have to undergo the ritual dismemberment, crucifixion and death prior to the resurrection of light and life. This is the dissolution of the existing self when the level of individual cohesion breaks down (the unity of the separate self and the mundane Sun), and is a stage that has to be endured before the next level of individual cohesion can emerge into being. The breakdown comes prior to the breakthrough, and is reflected by the triple alchemical process of *nigredo-albedo-rubedo*. To complete this process, he descends with his light down into the underworld kingdom and source of the dark powers. This can be seen as a regenerative function, where the creative aspect of the male potency seeds light in the darkness of the feminine womb, which can then later give birth to a revitalised unity; alternatively, the light penetrates the dark unconscious mind, illuminating its mysteries and secrets and purifying unredeemed energies and inhibited personality patterns. The hero then returns, or is resurrected, with an understanding of this mysterious process of transformation within life; this is often referred to as his theft of the magical elixir from the underworld, which he can then offer to the world as a resolution of the human dilemma. Essentially, the hero has reached his apotheosis, and realised the immanence of godhood, the fact that he is one with the universal Light.

There are several heroic attributions that recur through this mythic pattern, and these can also be linked with themes which are present within the twelve signs of the zodiac.

The hero as warrior is an archetype of force, associated with the birth of patriarchal power, wielding the renewing sword by shattering the crystallised structures of the status quo, breaking down the binding power of everything that is outworn and restrictive so that the creativity of new life can flow through, and the hidden potential be released. This is the dragon-slaying hero, and can correspond to the initiatory energy of Aries bringing the new life into existence.

The hero as the regenerative potency, fertilising the land and the creative spirit of culture, is reflected by the masculine virility of the Taurean bull and the association of the Persian Mithras and Celtic solar heroes with the bull.

The heroic confrontation with his shadow, the tanist and dark twin of his unintegrated and unrecognised unconscious self, is embodied by the symbol of Gemini and the challenge of transcending duality.

The hero's independence from his mother's embrace, and the breaking free from the psychological umbilical cord of the controlling mass collective consciousness to discover his individual path is indicated by Cancer.

The hero as king has the quest of defeating the existing powers of the established culture embodied by the ruling king, so that he can become the renewed king who inaugurates a new cycle. In this, he is challenged by a personal transformation to change his impulsive assertion of freedom into a determined effort to stimulate constructive social changes through reforms, new directions and reorganising the social structures. Yet as he begins to age, so his reformist plans and revitalised energies begin to wane and crystallise too, and he now becomes the epitome of the establishment, as conservative and conformist as the previous king. In due course, a new hero will emerge under the banner of 'the king must die, long live the king' to replace him with new vitality; and the cycle continues, similar to the seasonal cycle that was its inspiration. This urge for kingship embodies a Leo theme and the cyclic renewal of the lion as king of the beasts.

The hero as saint, ascetic and world renouncer can reflect the perfectionist tendency of Virgo, where withdrawal from life appears to offer the most effective means to attain that otherworldly perfection that is often dreamt about but rarely – if ever – attained on Earth.

In Libra, the balance of the 'god-man' is suggested, where the successful hero is centred at his inner source, revealing the harmony and transcendence of that balance, reflecting the World Axis by being a microcosmic mirror of the universal macrocosm. The God-man, the 'light of the world' reveals the meaning of existence and human purpose.

The resurrected hero emerges in the Scorpionic initiation and death rebirth drama like the Phoenix rising from its own ashes and the ongoing renewal of universal life.

The philosophical hero, custodian of cultural morals and teacher of ideals and social direction, is the theme associated with Sagittarius.

Capricorn is the heroic Law-giver (like Moses) the wielder of social power and influence, who imposes a revelatory message which reshapes social expression into a higher solar image.

The hero as a model for man's destiny, where the hero manifests in the present the future collective potential as a guarantee of man's evolutionary path, is reflected by the futuristic tendencies of Aquarius.

The hero as saviour and world redeemer through self-sacrifice is the Piscean pattern of the path, and is one of the most commonly recognised of the heroic traits, especially embodied in the Christian teachings. This theme includes the 'innocent heroes' who are unaggressive, and yet through courageously asserting their path become social and sacrificial victims, passing through social ignominy and death, after which their ideas, ideals and teachings are resurrected more powerfully than during their lives, and then spread influentially throughout the world. For their ideals to live and flourish, the heroic inspiration has to die.

Within the heroic myths, the role of the father has a peculiar ambivalence, as in the examples of two solar embodiments, Christ and Arthur, the father is absent or a mystery surrounds his identity. This poses the question of 'Who am I? Who is my father?', and ultimately the quest is to discover the answer to this ignorance. The eventual success of the hero through every test sees him returning with the symbols of the sword or sceptre of kingship and his book of the law; the hero is now a living representative of the unknown father, and is a teacher for mankind. He has a mission and is an emissary, stating his unification with his father in the terms of 'I and my father are one'.

Esoterically, this reflects the life process of Alpha and Omega, the beginning and ending of the world, and the interplay between light and darkness or conscious–unconscious levels of reality. In some myths, the Son attains at-one-ment with the Father, and in others the Son slays the Father, like the renewal of the kingship cycle where the hero kills the tyrant king and then assumes the crown. The Oedipus legend reflects this archetypal pattern, and in the Christian tradition, Christ replaces the power of the Old Testament Jehovah and the Ten Commandments by his superseding and synthesising new commandment of 'Love thy neighbour as thyself.'

What is the value of identifying these aspects of the heroic archetype? And what have they to do with astrology? The simple answer is that through attuning to our inner Sun, we can contact these, and be affected by their presence within our psyche. As Jung suggested, each individual life can be unconsciously founded on a particular mythic and archetypal structure, and it may be vitally important for us to discover which one(s) we resonate with, because in doing this we can begin to live more consciously through co-operating and adapting to that pattern. This may serve as an integrative power which also guides us on our path, and that could be of inestimable value. As has been considered, each sign reflects certain correspondences to certain heroic patterns, so it may be that our own Sun-sign conveys information as to the type of heroic path and endeavour that we should actualise on our personal life-journeys. This may be worth additional contemplation and investigation to see if our tendencies are reflecting specific heroic solar paths.

Three additional mythic structures will be considered as embodying heroic archetypes that can serve to inspire and guide us. These are the Albionic legends of Arthur, his knights and the Round Table; the twelve Labours of Hercules; and the Horned God of Wicca.

ARTHUR AND THE ROUND TABLE

One of the most potent British myths is the set of legends of King Arthur and his knights of the Round Table, which also serve as a synthesis of pagan-Celtic-Christian teachings. These stories still exert a great fascination today, and are now becoming a source for the revival of the spirit of Albion and a resurgence of interest in the native Celtic and shamanic culture that was overshadowed by the powerful wave of Christianity that cast a veil over the British spiritual roots.

The story of Arthur, his birth, childhood and emergence into adulthood by claiming his sword of rulership, followed by his acceptance of his mission, is in accord with the archetypal pattern of the solar hero-king. Although the Christians attempted to 'take over' the Arthurian myths by portraying him as a fifth-century king fighting under the banner of Christ to prevent Britain being overrun by the darkness of paganism after the occupying Roman troops withdrew, studies of the legend reveal symbolism that connects Arthur to much older Celtic cultures and spiritual teachings. Similarly, the Grail has become identified with the blood of Christ, yet this too has more ancient roots in the Celtic Cauldron of the Goddess.

While Arthur has become the embodiment of the British hero, the once and future king of these isles, the image that has served as a central symbol for the myth is the Round Table, or the King's High Table, located in the great beamed hall of Camelot. This table repeats the circular pattern of the solar glyph, and represents a microcosmic circle of light, unifying the purpose of the fellowship of knights who gathered around its magnetic centre.

Esoteric teachings consider that inscribed on the surface of the Round Table are the twelve signs of the zodiac, representing the collective wisdom and experience of humanity. Each knight becomes a representative of the qualities and gifts of their particular sign, offering them in service for the collective good of the kingdom. The Table becomes the rallying point for the highest group ideals of the society, as suggested by the elevation of Arthur's knights as the noblest warriors in the land, whose unity of thought and social influence directed by the King's power were a shining example for the people. The light that flowed through Arthur and his companions brought peace and prosperity to his kingdom.

One British esoteric school utilises this powerful symbol of the Round Table in its magical workings. The Table is visualised, and the meditator uses this image to cross the division between his conscious and unconscious mind as a means to open and expand his consciousness, synchronising together his two brain hemispheres. He sits at the siege of his Sun-sign, and the Table's circle or wheel of light begins to unify and integrate his psyche. Like the fabled magician, he evokes the power at the centre of the magical circle, becoming the sun of his own inner solar system. This power flows to him by the mediation of a veiled golden grail, which is receiving a downpouring of spiritual energy from the Sun of Tiphareth (see Chapter 8) which materialises above the centre of the Table.

While the twelve signs of the zodiac were represented by the Round Table, there was a thirteenth seat, the Seige Perilous, which remained empty until the arrival of Galahad, the future Grail King. This pattern of the Table indicated the lunar influence of the calendrical thirteen-month year. The Siege Perilous indicates the presence of the Eternal Feminine principle, the unintegrated Moon Goddess among the masculine solar dominance of Arthur's court.

After years of relative social peace and stability, Arthur grew older and his rule became that of the establishment, radical changes had faded away in favour of preserving the gains already achieved, and his light began to slowly wane. The unity of his companions started to fragment as the knights lacked any inspiring and challenging missions to pursue until the miraculous image of the Holy Grail appeared to them, and they decided to set off on a quest to discover its mystery.

Galahad arrived at court and claimed his Siege Perilous, which could be interpreted as the symbol for zodiacal synthesis, the potential of the whole universalised man, parallelling the relationship of Christ and his twelve disciples. After many trials, Galahad attains his transformative vision of the Grail, realising his spiritual unity. The Grail is primarily a symbol of the Goddess, and the knight's quest can be perceived as the masculine search to discover the inner feminine anima present in the unconscious mind, in order to become integrated.

Meanwhile, Arthur's rule was challenged by his own secret son, Mordred, who reflects the hero-king pattern of the renewal of the cycle, and also the shadow-dark self projection; both were mortally wounded in their final conflict, and the reign of Arthur's solar light was extinguished on the physical plane, yet still shines through legend and within the inner realities.

There are often attempts to make correspondences between certain knights and the cycle of Arthurian myths to the zodiacal signs. Often the knights are considered to display higher qualities which are characteristic of an attunement to the solar purpose. These can include qualities of courage, loyalty, nobility, gentleness, sincerity, virtue, chivalry, honour, charity and service, and are attributes that all can aspire towards.

Within the Arthurian cycle, the birth of Arthur has been connected to Capricorn, the time of the Winter solstice and the birth of the light and the Christ-child, a traditional time for the emergence of the solar hero. Galahad is the winged hero of the future Aquarian Age, setting an imprint of the archetype of the new man. In Taurus, the marriage of Arthur and Guinevere is consummated, the May Queen and Beltaine ceremony which failed to generate the successor to Arthur legitimately, and which by implication led to the wasteland spreading across the kingdom as the renewal of the nature cycle was not fertilised by the solar power.

Creating astrological correspondences to the Arthurian cycle can be an interesting and evocative exercise, and there can be several ways of developing such concepts and associations, although there can be no definitive version. All archetypal and mythic structures are extremely reflective, recurring in repetitive stories across cultures, and so attesting to their power to impress listeners on a collective level. One message of the Arthur legend, is that each man has to awaken his own solar light (or Christ consciousness) so that he becomes the living demonstration of the spiritualised hero-king; within everyone, that archetype resides.

The Labours of Hercules

In the Greek legends of Hercules (Herakles), the heroic path of the aspirant to the mysteries of life is portrayed, yet this is an arduous ascent which is fraught with mistakes and misunderstandings, much ordinary life when our unconsciousness creates many of our problems and suffering.

The wonder-child nature of Hercules is evident in the tales of his infancy. One story relates his slaying of the two serpents that attempted to kill him; these are the resistant forces of life, manifesting as the serpents of matter and illusion which were intent on destroying the solar child before his inner light burst free of their spellbinding influence. Another tale refers to Hercules being one of two twins with different fathers, one a son of an earthly father, and the other of an Olympian god. Hercules killed his earthly twin or material nature, because he had become aware of his duality, and this was the start of his quest for at-one-ment and the realisation of his heavenly father and spiritual nature.

The myth of Hercules is stained with death, killings and images of violence, as if the warrior aspect of the hero is the conditioning archetype. It is a dramatic and often tragic story, in which even the goddess Hera induced divine madness in Hercules, which resulted in an unleashing of his power without awareness of what he was doing; the consequences of this was his slaying of his own children, under the illusory belief that they were his enemies. Through this experience, he realised his own darkness and lack of wisdom, and feeling mortified he travelled to consult the Delphic oracle for advice over his future life and the means by which he could make restitution for his actions.

At Delphi, he was guided to submit himself to the instructions of Eurystheus for a period of twelve years. To redeem his life, he was given twelve consecutive tasks, each representing a year and one sign of the zodiac; collectively, they indicated a major lesson that he needed to learn.

The Hercules that started his labours had a temperament that symbolised the Fixed Cross of astrology, of Taurus, Leo, Scorpio and Aquarius. Alice Bailey's *The Labours of Hercules* states:

> Tradition tells us that he was physically bullnecked, as well as psychologically stubborn and ready to attack any problem and to rush blindly into any undertaking. Nothing could turn him from his purpose . . . and that he rushed headlong into them. Nothing deterred him, nothing frightened him, and one-pointedly he went his way. He was pledged to the spiritual life.

Although most temperaments may not fit this description of Hercules, we have our own particular tendencies to deal with; as prospective heroes we face similar tasks to complete, those trials to defeat our inner and outer monsters, those spiritual treasures to attain, and those services which can be freely given in life. All of these issues are reflected in our planetary natal chart as we strive to encompass the lessons of the zodiac. The external world becomes our temple of initiation, and our inner psyche the hidden initiation chamber.

What Hercules is asked to follow – and as aspirants, we are too – is the *Way to the Heart of God,* which enters the transformative circle of light through the Twelve Great Gates of the Zodiac. Each single path that we can complete leads us via a Great Gate into the light, where we receive in understanding the gift and lesson of each sign. Then, returning back into the world, we commence our next labour, which if successful, will enable us to pass through another Gate; eventually, we return to the light along all twelve paths and, transfigured, our wisdom radiates from our heart and mind. The Pathways are an evolutionary forcing process which unfolds the power, majesty and gifts of our soul/solar centre, an awakening which 'serves as a psychic resolvent, eating away all dross and leaves only the pure gold behind'.

Hercules has the task of expressing the positive and creative characteristics of each sign, which perpetually renews his self-knowledge, and offers opportunities to demonstrate the power and gifts of the signs. He transcends the lower and separative tendencies of the signs, and in so doing reveals his control of his own destiny, becoming a Master of Fate. One lesson that he offers to us, is that it is only in unconscious man that our stellar natal pattern controls our lives through unrealised manipulation of our tendencies; and that in the struggle to attain greater consciousness through the illumination of self-knowledge, we can claim the power to transform these lower tendencies, elevating them to spiritual influences and resolving dilemmas and contradictions within the psyche.

The Bailey book is highly recommended for those who wish to study these Labours from an esoteric astrological perspective, and gives considerable detail regarding the nature of Hercules' labours. All that can be indicated here is a summary of the esoteric lessons and realisations that Hercules achieved, which are steps on the path confronting everyone.

In Aries, the task is the Capture of the Man-eating Mares, and this is the start of the quest at the vernal equinox and the commencing of the new zodiacal year. Here he becomes aware of the creative power of thought and words, and the need to adopt a higher perspective and vision; it is a point of reorientation, where he is faced with the consequences of his actions, and needs to discover the right use of his creative mind and his will-power.

In Taurus, the task is the Capture of the Cretan Bull, which reflects the physicality of his lower nature, and the powerful attractions of personal desires and his polarised sexual nature. He needs to gain greater self-control, transmuting his energies towards aspiration rather than allowing their dispersal through separatist activities; in so doing, he evokes the strength of his will and consciously determined higher purpose.

In Gemini, the task is Gathering the Apples of the Hesperides, and this path shows starkly the nature of duality and its operation within the lower mind, which, through the intellectual tendency of differentiation, separation and analysis, creates the adversarial pairs of opposites. He needs to deepen the integration between soul and form, to allow light to descend into his world, so that the higher unifying vision predominates, resolving the conflicts of opposites. The perception of the many has to be replaced by the knowledge of the one.

In Cancer, the task is the Capture of the Doe or Hind, where his identification with form and the mass consciousness has to be dissolved through self-awareness and conscious relationship to others. Through a more empathic intuition, he sees that the way forward is through serving all on his path.

In Leo, the task is the Slaying of the Nemean Lion, and the lesson concerns asserting his power and independence, as he stands free from the constraints of the mass mind. His challenge is to become a leader of men; not as a ruler, although that can be a temptation, but as a pioneer, courageously forging new evolutionary paths for others later to follow. He needs to resist the tendencies of the separate self by subordinating them to his higher solar nature.

In Virgo, the task is to Seize the Girdle of Hippolyte, and this is a transition stage when he realises the immanence of the Christ child contained within him, spirit encased in matter, and now emerging into liberation. The lesson is that this work will become the reason for his endeavours, and that he should serve and nurture the spiritual birth within all nature; this is his heroic purpose and meaning for existence.

In Libra, the task is the Capture of the Erymanthian Boar, where the lesson is contained within the balancing of opposites, the equilibrium of spirit and form. This point is a preparatory pause, an establishing of everything that the hero has achieved so far. Treading the Middle Path, he may feel that the vitality has gone out of life, as the pull of his old nature has been neutralised, and his attempts to develop his higher nature appear quiescent.

In Scorpio, the task is the Destruction of the Many-Headed Hydra, and this constitutes a great crisis and turning point. Passing this test requires his cleansing and freedom from the mists of multiple illusions and glamours distorting his perception of himself and the world. This is a point of triumph, and the later stages of the path stand revealed to him now.

In Sagittarius, the task is Killing the Stymphalian Birds, and the lesson involves the renewing of his focused direction, aspiration and willed activities, a consecration to his path. The challenge is his need to learn how to apply his newly cleansed mind and power of speech and thought, because their potency and creative ability is increased, and can therefore be more dangerous if tainted by unconscious action. He is asked to become more responsible in all forms of his social expression and inner nature; he knows, and has little excuse to be lax.

In Capricorn, the task is the Slaying of Cerberus, the Guardian of Hades, and this is the challenge of working impersonally in the world, the start of world service by expressing the solar qualities for the benefit of the group. This requires the descent into the underworld of Hades, as a further phase of purification, and is a journey made by all solar heroes and initiates, as all are concerned with the release of those imprisoned in the dark underworld of their unconscious minds. It is in Capricorn that the Sun-gods are born, and to which they return to save humanity.

In Aquarius, the task is the Cleansing of the Augean Stables. The challenge is to demonstrate unselfish service, group co-operation and self-sacrifice for the well-being of the whole; he becomes a world server. There is no glamour to this role, as the Augean

Stables reveal. He had received his vision from the mountain top of initiation, as the glory of spirit blazed forth, shedding golden light across the world; now, he has to return into the filth of animal stables, uncleaned for years. This is symbolic of the world state: problems everywhere, filth, degradation, suffering, conflicts, war, poverty, ignorance, perversions, inhumanity. Into the seething mass of humanity, the initiate is cast again from the heights, and his mystical sensitivity shrinks from the magnitude of the task that faces him. But it is here that he must work, persevere and shine his light.

In Pisces, the task is Capturing the Red Cattle of Geryon, and here the hero is transformed into the world saviour, whose mission is to raise the level of all humanity, to attract them magnetically to take a few more faltering steps towards the light. Spirit is liberated from the chains of matter, and the light shines forth without dilution or distortion. The solar quest of the hero has reached its human end.

The Horned God of Wicca

The Divine Masculine principle of our native tradition of Wicca portrays the solar king as the consort of the Goddess, and he is known as the Horned God, representing an alternative perception of this power which in several ways forms a more suitable image for contemplation and potential inner contact for modern man than do the more violent warrior images.

The Horned God is associated with the cycles of nature and is a god of fertility and regeneration, the sower of the seed and the rebirth of the grain. He is known as the Lord of the Winds, wielder of the powers of nature and the elements, and as the Lord of the Dance, the generator of the spiralling seed energies of life, that are perpetually being reborn in new forms and constantly changing, and yet which through ceaseless motion, imprison life in the thraldom of matter.

He embodies unrestricted male sexual potency, the priapic tendencies of the procreative Pan and the impulse for union with the Goddess. His specific animal associations include the stag, stallion, bull and goat. His feelings and passions are strong and virile; not for him is the traditional male tendency of lukewarm emotions, repression and denial. The vitality and power of his feelings is acknowledged and honoured as a sign of life coursing through his nature, unrestricted and overflowing as evidence of his verdant potencies.

Through his dispersal into nature, his sexuality displays an integrative and connecting force, touching the mysteries of universal life as he oversees both the giving of life and the taking of life in the natural order of the world. Through his intimacy with the Goddess, he reflects a deep and holy communion that can be contacted by all those who seek to summon him from the tangled thickets of haunts in the wild woods.

Due to the Horned God's inner union with the Goddess, he expresses the integrated anima nature of the fusion of both masculine and feminine principles within his divine psyche, similar to the Greek gods of Apollo and Orpheus. In this sense, he can provide a role model for contemporary man, as he displays his sensitivity, gentleness and nurturing qualities as equally as his other personae. Men often have great difficulty in accepting and dealing with the power of their feelings and emotions, as it is an aspect to their being that can be culturally inhibited by social pressures to conform to several male stereotypal images, the stiff upper lip of the English, the macho power trips, the need for control over potential violent actions. Yet it is through such types of repressive social influences that many men learn to ignore and shut off their emotions as they mature to adulthood; and then later, when their imprisoned emotions finally overflow under the stimulation of love, or the failure of relationships, such men can find it extremely difficult to deal with their emotional vulnerability. The Horned God of Wicca offers an example of an integrated male, who is secure enough in his masculinity to include traditionally positive feminine qualities, with no diminution of his power; indeed, his nature is amplified and heightened.

It is only by forming an inner relationship with the anima within the psyche that man can become whole; he has to transcend the cultural pattern of conquering nature that has dominated male expression over the centuries, replacing it by a feminine archetype of inclusiveness and sensitivity, which then expands to encompass all levels of relationship with the world. In shattering the limitations of a partial male image, man can become liberated into a new perspective and experience of existence. By the evocation of the Horned God, the process of change can be quickened, and with the releasing of emotional vitality a corresponding increase in the power of creativity is often discovered.

For men, the astrological types that appear to find it easier to contact and absorb the anima archetype are related to the element of water. Cancer, Scorpio and Pisces are the water signs, and these are individuals who have deep emotional resonances, and for whom an emotional and feeling response to life is a more immediate reaction. Learning to live with their emotional sensitivity becomes a priority for them, so there is less of an innate distancing from that aspect of their being. Dealing with emotional depths, passions and fluctuations connects them more to the waxing and waning process of the feminine principle, and so they can find it easier to integrate their inner opposites for wholeness, once they face the full force of their emotional power.

As the Horned God of the Land, he embraces the physical level of reality, the innate instinctual wisdom of the body of nature. He is a God who is undivided, spirit and matter are fused through the lighted consciousness of mind and he embodies a unification of polarities. He is the bright vitalising force of light and life, and is the darkness of night and death. He becomes the Ever-Dying and Ever-Resurrected God, who has to surrender himself into death in order to be perpetually renewed. He offers the transformative process of self-acceptance and relaxation into the natural cycles of life, where our emotions and reactions have to be surrendered for cleansing and purgation; stripped of our psychological supports, illusions and glamours, we can stand free, ready for our destined rebirth where, having experienced the loss of everything, we now discover to our surprise that all is returned. The difference is that we have been renewed in the emptying, and we have only been relieved of anything that is inessential and inimical to our well-being, even though previously we would have considered it to be personally important.

The promise of the Horned God is that he offers a great healing to us with his outstretched hand of friendship. As he stands, half-hidden by the overshadowing trees of the wood, his antler-horns highlighted by the reflected light of the full moon, his vitality and power flows out to us and into the land. If we are afraid of confronting the mysteries of our nature, then he will become a Devil and we will reject him; if we feel the responsive pulse of quickened life within ourselves, then we step forward to follow him deeper into his kingdom. Taking that path transforms us into his role as the Hunter God, who is the seeker on a quest for knowledge and union; as each step is made, our cleansing deepens as we pursue him. Through the trees his image appears, fades and disappears; we are scratched and bruised as we run through the wood, desperate to keep him in our sight. Sometimes the moonlight flickers as clouds cross its face, and in the darkness we stumble and lose our footing, fears scattering across our mind like frightened birds. Then, in the distance, we see a glint of light, and the hunt is renewed. After what seems like an eternity in this otherworld, we emerge into a grove of oak trees. The night is silent. He stands alone, waiting. His hand is open and outstretched to us; we claim our hunter's rights and grasp his hand, and at that moment he is gone. We stand alone, but his power remains with us, and we realise . . .

Through our quest, we became the Hunter, the seeker for union and rebirth. Our masculine Logos, the power of mind, desires reconnection to Eros, the impulse for emotional merging and union with life. Our tendencies for analytical differentiation have to be elevated through the vision of inclusive synthesis for the whole pattern of mystery to be unfolded. In hunting the God we also discover the Goddess within, as our transformative quest takes us through all aspects of our psyche until we can stand face to face with our God, and realise that we are one. In dying to our old life, we are reborn into our new one; there is no other way.

This is the annual cyclic pattern of the Horned God, the 'wheel of the year' which symbolically we all participate in, and which we can experience as an inner process if we respond to his beckoning.

The child of light, the solar consort, is born at the Winter Solstice, as the light slowly increases by the Sun's moving northwards again after the annual longest night of darkness.

At Brigid or Candlemas (2 February), the light increases, and signs of the new verdant growth beneath the ground are observed, a promise of the renewal of life.

At the Spring Equinox, the Horned God appears in the disguise of the Green Youth, revelling in his vibrancy and vitality by his dancing and courtship of the Maiden, an aspect of the Goddess.

At Beltaine (1 May), the marriage of the adult solar god with the lunar goddess is celebrated by all in ritualised procreation.

At the Summer Solstice, the union of the marriage is achieved, as the 'Summer-Crowned King' reaches his ascendancy, and at the peak of his power he receives the rose crown, with its flowering bloom and sharp thorns; his blood drips on to the land, his seed potency is spent and his consummation is the apex of his fall and descent into death. The light begins to wane.

At Lughnassad (1 August), the mourning of the passing away of the verdant King and Horned God occurs.

At the Autumn Equinox, the God is said to be sleeping in the dark womb of the Goddess, sailing on the inner seas of the feminine tides.

At Samhain (31 October, Hallowe'en), he reaches the Land of Shining Youth, where he will rest and grow youthful again, regaining his power in the dreamtime, until the time arrives for his rebirth.

At the Winter Solstice, the child of light is reborn and the cycle continues.

The heroic paths are journeys towards the light, and include a radical redefinition of what our self and nature really is; the climax of the quest is the raising of our humanity to divinity, and the descent of divinity to humanity. We become Sons and Daughters of Light.

Such legends, myths and archetypes as Arthur and the Fellowship of the Round Table, the Labours of Hercules or the Horned God are all reminders of our need to search and live out our potential. In the silence of night, we dimly hear the horn alerting us to awake, and, like the Prodigal Son returning to the Father, struggle to return to our source. In our sleep, we can turn over, snuggle down under the covers and pretend that we never heard anything. Choosing ignorance, allows sleep to descend again; but the call will persist until it is acknowledged.

As astrologers, or serious students of this branch of the collective wisdom, we work with astrological archetypes and the patterns of the human life process as reflected through planetary transits or natal positions. Our major aim should be to use astrology to generate more light, on our own nature, for clients, and within the collective mind of humanity. Through greater consciousness we can include more of our totality into our lives, experiencing the abundant life that has been promised as a quality of the spiritual kingdom.

Our responsibility has to be embodying this light in our lives, through example and evidence of our themes of integration, meaning and purpose. We have to walk our own heroic path towards enlightenment; otherwise, in our own darkness, we act merely as the blind leading the blind, which is fundamentally dangerous. In Jungian terms, the Self is symbolised by the luminous and numinous Sun or Star, and it is the reality of this centre that seeks awakening within us. As the Hindu Krishna declares, 'I am the Self, seated in the heart of all creatures. I am the beginning, and the middle and the end of all beings.' This is the heart of the spiritual sun, whose residence can be first seen through the doorway of the mundane sun, the position of our natal sun in astrology. Through the path of becoming our solar self, we move from the periphery of our circle of consciousness towards our secret centre. Realisation or enlightenment occurs when we stand at the symbolic central point of our natal mandala, the birth chart, and from that unified perspective, see all aspects of our nature (planets, signs) dancing in harmony to the melody of Apollo the Sun God's lyre.

CHAPTER 8

The Esoteric Sun: The Heart Mandala of Light

> O Thou who givest sustenance to the universe
> From whom all things proceed
> To whom all things return,
> Unveil to us the face of the true Spiritual Sun
> Hidden by a disc of golden light
> That we may know the Truth
> And do our whole duty
> As we journey to Thy sacred feet.

THE PRAYER OF THE VEDIC GAYATRI reveals the esoteric insight into the nature of the spiritual sun, and the reverence shown to the creative power of the 'heart of the Sun'. It is this inner nature and spiritual source that can be discovered by all who journey into their own centre; as the physical sun gives life to our solar system, so does the spiritual sun give resurrection to the path of enlightenment.

The astrological symbol for the Sun, a circle with a point at the centre, contains considerable esoteric teaching. The circle represents the universe, infinity, self-complete and without beginning or end, the primal source of the original atom, where universal matter–spirit was enfolded. The circle is the original cause, the One from which the many emanate, the underlying unity within manifestation. The nature of the universal circle is unknowable, apart from its providing the root of all Life, and could be considered to be creative space, without dimension and self-existent. The circle is the Cosmic Mystery, which we are formed from and in which we live. The deeper we penetrate into the mysteries of matter, the more matter dissolves into spirit; and as our scientific knowledge 'grows', so does our ignorance as the mystery recedes beyond our eager grasp into a greater paradoxical simplicity-complexity, capable of uprooting our mental preconceptions as to the nature of the universe and reality. We cannot remain an objective, separate entity scientifically studying the foundations of life; we need to become more conscious of its activity through us, and by a transformation of consciousness embody the mystery ourselves.

The point or dot at the centre of the circle indicates the mystery of differentiation, the commencement of life from the overflowing creativity of the circle, the seed produced by the union of 'matter–spirit' within the primal cause. The point can be conceived as the first emanation of light emitted from the First Light, a life-giving energy from the unlimited divine source. It can be the opening through which universal manifestation is born from the depths of the eternally unmanifest. It can be the nuclei of the atom, from which the building blocks of our physical body and reality are composed, the seed of our potential expression of human–divine consciousness. The circle-point indicates the relationship of the separate individual with the greater whole of the universe, that of material existence to spiritual reality, the axis of life between the many and the one. The path to realise this potential is revealed through the conscious awareness of divinity hidden within matter, and the interrelatedness of universal life.

For the individual, the circle can represent a separative barrier, isolating them in self-centred consciousness from life. Esoteric teachings point to the realisation that while we are separate we are simultaneously all one, and all spiritual paths lead to the vision of that truth. Viewed from that perspective, the point then becomes an aperture to the inner reality, where the path leads inwards through the centre of the self to contact the spiritual dimension. The light of illumination shines from within outwards, and then is reflected within everything. The Sun symbol then serves as a dual indicator of the human nature; there is the lower self-centred perspective, seeking to grasp for the separate personality, and caring little about the well-being of others or the planet; and there is the higher self-centre, connected to the unity of the universe through spiritual awakening. This is the evolutionary path of humanity, seeking the Sun-path from self to Self, and the eternal quest of moving closer towards the light.

The astrological Sun symbol offers considerable depth for metaphysical speculation, but it is easier to apply it on the level of the individual search for Self; in the natal chart, it is a major signpost as to the direction of the journey and the sphere of life which is most intimately involved. This is the dual path, the evolutionary outwards and external one, and the involutionary inwards return. The relationship between the periphery of the circle and the central point is the path towards the inner Self. Like a mandala image, the intention is to focus on the centre of individual existence, meaning and purpose; in finding that heart, light is simultaneously discovered.

THE SEVEN RAYS SYSTEM

In the occult system of the Seven Rays, founded on the works of Blavatsky and especially Alice Bailey's transmission of the Tibetan Master's teachings, the Sun is associated with the Blue Ray, Ray 2 and the energy of Love-Wisdom. This is considered to be the vibration which two great spiritual teachers embodied: Gautama Buddha, the Wisdom aspect, and Jesus Christ the Love aspect. The concept of Seven Rays is derived from the one light crossing the 'prism of space' and being split into the seven colours of the spectrum. It is interesting to note that mythological symbolism connected to the Sun has the solar chariot drawn by either seven horses or a seven-headed horse, and the seven-stringed lyre of Apollo represented the keys to universal understanding.

The 2nd Ray is perceived as the energy of the Heart, and portrayals of Christ often have radiant beams of light and love emanating from his heart, his love encompassing all. As the Sun is traditionally the ruler of the heart, this is equated with the role of the physical sun whose fiery nature illuminates and enlivens the solar system. Love is felt as the fire burning in the human heart, and this corresponds to the sacred divine spark in the core of the atom, whose incredible power is now revealed to man by splitting the atom and nuclear fission. Many spiritual teachings emphasise the awakening of the heart as leading to the birth of the spiritual self, and this is stimulated by many meditative and visualisation techniques focused on the centre or heart of the body, designed to evoke a shift in energies. Meditations on evoking 'The Master in the Heart', or the Holy Grail and the Round Table, or several breathing and mantric chants, open the heart centre or chakra.

The ancient wisdom of the Sun worshippers intuited that the Sun corresponded to Love, seeing that it evoked the aspiration to draw closer to the brilliant source of light which illumines everything, and as the Gayatri stated, 'From whom all things proceed, To whom all things return.' This understanding emerged from the belief that from the union of the Universal Father–Mother (spirit – matter) came the Son/Sun, the Light and the Shadow, and the root of the twin concept mentioned in the mythological Sun chapter.

It is through the heart that bridges are made between people, and boundaries are dissolved through feelings of goodwill and a sense of human fellowship. It is through love that the world becomes enlivened, individuals feel that they belong and are needed, and that families and marriages are helped to remain cohesive; when love is impersonally applied it can work towards a global unity of diverse peoples and ways of life, refusing to fall into separative antagonisms towards those who think and live differently. Love transcends artificial barriers. As Alice Bailey states, 'Only from the heart centre can stream those lines of energy which link and bind together.' This is the magnetic and radiatory energy of the heart upon the environment, an energy that fuses together and heals through unity being experienced between people and their world.

The exoteric Sun, connected to the separative human body and personality, is a centralising and cohesive influence which maintains the egoic self, and is the function which is most recognised in the majority of people, identifiable through the exoteric Sun-type personality revealed by the natal Sun-sign. The esoteric Sun is discovered on the entrance to the spiritual path, at the symbolic Oracular Temple of Delphi, where the door only opens inwards to those who 'know thy Self'. Once past that threshold, the egoic self is balanced by the inclusive self, and the qualities of unification and merging are unfolded to become a channel for life, light and love.

Impersonal or universal love becomes a state of being which is as easily expressed as natural breathing, and is not dependent either on loving other individuals or being loved by them. Penetrating through the centre of the circle leads the seeker to 'the Heart of the Sun', which is the recognition of the inner point of Life within all manifestation, and standing within that light, he realises significance and meaning by the illumination of his mind. He enters the company of the Enlightened, the White Brotherhood or Hierarchy. Emanating outwards into the world of man is the constant stream of magnetic energy, seeking individual resonance and summoning the 'pilgrim home to the love of God'. It is the inner response to this call from the 'Heart of the Sun' that awakens in the depths of the mystic and spiritual seeker, and which enflames the development of collective humanitarian movements for the betterment of mankind.

The 'Old Commentary' in *Esoteric Astrology: A Treatise on the Seven Rays, Vol. 3,* by Alice Bailey, indicates the nature of the inner calling.

> The Transcendent One said: I am alone. I must arise and seek with ceaseless urge, that which produces completion, round out my circle whole, intensify My life, and make Me truly One, and this because I recognise the Two. I must have union with my other self, the self I dimly sense. Unto My heart I drew that other One and drawing thus I gave enlightenment; I dowered with enrichments; I freely gave.

Positive keynotes of the astrological Sun include: Will, Individuality, Independence, Presence, Magnetic Vitality, Intellectual Clarity, Autonomy, Creativity Personal Expression, and a firm Centre. If negatively expressed, these can become: Selfishness, Egotism, Pride, Domination, Force, Aggrandisement, Possessiveness. There is a need for personal egotism to be transcended, so that the inner qualities of the 2nd Ray of Love-Wisdom shine through, and this is the task for solar initiates, so that by their creative visualisation, light is directed into the dark corners of their nature, life and the ongoing planetary creative process, thus transforming, redeeming and purifying matter. The role of Lightbearer is assumed.

The Ray of Love-Wisdom is a building energy, seeking to transform the receptacle of matter into a medium of expressing divine love. It has a synthetic and inclusive quality, and operates through a high intuitiveness and empathy. In the world, its influence is displayed in acts of altruism and humanitarianism, where as a consequence of its magnetic, radiating and inclusive beneficence, the birth of the planetary fellowship of Aquarius is slowly forming and creating the new worldview for the next millennium. The characteristics of this Ray include attraction, love, wisdom, magnetism, balance, expansion, inclusion, relationship, absorption, illumination, centralisation, sympathetic understanding, comprehension, synthesis, intuition, honesty, loyalty, building and a search for truth.

Occultly, it is from the Spiritual Sun that all great teachers emerge into the world. Christ declared that 'I am the Light of the World' and that 'I and my Father are One'. Through his mission to release the cosmic principle of love into the world, by pursuing his sacrificial role to his mutilation and death on the cross, he demonstrated the magnetic nature of will by his love and radiating activity that spans time and space. It is a quality of the 2nd Ray that transmits this magnetic will, which brings into relation the pair of opposites (spirit – matter), drawing them together to form a united whole; one term for this is the sacred at-one-ment.

The Sun is 'the Great Illuminator', and is the inspiration for the spiritual seeker to discover the path which leads into a progressive sequence towards an ever greater and more inclusive light. In this Seven Rays system, the triple nature of the Sun evokes three fires within the individual.

The first is *fire by friction,* which is operative within the personality, related to prana (the animating and vivifying life-energy) and the etheric body, and corresponding to the physical Sun. This inner friction is felt as the multi-faceted 'I', which directs personality changes according to circumstances and moods, and is the root of self-contradiction and lack of self-knowledge. Another aspect of this is on the astral level, the realm of desires, where man's path is determined by the nature of his dreams and desires. Friction occurs as conflicting tendencies clash within the personality, and as the egoic self slowly awakens to the nature of global relationship and the promptings of his higher self. This energy is located at the base of the spine.

The second is *solar fire,* which is operative within genuine spiritual aspirants and initiates, and related to the soul or unifying level of man, awakened on the path of enlightenment. This corresponds to the heart of the Sun, and the esoteric planetary White Brotherhood, and is activated on the higher mental nature. This energy is located in the heart, which is opened at the time of the 1st Initiation (and considered in my *Phoenix Rising* book). Contacting this solar fire is an underlying intention of this exploration of the Sun, where the spiritual dimension is more openly studied.

The third, and highest fire that can be experienced by man is *electric fire*, which is operative within the higher Adepts and Masters of the Wisdom, and is activated when the mediating soul is no longer required and dissipates, leaving a direct channel between spirit and matter through monadic consciousness (constant awareness of unity and oneness). This is related to the spirit or atma in man, and corresponds to the central spiritual Sun, and the energy is located in the crown centre, the sahasra chakra of the thousand petalled lotus (Kether in Qabalah). Teachers of the stature of Christ and Buddha embody this level of evolution.

What is the point of these 'fires' within the human nature? The response is that the aim is a sequential revelation of light, 'carrying the initiate closer to the Heart of the Sun, wherein all things are known and felt, and through which all forms, all beings and all things can be bathed in love' (Alice Bailey, *The Rays and the Initiations, Vol.5, Treatise on the Seven Rays*).

The spiritual energy of the Sun reaches man through the mediation of his higher self, soul or solar angel. This stimulates increasing self-consciousness, and the awareness of the essential duality of his reality, and through inner friction and the unfolding of goodwill to others, the path of relationship between the egoic and higher self begins to be explored, leading to the solar transformation.

The Sun is the principle influence within astrology, and is considered to be the planetary representative of the self. Yet often this is restricted mainly to the twelve personality types approach, and the more advanced and spiritual dimension is ignored. In the older spiritual paths, this was not the case, and an understanding of the role and function of the Sun was vital for personal progress. The Sun is the supreme planetary deity, and should be recognised as that again, and astrology can perform its part in restoring this archetype of light and resurrection back into a living reality through astrological guidance, similarly to the invocation of the Moon (see my *Queen of the Night*) to create a new balance within the individual and society beyond dualistic perceptions.

The planets are the distributing agents for the energies emanating from the zodiacal constellations, and consequently are 'awakened' or discovered when man reaches the appropriate point of development and response. This is true both on the collective level, and on the individual scale, where planets exist in the 'dark unconscious' and act as his 'fate' until he can register their activity more consciously, and choose to become sensitive to their influences, working with them co-operatively to build a deeper inner harmony or to transform his limiting worldview.

One expression of this is the Sun exalted in Aries, which has a characteristic of being an initiating energy. Esoterically, Aries is the first sign of the zodiac, the beginning of the annual solar-zodiac year, and is the initiator of the great universal process of involution-evolution; the Sun represents the life of the spirit which descends into matter only to eventually rise again in transcendent glory and victory over 'death'. In Aries, the life energy is 'swung into activity', as latent patterns become manifest and the hidden creative potency is released, transforming the darkness into light over aeons of time. The Great Work of Infinity is the ceaseless task of making the unconscious conscious; and in our own small way, we participate in this endeavour.

The intent of the twelve constellations transmitted by planetary mediation is less the forming of twelve personality patterns, and more the stimulation of the soul-solar fire within the human form. This results in modified subjective activity, which moves closer to an awareness of the unity of all life, and eventually has repercussions in choices and expression in the world. There are two stages to this effect. The first is the domination of the personality by the Sun-sign characteristics, which gradually attune it to respond to the spiritual Sun, and this evokes the latent possibilities for that life to be manifested; this has been termed 'the potency of the Sun of Probability'. The second is an increasing response to the energies concealed by the Rising Sign, which evokes new opportunities by intensifying inner development and the evolutionary return; this has been termed 'the potency of the Sun of Possibility'.

Perhaps by opening ourselves more to the positive dimension of our Ascendant, we can enrich our lives more through merging two energies by the unifying quality of the Sun. As the Ascendant sets the house divisions, it determines the planetary positions in natal and transit charts, and so indicates the current life potential and challenges. Esoteric teaching suggests that the Ascendant holds the secret of future development and the higher life purpose which will evolve from the attunement to the spiritual Sun. The energy of the Ascendant may hold a key to the right relationship between personality and Self, and considering this may open doors for further individual exploration of their inner nature.

THE QABALAH AND THE SPHERE OF TIPHARETH

In the wisdom of the Qabalah, the sphere of Tiphareth corresponds with the Sun. On the Tree of Life, this is positioned at the centre of the Pillar of Equilibrium, above Yesod (the Moon sphere) and is the balancing path between the outer Pillars of Mercy and Severity. Examining Tiphareth is useful in becoming aware of the higher dimensions of the astrological Sun, as many of the themes associated with this Sephirah are noted in the mythological and astrological solar patterns.

Tiphareth is Shemesh, the Sphere of the Sun, and has images of 'a majestic King', 'a magical child', and 'a sacrificed god', indicating three aspects of the Wise One – the Self. The Vision of Tiphareth is that of the harmony and beauty of nature, through a holistic insight into its spirituality. By this perception, an at-one-ment with the universe is attained, joining the 'Outer Robe of Concealment' with the 'Inner Robe of Glory', matter and spirit. The Virtue of this sphere is 'Devotion to the Great Work', and this leads through the mystery of the crucifixion phase of the sacrificed god. The Vice is Pride; and in the human body, its physical correspondence is to the breast and heart. Symbols which are associated include the Rose Cross, the Calvary Cross, the truncated pyramid, the cube, and the lamen which contains an image of the Sun in splendour.

Tiphareth assumes a central role on the Qabalistic Tree, serving as a keystone and integrative sphere. Above Tiphareth lie the spheres associated with the higher Self, those of Geburah,

Chesed, Binah, Chokmah and the spiritual Source of Kether, the nucleus of the Divine Spark. It is a point of transmutation between these planes of force and the lower planes of form, and is considered to be the 'child and son' of Kether, and the 'King' of the human reality and world formed by Netzach (nature forces, elemental contacts, feelings, Venus), Hod (ceremonial magic, occult knowledge, intellect, Mercury), Yesod (psychism, etheric nature, emotions, Moon) and Malkuth (the physical kingdom). These comprise the lower self of the personality.

The function of Tiphareth is as a focusing point, a centre of transition and transformation for the rising of consciousness along the Path of Equilibrium. It is a mediator, receiving, transforming, transmitting and distributing the primal spiritual energy of Kether, operating like a two-fold switch, transferring the higher energies down, and magnetically attracting the lower energies of the human nature to return towards spirit. Tiphareth embodies the hermetic axiom of 'As above, so below' and the nature of relationship between the macrocosm and the microcosm. This is achieved by a rhythmic interplay between levels, and is equated with its correspondences to the chest, heart, lungs and solar plexus, where the activity of breathing connects the individual to the universe and the descending–ascending flow of the life energies.

Tiphareth mediates between God–Spirit–Kether and the material worlds, and is the most contactable manifestation of God-in-form within the range of human consciousness. This is through the medium of the Divine Son, who by his existence is a pointer towards the even greater reality of Spirit. As Christ declared 'Whoso hath seen me hath seen the Father.' The concepts of solar mediators and redeemers comes from this integrating and unifying quality of Tiphareth–Sun, where the matter of form and the lower self are stabilised and equilibrated in order to reflect the higher reality.

This is the root of the many religious legends of the wonder child who matures to face his adult destiny as a 'Redeemer', by reuniting the lower kingdom to its higher source, and through many trials and tribulations is led towards the sacrificial crucifixion. The Redeemer attempts to open blocked channels of energy between levels, to restore the successful flow of inspiration and transformative spiritual force into matter so that unbalanced energies are reintegrated under the higher imprint of unity. In the process, the 'sacrificial King' loses his material life for love of the people. This is the process of the Christian doctrine, and the symbolism of Christ's death, resurrection and regeneration, implied by the spilling of his blood into the land on Mount Golgotha. Through the transformation of crucifixion on the cross of spirit–matter, form is transcended by the releasing of the contained spiritual forces, and form is changed from a static pattern of limitation to one of kinetic movement and openness to spirit, making it available for the regenerative Great Work of redemptive purification.

This is the task of the White Lodge, the Tiphareth world of initiated adepts and teachers, which is only entered by those who have undergone the 'death of initiation', becoming the initiate or 'the living dead man', reborn to conscious awareness of the higher realms. Tiphareth is the sphere of pure self-consciousness, of the timeless 'I am', reflecting the esoteric heart of the Sun; in its lower expression, it reflects the misidentification of the egoic self with the individual form and contents of consciousness. From the perspective of the solar consciousness, there is no birth, death or rebirth, only the eternal now, and it is the centre of all experience and awareness, remaining constant as the point at the centre while watching everything changing within the periphery.

Healing is associated with the solar force, and all healing gods are manifestations of Tiphareth. The Archangel Raphael is 'the spirit that standeth in the sun', and is the angel of healing, working with the sun and the life-force to create balanced health in the individual. This was the technique used by ancient initiates of the therapeutic priesthood who manipulated solar force to restore vitality and radiant well-being. Often disease and physiological disorder is activated by blockages in the energy flow of the body, and this can be related to circulatory problems or restrictions of the solar plexus area. The therapeutics attempted to open any closed body channels, so that receptivity to the vitalising solar and spiritual forces was renewed. The Greek healing cult of Aesculapius was founded on sun worship and solar magic.

Tiphareth is sometimes referred to as the 'Christ Centre', the 'Centre of the Inebriating God and Giver of Illumination'. The experiences associated with Tiphareth include the blinding lights of mystical exaltation, such as the conversion of Paul on the road to Damascus, or the transfiguration of Jesus. These involve the movement of consciousness beyond form identification, due to an overwhelming inflow of spiritual force, which awakens the self to realise a new dimension to its nature. One challenge of the Tiphareth experience is to forge a bridge between the new level of consciousness and the old familiar perception and mode of living, to fuse them together in a new way of living; or the danger is that the brilliance of light becomes blinding rather than illuminating.

Through the perception of Tiphareth, the psychic symbols generated by Yesod (the Moon) which form the 'Treasure House of Images', those archetypal symbols of astrology, tarot, etc., stand revealed in their real liberating light, becoming transparent instead of veiling the hidden reality behind them.

Certain paths to evoke a response from the solar centre use the imagery of inebriation. The Dionysian Mysteries are one example of stimulating an ecstatic state of consciousness as the inflow of higher energy raises the aspirant to the 'divine inebriation'. The mystical Sufi sects also speak of 'becoming drunk on the Divine Love, Divine Light and the Mystery'.

Tiphareth is the Sun of the inner solar system, a higher level of consciousness than is still normally experienced by the majority. It sits at the heart of the psyche, at the dividing veil of the conscious and unconscious mind, and Janus-like, looks to the spirit and to the personality. The astrological Sun stands likewise at the junction of the psyche, connecting us to our spiritual nature if we choose. In the natal chart, the Sun indicates the essence of our 'type', our fundamental characteristics, as well as the area of life that it should manifest through, revealed by its house position. These twelve human 'types' are twelve groups, or twelve faces of the Cosmic Archetype of Man, and our Sun-sign is not individual in nature, but indicates our group contribution and function, our gift to the collective well-being and evolutionary development.

Through our inner Sun, we can journey ever deeper into our hidden nature, liberating our solar potential and walking a path of light. By being true to that innate Sun pattern, we can 'follow our Star', much as the Three Magi, those Wise Astrologers were guided to the birth of the Wonder Child in the cave. One key to the individual task facing us is often revealed by the Sabian symbols, especially in the interpretations by Dane Rudhyar, where we can establish the imagery of our 'personal cross to bear' by the Ascendant/Descendant and Midheaven/Nadir axes, which imply a cross formed by the horizon and meridian. The degree and sign of these four points on the natal chart is then symbolically interpreted in terms of the Ascendant – 'What is the point or meaning of this life?'; Descendant – 'Where is this leading me?'; Midheaven – 'Why am I passing through life, what role am I playing in the human drama?'; Nadir – 'How can I achieve the best results to fulfil my way of destiny?' Working with such Sabian imagery through meditation and contemplation can provide one way to tune into your own solar path, and can be very illuminating for those who are comfortable with visualising creative imagery.

The esoteric perception of the astrological Sun may not be easily assimilated, especially if you are unfamiliar with the Seven Rays and Qabalistic paths. Yet it reminds the astrologer of greater depths to a planet that can easily be mentally dismissed in terms of superficial Sun-signs and daily newspaper horoscopes. The ancient formulators of such esoteric teachings ensured that they did not lose sight of the solar potential, and as astrologers we would be wise to follow their example, and reconsider how we can personally work with this centre in our own natal charts and evoke its unifying and integrative function within our psyche. Perhaps as custodians of the star-lore, the ancient stellar wisdom, we should begin to live our lives from the higher vision of the solar angel. That is the challenge confronting each of us, and one which we should not evade. Working within the tradition of astrology, part of our collective responsibility is to live as a channel for these transformative planetary energies to influence our reality positively, so that we become conscious, constructive Masters of our Fate, instead of unconscious victims.

CHAPTER 9

Communion with the Sun

ASTROLOGY SHOULD NOT BE just the learning of traditional astrological attributes of various signs, houses or aspects, and the dissemination of these through interpretations of natal charts; this is just its superficial facade and the real intent and purpose of the wisdom of astrology is to guide seekers towards their inmost centre, where humanity and divinity merge in union. As astrologers, our group challenge and direction is to attain this goal; we have to embody the integration that we believe is the destined future for humanity, serving as guides to this lighted path. As students of this ancient wisdom, we are also custodians of its preservation and evolution to meet modern needs, and the value of astrological insights should also be displayed by ourselves in the midst of daily life, by our nature and social contribution, because that is the real spiritual crucible and testing ground.

One of the values of astrological study can be found by its influence in deepening understanding, even by focusing on the twelve primary psychological types of humanity, symbolised by the natal Sun sign. This enables the astrologer to expand beyond his own individual focus to look again at the world through different types of perception, worldviews, innate responses and psychological screens and filters. The limitations of the astrologer's own type can be dissolved, as their patterns of perception become temporarily transcended through opening to the different zodiacal archetypes. Tolerance and insight into the nature of people should be one result of this process, and these are qualities that could become transformative in society.

As we may recognise, astrology is not really about looking out to the heavens for guidance; this is just a technique to align the macrocosm and microcosm to create a reflective mirror (the planetary positions) that enables us to look inside our inner personality and psychology and to study our complex behavioural patterns to enhance understanding. This is similar to the difficulty in seeing our own faces; we can only do this when using an external mirror to reflect our image back to us. So astrology initially looks out into the universe to gain enlightenment as to our individual human natures.

The Sun is the centre of both our outer and inner universes, but to discover our inner centre, we need to journey beyond its surrogate reflection as the separated ego structure, to penetrate into the secret heart of our being. The challenge is to awaken the golden dawn of sunrise within ourselves, and not just see the physical sun rising in the East.

The heroic path and solar journey commence when those whispers to become something and do something can no longer be ignored. Questions of 'Who am I? What am I doing here? What is my purpose? What is the meaning of my life?' remain as uncomfortable shadows in the midst of everyday existence. The resolution of these existential issues is only found on a path of transformation; otherwise, existential angst persists, as does the 'nausea' that Jean-Paul Sartre experienced in his life at the lack of meaning and connectedness, and which Colin Wilson explores in several of his books, especially in *The Outsider*.

While the solar path may descend deeply into the darkness and shadows of the underworld – the realm of the Goddess – confronting the seeker with his unredeemed nature and the consequences of separative attitudes, this is only to culminate in the liberating inner death of the initiate and the subsequent resurrection into light for the triumphant hero. Our journey leads us to a personal experience of this archetypal pattern and path, recognised as an initiatory way by all ancient cultures. It is through following the gleams of light towards our inner Sun that we begin to transform, unite and integrate our disparate personality, in a parallel manner to the Sun's cohesive power over the planets. As our journey proceeds, it is as if each planetary tendency becomes rearranged under the aegis of the solar centre, so that their positive qualities can be released through the individual into society.

Historically, humanity has passed through long periods of matriarchal and patriarchal cultures conditioning social attitudes, reflected in religious forms by the relative powers of either Goddesses or Gods. In recent times, since the early Western Industrial Revolution and the discovery of Uranus (as a cosmic time-keeper), the forces of patriarchal and masculine social domination have become less positive; scientific technology and man's greed have hastened the exploitation of the planet beyond safe sustainable levels, and unless checked and reversed, we will rush like lemmings over the cliffs of ecological and cultural disaster. Our solar expression is now being distorted, and becoming dangerous; its supremacy is ending. As a natural corrective to this, the power of the feminine is rising, with environmental and global issues of collective responsibility being recognised, and concepts of planetary and social nurturing quickly forming as preferable directions for the future.

Yet replacing the solar culture by a lunar culture is not the whole answer either. It is vitally necessary for the collective feminine perception to modify our solar tendencies, and to rebalance social equilibrium, but as we stand on the brink of a new millennium a new direction and archetypal pattern is being born, which moves us beyond polarities into a higher state of integration.

The human being is separated into male and female, which, when these two opposites are temporarily mated, generate new life in a child. Our religious divinities have similarly been separated in the common mind over centuries, as either all-powerful Gods or Goddesses, becoming polarised Deities, reflected by the astrological symbolism of Sun and Moon.

While to some it may appear that culturally we are embarked on a struggle between patriarchal and matriarchal tendencies for the future well-being of the world, these are in fact the death-struggles of such dualistic attitudes fading away. At the end of the Age, all the gods and goddesses come back, resurrected from their graves, and recapitulating what has passed and formed the present. Certainly, a temporary transition phase is urgently required where the feminine powers are released again into society, awakening people to the necessity of love, care and concern for the whole planet on every level of manifestation, but this is not the end of the process that humanity is now entering.

As the solar hero enters the innermost depths of the lunar underworld on his quest for Self, the transformation occurs. He does not return unchanged; he has, in fact, died to his old self. Within that dark chamber or vault of his nature, the God and Goddess have united as one. The hero re-enters the world as a *Son or Daughter of Light* a psychological androgyne whose transformed consciousness reflects the positive qualities of both the masculine and feminine archetypes; the realisation is that the Self is beyond polarities and is One, not dual.

This is the stage that humanity is starting to confront as the future evolutionary step, where a new Aquarian vision of both human and divine nature needs to be attained. No longer can we afford dualistic attitudes; if we perpetuate them, then the planet will be torn apart on the horns of our dilemmas and inner schisms. We have to awaken to our humanity, not just our masculinity or femininity, but to move beyond such limiting patterns. We seek not only the 'new woman' or the 'new man', but the *new human* which is in gestation in the planetary womb.

Communion with the spiritual Sun is union with the Self; that is the real purpose and secret of the hero quest, whether it is pursued by man or woman. Our journey takes us into the heart of the encompassing circle of our psyche, where the point resides; from there we can radiate light and influence, to make our heroic mark on the world.

The view from that centre is of light as the foundation of all life, and as Christ stated on behalf of all lightbearers, 'I am the Light of the World.' The image for Aquarius is of the man holding an inverted vase, and one key phrase for this is 'Water of Life am I, poured forth for thirsty men'. We can see this as a stream of light entering the world, dissolving our fallacious separative thinking, cleansing the Augean stables of the collective mind and emotions, revealing meaning and purpose in life.

As we go in search of the Lord of Light, remember that the hero has to return back into the world carrying his burden, from which he will release those energy streams of light, love and renewed life into the Earth. We can share this sacred task of the Fellowship of Light.

Index

Adam Kadmon 171–2
Aesculapius 225
Akhenaten 4, 14
alchemy 198
Anaxagoras 2
androgyne 36
anima 21, 38, 39, 203, 210, 211
animus 21, 38, 39, 44–5
Aphrodite 4
Apollo 17–18
Aquarius 190–1, 200, 208–9, 231
archetypes 171, 201
Arianrhod 22
Aries 173–5, 199, 207, 222
Artemis 18
Arthur, King 22, 194, 197, 202–4
Ascendant, esoteric view of 223
Asclepius 18
aspects to Sun 55–7 *see also* *individual planets*
astrology
  esoteric 223
  nature of 8–9
  role of 195, 213–14, 228–9
atomic theory 8, 10
authority 37

Bach, Dr. Edward 132–7
Bailey, Alice 205, 217
Blavatsky, H. P. 217
Buddha 221

calendars 3–4, 4–5 *see also* festivals, pagan
Cancer 178–80, 199, 207, 211
Capricorn 188–90, 200, 204, 208
cell, human 7
Celts 20–2, 199 *see also* Arthur, King; Druidism
child heroes 196–7, 205
Christ 196–7, 200–1, 220, 221, 224–5
circle, symbolism of 215–17
Copernicus 2

Dali, Salvador 141–4
Delphi, Oracle of 18
destiny 25
Dionysian Mysteries 18, 226
Druidism 5, 21

ego-Self relationship 23–5, 27, 34, 216–17, 221
elements
  Air 30
  Earth 30–1
  Fire 31
  Water 29–30
equinoxes 5, 6–7, 48
Eros 37, 38
Eurydice 18–19
Eurystheus 205
exaltation 222

family life 35–6
father
  archetype 35–7, 200–1
  authority, and 37, 45
  early relationship with 29, 42–5
  house association 36
festivals, pagan 212–13

Galahad 203, 204
Gemini 176–8, 199, 207
genetics 9
Goddess *see* Moon Goddess
Grail, Holy 22, 194, 202, 203
Gwydion 22
Gwyn ap Nudd 22

healing 225
heart 52–3
heliocentric view 2
Helios 17
Hera 205
Hercules 17, 19, 204–9
heroic quest 194–201, 229 *see also* Arthur, King; Hercules; Horned God
Herne the Hunter 22
Hinduism 12–13
homosexuality 35
Horned God 209–14
Horus 4, 15, 16–17
houses, natal, Sun in 146–8
  1st 148–9
  2nd 149–51
  3rd 151–3
  4th 153–4
  5th 155–6
  6th 156–8

7th 158–60
8th 160–2
9th 162–4
10th 164–6
11th 166–8
12th 168–70
immune system 54
individuation 26
ionosphere 2
Isis 4, 15
Ishtar 4

Jupiter
midpoints of Sun and 51
solar aspects to
conjunction 81–3
sextile 83–5
trine 85–7
square 87–9
opposition 89–91
see also Zeus

Kepler, Johann 2
kingship 4, 20, 21, 22, 199, 225 *see also* Arthur, King

Leo 180–1, 199, 207
Libra 183–5, 200, 208
light 7–8, 17
Logos 37, 38
love 218–19
Lugh 20

Mars
midpoints of Sun and 51
solar aspects to
conjunction 72–4
sextile 74–6
trine 77
square 78–9
opposition 80–81
masculinity 44, 196, 230 *see also* animus; father
matriarchy 4, 230
Mercury, solar aspects to 51, 69–71
Merlin 22
midpoints 49–52
Mithraism 13, 199
Moon
midpoints of Sun and 51
solar aspects to 36, 37, 51
conjunction 57–9
sextile 59–61
trine 61–3
square 63–6
opposition 66–9
Moon Goddess 21, 203, 210, 230
Mordred 22, 204
Moses 197
Myth, living according to 201

Neptune
midpoints of Sun and 52
solar aspects to 31–2, 33, 34, 37–8, 56
conjunction 112–15
sextile 115–17
trine 117–118
square 118–21
opposition 121–3
Newton, Isaac 2

Oedipus 201
Orpheus 17, 18–19
Orphic Mysteries 18
Osiris 4, 15, 16–17

paganism 5, 209–14 *see also* Druidism
Pan 209
parents, early relationship with 29, 38, 42–5
Pisces 191–3, 200, 209, 211
Planck, Max 7
Pluto
midpoints of Sun and 52
solar aspects to 31–2, 33–4, 38, 56
conjunction 123–5
sextile 125–6
trine 126–8
square 128–30
opposition 130–2
polarities, integrating 10, 36, 203, 210, 231 *see also* anima; animus
purpose, sense of 27–8

Qabalah 223–7
Quantum theory 8

Ra 4, 14, 14–15, 15–16
Raphael, Archangel 225
Rays, Seven 217–23
relationships 37–9
resurrection 198,225
Rudhyar, Dane 227

Sabian symbols 227
Sagittarius 186–8, 200, 208
Sartre, Jean-Paul 229
Saturn

authority, and 45
function 40–1
midpoints of Sun and 51
polarity with Sun 39–46
solar aspects to 36, 39, 41–3
conjunction 92–3
sextile 94–5
trine 95–7
square 97–9
opposition 99–101
Scorpio 185–6, 200, 208, 211
Sekhmet 17
Selene 17
Self, higher *see* ego-Self relationship
self-confidence 28
Self-ego relationship *see* ego-Self relationship
self-sufficiency 28–9
Set 15
signs, zodiacal *see* zodiac, signs of
Sol 1
solar centre, contacting 10–11
solar myths
Celtic 20–2
Egyptian 14–17
Greek 17–19
solar returns 46–7
solar transits
house 47–9
natal Sun, to 46–7
solstices 5–7, 21, 48, 204
Stonehenge 20–1
Sufism 226
Sun
composition 2
distance from earth 2
glyph for, symbolism of 215–17
gravity 2
measurements 2
orbit 3
worship 12–13
Sun-gods 12–13, 22
sunlight, benefit to health 54

Tarot 39
Taurus 175–6, 199, 204, 207
Thoth 15
thymus 53–4
Tiphareth 223–7
Tree of Life 223–4

Uranus
discovery of as herald of change 230
midpoints of Sun and 51–2
solar aspects to 31–3, 36, 38, 56
conjunction 101–4
sextile 104–6
trine 106–7
square 107–9
opposition 109–11

Virgo 181–3, 199–200, 207–8
visualisation 54
Venus, solar aspects to 37–8, 51, 72–4

Wicca 209–14
Wilson, Colin 136–41, 229

Zeus 17
zodiac, signs of 25, 171–3, 203, 204, 205–6 *see also individual signs*
Zoroastrianism 13